Media
Materialities

BCMCR
New Directions in Media and Cultural Research

Series editors: Oliver Carter, Kirsten Forkert, and Nicholas Gebhardt
Print ISSN: 2752-4515 | **Online ISSN:** 2752-4523

The Birmingham Centre for Media and Cultural Research's 'New Directions' book series aims to advance research and teaching in the broad range of media and cultural studies and to serve as the focal point for a community of scholars who are committed to critical inquiry and collaborative practice. Books in the series engage with developments in the field, showing how new theoretical approaches have impacted on research within both media and cultural studies and other related disciplines. Each volume will focus on a specific theme or issue, as well as exploring broader processes of social and cultural transformation. The series is committed to producing distinctive titles that challenge traditional disciplinary boundaries and question existing paradigms, including innovative scholarship in areas such as the creative industries; media history, heritage and archives; games studies; gender and sexuality; screen cultures; jazz and popular music studies; media and conflict; song-writing studies; and critical theory. The editors are also keen to encourage authors to experiment with non-standard approaches to academic writing.

In this series:

Under the Counter: Britain's Trade in Hardcore Pornographic 8mm Films, by Oliver Carter (2023)
Media Materialities: Form, Format, and Ephemeral Meaning, edited by Iain A. Taylor and Oliver Carter (2023)

Media Materialities

Form, Format, and Ephemeral Meaning

EDITED BY
Iain A. Taylor and Oliver Carter

Bristol, UK / Chicago, USA

First published in the UK in 2023 by
Intellect, The Mill, Parnall Road, Fishponds, Bristol, BS16 3JG, UK

First published in the USA in 2023 by
Intellect, The University of Chicago Press, 1427 E. 60th Street,
Chicago, IL 60637, USA

Copyright © 2023 Intellect Ltd
All rights reserved. No part of this publication may be reproduced,
stored in a retrieval system, or transmitted, in any form or by
any means, electronic, mechanical, photocopying, recording, or
otherwise, without written permission.

A catalogue record for this book is available from
the British Library.

Copy editor: MPS Limited
Cover designer: Tanya Montefusco
Cover image: Eastronic portable radio.
Photograph courtesy of Sam Coley (2021).
Production manager: Debora Nicosia
Typesetter: MPS Limited
Indexer: Janet Adams

Hardback ISBN 978-1-78938-817-6
ePDF ISBN 978-1-78938-818-3
ePUB ISBN 978-1-78938-819-0

Part of BCMCR New Directions in Media and Cultural Research
Print ISSN: 2752-4515 / Online ISSN: 2752-4523

To find out about all our publications, please visit our website.
There you can subscribe to our e-newsletter, browse or download our current
catalogue and buy any titles that are in print.

www.intellectbooks.com

This is a peer-reviewed publication.

Contents

List of Figures   ix

Acknowledgements   xi

Foreword   xiii
  Nicholas Gebhardt

Introduction   1

SECTION 1: FORM   17

Short Take 1: My Notebook   19
  Lee Griffiths

1. Investigating the Illicit: The Material Traces of Britain's Early   21
Trade in Obscene 8mm Films
  Oliver Carter

Short Take 2: 'Press the Start Button'   41
  Harrison Charles

2. On, Off, and in the Map: Materializing Game Experiences   43
Through Player Cartography
  Nick Webber

Short Take 3: Making Order Out of Chaos   67
  Hilary Weston Jones

3. The Solid State of Radio   69
  Sam Coley

Short Take 4: Materialities of Television History   91
  E. Charlotte Stevens

SECTION 2: FORMAT — 93

Short Take 5: Only Dancing. Again — 95
Philip Young

4. Between Analogue and Digital: The Cassette Tape as Hybrid Artefact — 97
Iain A. Taylor

Short Take 6: Patch Lead Possibilities — 112
Chris Mapp

5. 'Because It Is Not Digital': The Cultural Value of the Analogue Book in Digital Age — 114
Christian Moerken

Short Take 7: Materialities of Spatial Confinement: Trefeglwys Meets Beirut — 130
Dima Saber

6. Essentially (Not) the Game: Reading the Materiality of Video Game Paratexts — 132
Regina Seiwald

Short Take 8: Materialities and Craft Value — 151
Karen Patel

SECTION 3: EPHEMERAL MEANING — 155

Short Take 9: Still Angry: Still Feeding — 157
Matt Grimes

7. Stamp of Approval: A Prosopography of the English Midlands Videogame Industry — 159
Alex Wade and Adam Whittaker

Short Take 10: The Edward Colston Experience — 179
Martin Cox

8. Reframing Materiality in the *Caribbean Diaspora Podcast* — 182
Rachel-Ann Charles and Tim Wall

CONTENTS

Short Take 11: We're all Victorians Now   203
  Kirsten Forkert

9. You Can Look, Share and Comment, But You Can't Touch: 205
The Relationship Between the Materiality and Physicality of
Photographs in an Online Community Archive
  Vanessa Jackson

Short Take 12: Location, Agency, and Hashtag Activism During   228
the COVID-19 Pandemic
  Yemisi Akinbobola

10. Thirty-Seven Retweets   230
  John Hillman

Conclusion: Shifting Horizons of Possibility   247
  Susanna Paasonen

Notes on Contributors   251

Index   259

Figures

ST.1	One of Lee's notebooks. Author's own image.	19
1.1	*Chez M. Pirgeon*'s handwritten title card. Author's personal collection.	30
1.2	*Chez M. Pirgeon*'s processing errors? Author's personal collection.	31
1.3	The mysterious Paillard Bolex operator who makes an accidental appearance in *Chez M. Pirgeon*. Author's personal collection.	33
1.4	Title cards from *Chez M. Pirgeon*, *Hotel Sexi*, *La Dolce Vita*, and *Lavabora*. Author's personal collection.	35
ST.2	Harrison's Game Boy. Author's own image.	41
2.1	A player map from a Dungeons & Dragons adventure. From author's personal collection.	45
2.2	Player map showing rudimentary compass rose. From author's personal collection.	50
2.3	Player map of a level from *Bard's Tale II: The Destiny Knight*. From author's personal collection.	55
2.4	Two examples of players' pointcrawl maps. From author's personal collection.	57
2.5	Map of the Advanced Dungeons & Dragons adventure 'Tomb of Horrors'. From author's personal collection.	61
ST.3	Hilary's calculator. Author's own image.	67
3.1	Cover of Danish Philips radio catalogue, 1959. Courtesy of the Royal Philips/Philips Company Archives.	73
3.2	The Sony CRF-150, Surplus Tech Mart. Author's personal collection.	76
3.3	Philips Radiorecorder, 1966. Courtesy of the Royal Philips/Philips Company Archives.	81
3.4	Belle Epoque 1906 DAB Retro Stereo System, Auna. Courtesy of the Berlin Brands Group.	84

3.5	The author's Eastronic portable radio. Author's own image.	87
ST.5	The author's copy of David Bowie's *Cracked Actor* CD. Author's own image.	96
ST.6	The author's patch lead. Author's own image.	112
6.1	Designing an avatar in *World of Warcraft*, Blizzard Entertainment (dev.), *World of Warcraft*, 2004. Available at https://news.blizzard.com/en-us/world-of-warcraft/23737992/shadowlands-an-inside-look-at-the-character-creation-ui-redesign.	136
ST.8	Craftmaking. Author's own image.	151
ST.9	Crass's *The Feeding of the Five Thousand* vinyl cover (1978). Author's own image.	158
ST.10	Edward Colston's statue at the M Shed in Bristol. Courtesy of Adrian Boliston under Creative Commons Licence Attribution 2.0 Generic (CC-BY-2.0).	180
9.1	BBC Birmingham Canteen, 2004. Photograph by Philip Morgan.	213
9.2	Frank Carson giving an impromptu performance in the Canteen in the 1990s. Photograph by Paul Hunt.	216
9.3	Filming on location for *Witchcraft* (BBC 2, 1992). Photograph by Willoughby Gullachsen (Gus).	217
9.4	Crew shooting *Boogie Outlaws* (BBC 2, 1987). Photograph by Willoughby Gullachsen (Gus).	219
9.5	Polaroid from *Juliet Bravo* shoot (*c.*1980–85). Photograph by Janice Rider.	221
9.6	Brian Glover and Gwen Arthy on *Shakespeare or Bust* (BBC 1, 1973). Photograph by Graham Pettifer.	222
9.7	Brian Glover and Gwen Arthy on *Shakespeare or Bust* (BBC 1, 1973). Photograph by Graham Pettifer. Colour-corrected version	223

Acknowledgements

The authors would collectively like to thank all the colleagues at the Birmingham Centre for Media and Cultural Research (BCMCR) who contributed to this book and the wider intellectual project from which it was birthed.

BCMCR was established in 2009 to develop research as a core activity within the Birmingham School of Media at Birmingham City University. Founded by Tim Wall and Paul Long, BCMCR has grown from just 3 researchers in 2008 to 32 in 2021.

The Centre's primary mission has been to promote scholarship about all aspects of media and cultural studies, which includes collaboration and partnerships. It does this by supporting a large group of active researchers at all career stages and providing a variety of contexts for the exchange of ideas.

Such formal and informal exchanges – weekly research seminars, short writings and the occasional pub visit – shaped the direction of this book, which has certainly been a collective enterprise. We also acknowledge that the project was undertaken during COVID-19 and are grateful that the authors remained committed to their contributions despite the personal challenges we all faced at this time.

We particularly thank Nicholas Gebhardt, former Director of BCMCR, for his belief and support in the project, Feona Attwood for her much-appreciated proofing skills, Susanna Paasonen for her willingness to write the conclusion to this book, Grant Bollmer for taking the time to offer such a detailed and helpful peer review, and Tim Mitchell and the team at Intellect Books for making this such a smooth process.

Iain would like to thank colleagues past and present at Birmingham City University and University of the West of Scotland for their intellectual (and moral) support, and Holley, for pretty much everything really.

Oliver would personally like to thank Iain for being such a great co-editor who created the critical environment that eventually resulted in this collection. He also thanks, as always, Katie and Evie for putting up with the completion of yet another book, and allowing me to escape the occasional bedtime routine to do editorial work. I love you both.

Foreword

Nicholas Gebhardt

This edited collection marks the culmination of a year-long programme of research into the theme of materialities undertaken by members of the Birmingham Centre for Media and Cultural Research at Birmingham City University in the United Kingdom. The focus of this programme was to explore some of the ways in which the objects that surround us exist within and mediate our social realities, and to consider the theoretical challenges posed by the concept of materiality. In his influential three-volume study of the rise of capitalism, the French historian Ferdinand Braudel argued for the importance of material culture to the study of human societies. 'This rich zone', he explained, 'like a layer covering the earth, I have called for want of a better expression *material life* or *material civilization*' (1992: 23, original emphasis). For Braudel, material life is made up of people and things, and it is through studying the changing interactions between different populations, their daily habits and activities, and the things that shape those habits and activities that we can better understand the emergence of capitalist modernity (1992: 31).

The chapters and reflections that follow excavate this rich zone of material possibility, drawing on multiple perspectives and methodologies to disclose our shifting relations with the world of things. In taking up the problem of materialities in this way, each of the authors challenges us to engage more fully with our experiences of everyday objects – our passion for collecting, for holding onto things, for returning to them over and over – and so reconceive our sense of their meaning and significance. Their work is also testimony to the mission of this book series, which serves as the focal point for a community of researchers who are committed to critical inquiry and collaborative practice, to experiments with the forms of academic writing that cut across traditional disciplinary boundaries and question existing paradigms. The aggregation of objects and juxtaposition of modes of writing gathered in this collection speaks squarely to this mission by bringing renewed attention to the material dynamics of culture and testing the concepts we rely on to explain it.

REFERENCE

Braudel, Ferdinand (1992), *Civilization and Capitalism, 15th–18th Century: The Structures of Everyday Life*, vol. 1 (trans. S. Reynolds), Berkeley: University of California Press.

Introduction

In October 2021, Australian musician and composer Warren Ellis published a book entitled *Nina Simone's Gum*. Ellis tells the story of how, in 1999, following Simone's performance as part of Nick Cave's Meltdown Festival, and still reeling from the weight and emotive resonance of her set, he sidled quietly onto the stage, grabbed the towel that held Simone's chewed gum, and quietly left the venue. A friend gave him a yellow Tower Records plastic carrier bag to keep the sacred package safe, and Ellis locked it in his Samsonite briefcase, where it travelled with him for two years. After realizing the significance, and precarity, of his possession, Ellis placed the bag on the top of his home piano, before relocating it to a drawer, where it stayed until November 2019. Ellis (2021: 31) recalls opening the drawer:

> I went to the drawer in my attic and took out the Tower Records bag and removed the towel. I opened it. The gum was in there. It looked as I remembered, the sacred heart, a Buddha. That cute rabbit in the moon bashing rice to make *omochi* お餅 with a wooden hammer that the Japanese see when the moon is full. Africa. The welcome nugget. Sometimes I saw Christ on the cross, his knees bent to the side her tooth print was still visible.

In introducing a volume on the subject of media materialities, this example offers a compelling account of the emotive power, and cultural resonance, that materiality has within culture and society. It highlights how the literal ephemera of something so trivial and inherently disposable as a piece of chewing gum can, given the correct context, become the focal point for something deeply meaningful on a personal, cultural, and political level. Starting from this one, indistinct piece of gum, completely worthless and disposable in any other context, Ellis tells a compelling story which takes in racial politics, structural accounts of the music industries, artistic and creative practice, and personal, emotive, and mnemonic reflection on the passage of time. In 2020, the Royal Danish Library in Copenhagen displayed the gum on a marble pedestal in a velvet-lined, temperature-controlled viewing box as part of the Stranger than Kindness Nick Cave exhibition. Cave called it a 'genuine religious artefact' (Cave cited in Ellis 2021: 8). It was also made into a piece of jewellery and a statue.

All that, from a piece of chewing gum.

This example of Nina Simone, and her chewing gum, is a timely reminder that the significance of materiality to the study of media extends itself far beyond the world of text, form, and format, which so often form the basis of media and communications scholarship. It highlights the complexity of our relationship with material things, and the deep entanglement between the mediation of meaning to a mass audience on one hand, and the complex entanglements of personal, mnemonic significance on the other. It highlights that even a mass-produced artefact, created with its very disposability in mind, contained the capacity to 'reveal the continuity of the self through time, by providing foci of involvement in the present, mementos and souvenirs of the past, and signposts for future goals' (Csikszentmihalyi 1993: 23).

It is in this same vein of attentiveness to the seemingly ephemeral, and the potential duality of objects and artefacts as at once mass-produced commodities *and* deeply personal mementos, that this collection is presented. The study of media, culture, and society has long been intimately and, arguably, inextricably entangled with the material world in which meaning is produced and consumed. To discuss the mediation of ideas and meaning is to consider the means through which the transient and evasive nature of ideas and meaning becomes fixed through material means. As such, we believe that the notion of 'materiality', or 'how the material character of the world around us is appropriated by humanity' (Graves-Brown 2000: 1) should be a more pervasive one in fields of study which take media and culture as their focal point. The work collected in this book aims to capture a snapshot of contemporary thought and a discussion on the role that materiality plays in our understanding of an ever-changing media landscape. We argue that attentiveness to the materiality of media and awareness of material culture studies approaches to understanding its meaning has a significant amount to offer scholars of media and communication.

Such considerations of material meanings and their relationship with theoretical concepts and positions should, we believe, be quite timely ones for scholars of media, culture, and society. News cycles are currently dominated by discussions of shifting environmental realities such as the current global climate emergency, with accounts of destruction and displacement as a result of global conflict, and debates around rapid technological advancement and its cultural and economic impact. Sociopolitical logics of competition, control, and scarcity create pressure towards what John Law and Annemarie Mol (1995: 283) describe as 'material inflation' or 'material instability', whereby the relationships between cultural and political meanings and material consequences become volatile. Rapid developments in the

INTRODUCTION

technologies of mediation have seen a wholesale change in consumer expectations around the media that they consume, and an increasing shift towards online and on-demand content, resulting in what Vlad Coroama et al. (2015) have referred to as the 'dematerialization' of media – a move away from physical artefacts, and analogue platforms and processes of consumption, and an ever-accelerating digitalization of media. This move towards dematerialization has become an increasing focus of scholarship in related fields, such as popular music studies, in which the shift from the consumption of physical formats to the prevalence of cloud-based subscription models (see Maguadda 2011; Anderson 2016; Krohn-Gimberghe 2020) have been at the heart of many recent debates in the field. However, while the suffix 'in the digital age' has become commonplace across media scholarship, such overt connections between digitality and dematerialization have been less forthcoming within media and communication studies. As such, a reconsideration of the relationship between sociocultural meaning and the material world in which it is situated takes on a new sense of significance and urgency for scholars of media, culture, and society.

Beyond that intellectual project, this book is also an attempt to capture not only the outcomes of the research projects and critical reflections which are contained within its full chapters, but also to say something about the conversations, debates, and thought experiments which led to them. As the first edited collection in the Birmingham Centre for Media and Cultural Research book series, we as editors were keen to try and capture something of the intellectual environment from which this work emerged, and to develop an organizing structure for the book, reflecting the many voices whose ideas have gone towards shaping the chapters which constitute this collection. Over the course of a year, Centre colleagues wrote a number of short pieces that reflected on the concept of materiality and its relationship to their own work. We have included a selection of these throughout the book for two reasons. First, they serve as an organizing structure to the book, reflecting the diversity of voices whose ideas have gone towards shaping the chapters that constitute this collection. Second, many of the chapters began as short reflections on media materiality, before being expanded for inclusion here. Therefore, they are demonstrative of how a seemingly innocent engagement with a childhood radio, a gaming map or a series of photographs, for instance, can be developed into a detailed, critical interrogation of their material properties.

Media and materiality

This collection, then, aims to make the case for a greater, and arguably more plural engagement, from within the field of media and communications, with broad notions of materiality. However, in choosing *Media Materialities* as the title of this book, we recognize that the term 'materiality' comes loaded with a complex and often contested set of meanings, stemming from a variety of disciplinary approaches and perspectives. The polysemous use of the term across a range of disciplines, and indeed, often by different authors within the same discipline presents a particular challenge in developing an edited collection of this nature. The propensity for the loose or inconsistent evocation of materiality as a concept, and of its associated concepts of materialism, materialization, dematerialization, and (perhaps most questionably) that of the immaterial is problematic and must be treated critically. As Joseph Berger et al. (1972) have argued, it is difficult to build theoretical models in the absence of clearly defined and relationally situated concepts. Furthermore, and perhaps more significantly in the context of this collection, as Stuart Hall (1996: 232) has noted, the increasing adoption of the term 'immaterial' as being synonymous with 'non-physical' risks undermining the complexity of materiality within the fields of cultural production in which 'the word is [...] as "material" as the world'. As such, any discussion of 'materiality' as a singular concept must be tempered by a consideration of its broader use across a range of academic disciplines and everyday discourses.

With that in mind, before we can make a case for what a greater, and more plural attentiveness to notions of materiality has to offer the study of media, it is important to take a moment to outline exactly what we mean by materiality in the context of this discussion. Broadly speaking, materiality as it is evoked in this collection refers not simply to the physical qualities of a particular artefact, object, or space. To speak of the materiality of media is not simply to describe the physical appearance or qualities of a particular media format or device, but to engage with the relationships through which such material qualities are created and understood as meaningful within wider systems of society and culture. It is to reflect upon the power which physical tangibility affords to artefacts and spaces as sites of meaning, the 'inescapable situatedness' of human existence, and the objects and artefacts which shape and colour that existence, within corporeal experience (Kallinikos et al. 2012: 6).

It is important to note, however, that this particular framing of materiality in relation to tensions between human experience and corporeal fixities as a means of situating questions of social and cultural meaning within the physical world is far from universal within the academy. Indeed, within the field of media studies, such discussions have tended to stem from consideration of technologies of communication, and the agency afforded to such technologies to impact upon and shape what is being communicated. It has been six decades since Marshall McLuhan (1964) proclaimed that 'the medium is the message',

INTRODUCTION

suggesting that the media through which ideas are communicated and articulated hold equal, if not greater significance than the messages communicated through them. McLuhan's ideas, particularly around the agency of communication technologies and their capacity to exert influence on the social systems in which they are located, have cut to the core of materialist media theory. Contained within such debates is an underlying criticality towards assumptions that the meanings of what is communicated through technologies of mediation are purely the product of human agency or even the *predominant* product of human intentionality. Rather, the objects and artefacts which are produced and utilized within such processes point beyond themselves towards wider processes of sociality. In other words, 'materialities' in this context might be understood as the 'points in which the transition of these processes become visible and traceable, become ciphers for "materiality" as a kind of dynamic condition of existence' (Pottage 2012: 168).

The impact of McLuhan's interventions in the study of media cannot be understated, playing a substantial and extremely public-facing role in helping develop what is now understood as media and communication studies. In particular, *Understanding Media* provided a platform for the study and exploration of meaning in relation to the forms, formats, and technologies of mediation. His work demanded that critics, scholars, and others who sought to take media seriously must move beyond a narrow focus on the textual analysis of media content, and a greater sensitivity to the mediation of content through television, radio, print materials, and film. Moreover, it sought to expand our conceptualization of 'media' from a narrow range of forms and formats of content delivery and open it up to a plurality of objects and artefacts, from transportation forms such as trains and aeroplanes to clocks, and to electric light itself. For McLuhan, the message contained within any media technology can be reduced to 'the scale or pace or pattern that it introduces into human affairs' (1964: 8). In doing so, he sets the challenge for future scholars of media and communication to widen both the scope and the scale of the work that they produce and laid the foundations of much of contemporary scholarship concerned with the specificities of the forms and formats through which societal change is enacted and understood.

This is not to say that McLuhan's theoretical framing has not been subject to challenge, revision, and recontextualization over the prevailing decades. The influential work of Friedrich Kittler (1986, 1999), for instance, is critical of McLuhan's project of attempting to 'understand' media at all. For Kittler (1999: xxxix), the notion that 'the medium is the message' does not go far enough, instead stating that 'media determine our situation'. Any attempt to 'understand' media is inevitably doomed to failure, as while it may well be possible to understand the effects that media exert upon a given social system, the suggestion that we might understand media on their own terms relies upon an 'anthropocentric illusion' of meaning which stems *from*, not through, the medium in question (Kittler 1986: 166).

For Kittler, it is the technologies of media themselves which give structure to human bodies, human societies, and human agency, a theoretical position which has formed the basis of a broad range of the work which has followed it, notably, proponents of Actor-Network Theory, such as Bruno Latour (see Latour 1993, 2005) and John Law (see Law and Hassard 1999; Law and Mol 2002). Actor-Network Theory (or ANT) refers to the often-controversial branch of social and technological theory, which seeks to place the agency of 'non-human' actors at the heart of debates about science, technology, and society. The core principles underpinning ANT stem from a dissatisfaction with philosophical traditions in which objects are conceived as in diametric opposition to subjects, and where the latter is afforded primacy and agency while the former is not. Instead, ANT seeks to argue in favour of the agency of 'non-human actors' – described by Latour (1993: 13) as 'things, objects [and] beasts' – over that of other actors, taken to refer to humans, entirely symbolic entities, and entities which exist on such a scale as to subsume both human and non-human. Contained within this framing is also the possibility for what might be referred to as 'hybrid actants', or the suggestion that agency 'is not inherently either human or non-human; it is an emergent effect of the composition of humans and non-humans, or of their reciprocal engagement or co-variation as moments in the unfolding of an actor-network' (Pottage 2012: 168).

More recently, McLuhan's ideas, and their legacy within the field of media and communication studies, have been revisited and problematized from other, more humanistic perspectives. The work of Sarah Sharma and Rianka Singh (2022), for instance, highlights some of the challenges of disentangling McLuhan's work from the sociocultural assumptions and prejudices of its time. While his work 'ushered in the field of study of media *as* media', contemporary readings of McLuhan often struggle to move past the fact that his texts are 'peppered with frequent misogynistic, racist, and nonsensical commentary' (Sharma and Singh 2022: 2). In seeking to reclaim the validity and the use of McLuhan's theoretical ideas, Sharma and Singh argue for a return to the very human implications contained within his work, seeking to use the indisputably important claims contained within, while also adopting such insights to 'inspire a new critical project' which is sensitive to the implications of media theory for the subjective experience of the 'economics, politics, and bodies' that it speaks to (Sharma and Singh 2022: 2). In doing so, they note Sterne's (2011: 207) observation that we can 'honour the curiosity of scholars' such as McLuhan, whose contributions to scholarship and knowledge exist in tension,

INTRODUCTION

by current standards, with problematic personal beliefs and politics, 'without taking their findings as timeless truths'.

Media as material culture

This book, then, is not by any means an attempt to break from, or to argue in opposition to the line of materialist media theory outlined above. In taking the materiality of media as our focus, we remain indebted to the expansive work carried out by followers of the work of key scholars such as McLuhan (1964) and Kittler (1999), particularly in advancing the field beyond a preoccupation with media as purely textual and paving the way for our capacity to look seriously and critically at the significance of objects and artefacts to how we engage with and seek to understand media, mediation, and materiality. On the other hand, it is also important to emphasize that the work contained in this collection is not, necessarily, an extension of such theoretical positions either. While, as has been established, a rejection of the importance and agency of non-human things does not stand up to conceptual and critical scrutiny, attempts to *understand* our relationships with such things tend to reintroduce a humanistic dynamic into the way that we think about, describe, and debate the mediation of meaning through media forms and formats.

A core principle which underpins this collection is that the use of 'materiality' in a singular sense belies the ever-shifting nature of both the material world and the ways that we interact with it. The meaning of material things is never fixed or final, as these things themselves are constantly in motion (Hodder 2012). In turn, their social meanings remain in a constant process of negotiation and renegotiation between people, artefacts, and material spaces (see Appaduri 1986). To talk of materiality is not to speak of a fixed and stable sense of meaning, but rather of a particular set of meanings as part of a particular social system at a particular moment in time. One needs to only look as far as the polarizing political positions emerging from some of the issues highlighted above to see that material meanings are, and will remain, a contested space. As such, in this book, we seek to collectively explore, challenge, and problematize existing notions of materiality in relation to the study of media and culture from a range of perspectives which are not the focus of the kinds of materialist media theory scholarship outlined above. We seek to consider the plurality of *materialities* which emerge across the broad and variegated range of the term's use and to create spaces for conversation and debate about implications that this plurality of material meanings might have for the study of media, culture, and society.

In doing so, the broad approach which underpins this collection, and the materialities that are explored within it, has its roots in the methods and approaches of material culture studies. As we will highlight below in the outline of chapters, the authors contained within this collection employ a breadth and plurality of concepts and methods in their approach to the broad notion of media and materiality. However, these approaches are unified in their utilization of broadly qualitative approaches to researching and analyzing relationships between people and things, often drawing upon ethnographic and autoethnographic methodologies in their gathering and analysis of empirical data.

While it falls beyond the scope of this introduction to provide a full history of material culture studies – see Chris Tilley et al. (2005) and Dan Hicks and Mary Beaudry (2010) for more expansive accounts of the development of material culture studies as a field – it is important to establish here what we understand the core principles of this field to be, and to outline how we see it as useful in advancing and nuancing scholarship on media and communication. To that end, it is worthwhile to recognize the field's emergence from the disciplines of 'archaeology and socio-cultural anthropology, and especially in the place of intersection between the two: anthropological archaeology' (Hicks 2010: 25), and its subsequent garnering of interest from a broad range of 'archaeologists, anthropologists, sociologists, geographers, historians, and people working in cultural, design, and technological studies' (Tilley et al. 2006: 1). Broadly speaking, the field is concerned with the study of material 'things', with the word 'material' in material culture referring 'to a broad, but not unrestricted, range of objects', embracing 'the class of objects known as artefacts – made by man or modified by man' (Prown 1982: 2). As such, with regard to its empirical analysis, 'material culture studies involve the analysis of a domain of things, or objects, which are endlessly diverse', with its focus ranging to 'anything from a packet of fast food to a house to an entire landscape, and either in the past or in the present' (Tilley et al. 2006: 3). These approaches, rooted in anthropological study and other disciplines, do not aim to eliminate the significance of human actors, meanings, and motivations. Instead, they strive to comprehend and situate them within a broad, inclusive materiality that encompasses both the physical properties of objects and artefacts, and their relationship to human subjectivities.

As Daniel Miller (2010: 1) notes, material culture studies might be described and typified by its interdisciplinary approach, or as an 'undisciplined substitute for a discipline'. This broadness and variety of approaches are seen as being fundamental to the study of the relationship between people and material things, in that such relationships are continually changing and evolving. Chris Tilley et al. (2006: 1), for instance, observe that: 'As a field of research transcending established disciplines material culture studies are always changing and developing, redefining both

INTRODUCTION

themselves and their objects of study, cross-fertilizing various other "disciplined" ideas and influences: impure, contingent, dynamic'.

It should be noted that such an account of a research field which transcends 'established disciplines', is constantly changing and developing, and aims to constantly redefine both itself as a field of study and those objects which are studied. This description could equally and successfully be applied to the other field of study to which this collection is broadly addressed – media and communication studies; a field of study that has long been synonymous with interdisciplinary approaches (Marchessault 2014).

It is within this exciting and fertile interdisciplinary space that we believe that this collection has the scope to make a meaningful and important contribution to existing debates and approaches to understanding the relationships between media technologies, the artefacts which stem from them, and the systems of meaning that they produce. In spite of the many notable similarities with regards to interdisciplinarity of approach, and what we see as a clear opportunity for useful cross-fertilization of ideas within these two fields, it is noteworthy that the material culture of media forms and formats has been largely overlooked in the field of material culture studies. Likewise, as Tarleton Gillespie et al. (2014: 1) have previously noted, in spite of the contribution made by scholars outlined in the previous section of this introduction, 'in communication and media scholarship, the overwhelming focus has been on texts, the industry that produces them, and the viewers that consume them; the materiality of these devices and networks has been consistently overlooked'. It is not our intention here to argue against the centrality of textual meaning within the study of media and communication, nor the deep importance of the politics of representation and image which the field is built upon. Rather, in bringing together this collection, we take a similar stance to Grant Bollmer's (2019: 1) argument that attentiveness to the physical materiality of media forms and formats should be essential to any study of media, but also an understanding that such arguments should be made 'without discarding the past traditions of media and cultural studies – especially the critique of representation and identity'.

Structure of the book

As its subtitle suggests, this book is structured around three broad ways in which the changing materiality of media might be considered, understood and organized around a spectrum of physicality to ephemerality with regard to the objects of study for each chapter. Section 1 thinks through materiality from the perspective of concrete, corporeal media artefacts – the physical **form** of the objects of study, and the material meanings which extend from that form. Section 2 is concerned with **format** – books, cassette tapes, videogame materialities – and how the materialities of these formats are challenged, complicated, and arguably augmented within an increasingly digitalized media landscape. Finally, the third and final section explores media materialities from the perspective of changing meanings of places and spaces – both physical/geographic, and digital/conceptual – and the role of mediation in giving shape to otherwise **ephemeral meaning**.

In structuring the book along these lines, it is our intention to capture the complex and constantly shifting nature of material meaning in relation to the study of media. With the ever-increasing influence of digitalization upon the ways in which media is produced and consumed, this structure seeks to provoke thought, reflection, and debate around what we understand materiality to mean in this ever-changing media landscape. Starting with the stubbornly enduring material meanings of old artefacts, which arrive in the present 'bearing meanings which the distance of their travel and the manner of their acquisition have inscribed upon them' (Straw 2002: 165), the first section of this book sets out to establish the enduring significance of materiality, and the usefulness of material culture studies approaches, to the study of media.

We then move on, in Section 2, to question how such existing conceptions and experiences of media materialities might be problematized (or, indeed, reinforced) when considered in relation to the perceived (and often problematic) notion of the 'immaterial' nature of digital forms and formats. Such questions are timely ones. As Babette Tischleder and Sarah Wasserman (2015) note, contemporary experiences of media are often defined by the tensions between the perceived supersession of old forms of consumption by new ones (typified, for instance, by the shift in home media consumption from VHS to DVD to Blu-ray to digital streaming) on one hand, and the dogged tendency of the obsolete to persistently endure on the other. In addressing the overlaps, and indeed, the blurring of lines between analog materiality on one hand, and digital ubiquity on the other, this section aims to highlight the complexity of media materialities in relation to digitalization and to prompt discussion of how attentiveness to these tensions is becoming increasingly important to the study of media forms and formats.

Finally, in the third, and arguably most speculative section of the collection, we turn our attention to the role that media and mediation play in giving form to otherwise potentially ephemeral cultural meanings. This section addresses questions about the polysemy of meaning in an increasingly digitalized media landscape and a blurring of lines around what media materialities might look like now and in the future. As Leonardi (2010: n.pag.) identifies, 'in the case of digital artifacts, what may matter most about "materiality" is that artifacts and their consequences

INTRODUCTION

are created and shaped through interaction'. As digitalization, and its associated forms and formats, come to dominate the media landscape, this final section seeks to present perspectives on what materiality might look like in digital spaces and to prompt further discussion around the enduring material meanings contained within digital media formats.

Material reflections

In bringing together the chapters contained within this volume, we came to feel that the conventional structure of an edited collection was not satisfactory for the purposes that we had envisioned. For each chapter that we received and accepted for this collection, there were a great many more conversations, discussions, debates, and disagreements which cannot be adequately captured. As a result, in addition to the conventional chapters which represent the substantive output of this collection, this volume is also made up of a range of short takes, sketches, and reflections on the subject of media and materiality. These short pieces were created as part of *Material Reflections* – a year-long project which was developed by the editors to provide a route into the notion of materiality and to stimulate the ideas and discussions which culminate in this book. Colleagues from within Birmingham Centre for Media and Cultural Studies, as well as affiliates and creative practitioners, were encouraged to submit an image of an item or artefact which they closely associated with their professional, intellectual, and/or creative practice, and to reflect, in 500 words or less, upon its meaningfulness to them.

From our fairly open call for contributions, we received an incredible breadth and depth of responses. Some responses focused, as might be expected, upon objects and artefacts which relate directly to their practice as media scholars and makers. For instance, Sam Coley's reflection on his childhood radio (which formed the basis of what became his chapter in this collection) reflects upon how the format captured his young imagination and the ways in which this seemingly innocuous artefact may in fact have set him on the creative and intellectual trajectory which led him into a career as an award-winning radio documentarian. Likewise, Chris Mapp's contribution, which is reprinted as part of section two of this collection, reflects upon the significance of a single patch-lead to his practice as an experimental musician working in the field of improvised performance, and the options, opportunities, and possibilities that such physical connections represent.

Others approached the brief in a different way. Hilary Weston Jones's contribution, which features in the first section of this book, reflects upon the personal significance of a seemingly unremarkable plastic calculator, and the role that it played in her attempts to balance the editorial, creative, and logistical

11

demands of a career in television production. Similarly, Philip Young's short take provides a potent and emotive reminder of the personal significance that mass-produced objects can hold for us as individuals, and how the fragility and precarity of something like a CD offers a site of reflection upon our own precarity and fragility.

While these short takes provide a useful and interesting context to the research environment from which this collection emerged, their significance to the volume extends beyond the context. The purpose of this exercise was, in effect, to foster reflection upon the complex entanglements of materiality, media, and meaning that were so succinctly illustrated by the example of Nina Simone's chewing gum in the introduction of this chapter. To an extent, then, these short 'material reflections' and their inclusion within this volume can be seen as methodological, representing a particular approach to thinking through questions of materiality, ephemerality, and meaning in relation to a multitude of cultural artefacts.

The starting point for this process is to identify an object or artefact which has notable personal meaning to you. This might be an artefact which symbolizes an aspect of your professional, creative, or personal life. It may be a souvenir, memento, or other mnemonic token – something which connects you to a particular moment in time. It may even be something which, on the surface, is purely functional – a connecting cable for a piece of media technology, perhaps, or a notebook. From here, take the time to write a brief reflexive account of this artefact, and its significance to you personally. This account should be succinct (no more than 500 words), specific, and personal in nature, highlighting why you chose this artefact, what it means to you, and how that meaning is imbued upon the artefact itself through your personal relationship to it. From this process emerges the raw material through which a wider exploration of material meanings might emerge. In the same way that Ellis's (2021) work conjures a discussion of racial politics, political economies of music, and reflections on creative practice, all from a piece of chewing gum, *what might this otherwise unremarkable object have to tell us about the changing relationships that we have with material objects, mediations of meaning, corporeality, and ephemerality?*

It is from this same process of introspection, reflection, and extrapolation that the full-length chapters contained within this volume were conceived, developed, and concluded. In contextualizing these full chapters against shorter material reflections, our intention is to highlight the parallels of thought, argument, and meaning that exist between succinct acts of reflection on one hand, and extended chapters of critical, empirical, and theoretical discussion on the other. In approaching each section of the collection, and in reflecting upon the relationship between sections, we encourage the reader to consider these short material reflections not as interludes between chapters so much as illustrations, challenges, and segues

INTRODUCTION

which contextualize, extend, and augment the self-contained arguments of the chapters into the wider purpose of this collection as a whole.

Conclusions

The work collected together in this book aims to provide new perspectives on the increasingly complex relationships between media forms and formats, materiality, and meaning. These perspectives, while indebted to the work of the materialist media theories of scholars such as McLuhan (1964) and Kittler (1986, 1999), stem predominantly from an attempt to bring material culture studies concepts and methods to bear on the study of media forms and formats. Through an increased attentiveness to shifting and evolving material meanings, stemming from interdisciplinary, qualitative methods and methodologies, we believe that new approaches to understanding the changing meanings and significance of materiality as a concept in the study of media and communication can emerge.

As Susanna Paasonen notes in her conclusion to this collection, questions relating to the material meanings of media are seldom met with straightforward answers. But yet, these questions of materiality continue to matter. We believe that each of the chapters in this collection, the accompanying short takes and material reflections, and the dialogues that exist between and among them, has a significant amount to offer scholars of media and communication. It is our hope that these chapters can form the basis of the ongoing debates and discussions around the changing nature of media materialities that Passonen alludes to, and their ongoing significance within the field of media and communication studies. It is our additional hope that within these chapters, readers of this collection might, in turn, embark upon their own material reflections on the meaningfulness of media artefacts, and employ similar approaches in considering how reflexive approaches to seemingly incongruous objects might represent the starting point of more substantive explorations of the relationships between media, materiality, and meaning.

REFERENCES

Anderson, Chris (2016), 'Sonic artefacts: "Record Collecting" in the digital age', *IASPM@ Journal*, 6:1, pp. 85–103.

Appadurai, Arjun (1986), *The Social Life of Things: Commodities in Cultural Perspective*, Cambridge: Cambridge University Press.

Berger, Joseph, Zelditch, Morris, and Anderson, Bo (1972), *Sociological Theories in Progress*, New York: Houghton Mifflin.

Bollmer, Grant (2019), *Materialist Media Studies: An Introduction*, London: Bloomsbury.

Coroama, Vlad C., Moberg, Åsa, and Hilty, Lorenz M. (2015), 'Dematerialization through electronic media?', in L. Hilty and B. Aebischer (eds), *ICT Innovations for Sustainability*, Cham: Springer, pp. 405–21.

Csikszentmihalyi, Mihaly (1993), 'Why we need things', in S. Lubar and W. D. Kingery (eds), *History from Things: Essays on Material Culture*, Washington, DC: Smithsonian Institution Press, pp. 20–29.

Ellis, Warren (2021), *Nina Simone's Gum*, London: Faber and Faber.

Gillespie, Tarleton, Boczkowski, Pablo J., and Foot, Kirsten A. (2014), *Media Technologies: Essays on Communication, Materiality, and Society*, Cambridge: MIT Press.

Graves-Brown, Paul M. (2000), *Matter, Materiality and Modern Culture*, London: Routledge.

Hall, Stuart (1996), 'The meaning of New Times', in K.-H. Chen and D. Morley (eds), *Stuart Hall: Critical Dialogues in Cultural Studies*, 1st ed., London: Routledge, pp. 222–36.

Hicks, Dan (2010), 'The material cultural turn: Event and effect', in D. Hicks and M. C. Beaudry (eds), *The Oxford Handbook of Material Culture Studies*, Oxford: Oxford University Press, pp. 25–98.

Hicks, Dan and Beaudry, Mary C. (2010), 'Introduction: Material culture studies: A reactionary approach', in D. Hicks and M. C. Beaudry (eds), *The Oxford Handbook of Material Culture Studies*, Oxford: Oxford University Press, pp. 1–14.

Hodder, Ian (2012), *Entangled: An Archaeology of the Relationships between Humans and Things*, Chichester: Wiley-Blackwell.

Kallinikos, Jannis, Leonardi, Paul M., and Nardi, Bonnie A. (2012), 'The challenge of materiality: Origins, scope, and prospects', in P. M. Leonardi, B. A. Nardi, and J. Kallinikos (eds), *Materiality and Organizing: Social Interaction in a Technological World*, Oxford: Oxford University Press, pp. 3–24.

Kittler, Friedrich (1986), 'A discourse on discourse', *Stanford Literary Review*, 3:1, pp. 157–66.

Kittler, Friedrich (1999), *Gramophone, Film, Typewriter* (trans. G. Winthrop-Young and M. Wutz), Stanford: Stanford University Press.

Krohn-Gimberghe, Lukas (2020), 'The dematerialization of music: How streaming technology impacts music production and consumption', in M. Tröndle (ed.), *Classical Concert Studies: A Companion to Contemporary Research and Performance*, London: Routledge, pp. 296–308.

Latour, Bruno (1993), *We Have Never Been Modern* (trans. C. Porter), Cambridge: Harvard University Press.

Latour, Bruno (2005), *Reassembling the Social: An Introduction to Actor-Network Theory*, Oxford: Oxford University Press.

Law, John and Hassard, John (1999), *Actor-Network Theory and After*, Massachusetts: Blackwell.

Law, John and Mol, Annemarie (1995), 'Notes on materiality and sociality', *The Sociological Review*, 43, pp. 274–94.

Leonardi, Paul M. (2010), 'Digital materiality? How artifacts without matter, matter', *First Monday*, 15:6, https://doi.org/10.5210/fm.v15i6.3036.

Magaudda, Paolo (2011), 'When materiality bites back: Digital music consumption practices in the age of dematerialization', *Journal of Consumer Culture*, 11:1, pp. 15–36.

Marchessault, Janine (2014), 'Media studies as interdisciplinary exploration', *Journal of Visual Culture*, 13:1, pp. 82–84.

McLuhan, Marshal (1964), *Understanding Media: The Extensions of Man*, London: McGraw-Hill.

Miller, Daniel (2010), *Stuff*, Cambridge: Polity.

Pottage, Alain (2012), 'The materiality of what?', *Journal of Law and Society*, 39:1, pp. 167–83.

Prown, Jules D. (1982), 'Mind in matter: An introduction to material culture theory and method', *Winterthur Portfolio*, 17:1, pp. 1–19.

Sharma, Sarah and Singh, Rianka (2022), *Re-Understanding Media: Feminist Extensions of Marshal McLuhan*, Durham: Duke University Press.

Sterne, Jonathan (2011), 'The theology of sound: A critique of orality', *Canadian Journal of Communication*, 36, pp. 207–25.

Tilley, Chris, Webb, Keane, Küchler, Susanne, Rowlands, Mike, and Spyer, Patricia (2006), 'Introduction', in C. Tilley, K. Webb, S. Kuchler, M. Rowlands, and P. Spyer (eds), *Handbook of Material Culture*, London: Sage Publications, pp. 1–6.

Tischleder, Babette and Wasserman, Sarah (2015), 'Introduction: Thinking out of sync', in B. Tischleder and S. Wasserman (eds), *Cultures of Obsolescence: History, Materiality, and the Digital Age*, Cham: Springer, pp. 1–17.

SECTION 1

FORM

Introduction

This first section of the book concerns itself with questions of form, or, the meanings, ideas, and practices inscribed upon physical objects. At a moment in time which is increasingly defined by a focus on digital technologies, cloud-based content, and access-over-ownership, this section takes the physical form of media artefacts as its focus. In doing so, it aims to remind us of the ongoing significance of form and physicality to our understanding of the media world, and the opportunities that attentiveness to such corporeal qualities offers to those studying media and its evolving meanings.

As Jannis Kallinikos (2012: 68) notes, the dominant associations technology invokes still stem from inherent materiality, in which 'material embodiment is essential to technology'. The functions that an artefact embodies, whether by design or by cultural redesignation, are inevitably 'conditioned by [its] material constitution' (2012: 68). This opening section of the book offers a range of perspectives on the continuing centrality of these 'material constitutions' of form in relation to media technologies and explores them in the context of a range of conceptions (and *re*-conceptions) of media forms and mediated meanings.

We begin this opening section with Lee Griffiths's short reflection, and fittingly, with a blank page. Lee considers how his ever-present notebook provides a space for reflection and idea collection. Although Lee rarely refers to his notebook(s), he acknowledges how the act of collecting thoughts gives him time to be thoughtful. Following on from this, in Chapter 1, Oliver Carter takes an object-based material culture approach to study an illicit pornographic 8mm film titled

Chez M. Pirgeon. Carter questions whether the material properties of such orphaned films might reveal more about the clandestine conditions in which they were produced. From the study of a pornographic artefact, we move to the subject of games, with Harrison Charles recalling his Game Boy Color, the memories it evokes of his childhood and particularly his grandmother, while Nick Webber's chapter explores role-playing game character sheets and how these player-created materials serve as a document of gaming, chronicling experience and recording past.

If the gaming sheets help players make sense of their past adventures, Hilary Weston Jones briefly contemplates how her valued calculator evokes memories of her career working in television, helping her 'make sense of the chaos' that often enveloped her. The final chapter in this section focuses on another physical object, this time a transistor radio. Radio producer Sam Coley investigates the origins of his first radio, looking at the relationship between the physicality of radio and its intangibility. Coley interrogates radio's technological shift, being incorporated by other media technologies, with companies drawing on radio's nostalgia to influence the design of new devices. We conclude the section with E. Charlotte Stevens's engagement with 'letterzines', or 'letters of comment', that serve as traces of viewers' historical encounters with television shows. Stevens sees such materials as providing a window into the material realities of pre-digital television.

REFERENCE

Kallinkos, Jannis (2012), 'Form, function, and matter: Crossing the border of materiality', in P. M. Leonardi, B. A. Nardi, and J. Kallinikos (eds), *Materiality and Organizing: Social Interaction in a Technological World*, Oxford: Oxford University Press, pp. 67–87.

Short Take 1

My Notebook

Lee Griffiths

Figure ST.1 shows my notebook. I take it with me whenever I attend a lecture or seminar, and when I am listening to somebody presenting at one of these events, I take notes. The reason I take notes though is not in order to remember. My notebook does not function as a technology of memory, intended to preserve with perfect fidelity those thoughts which I might want to recall at some point in the future. I hardly ever look at the notes I have taken.

When I am listening to somebody present their research, I am often swept up in the current of their narrative. I can be struck by intuitions and impressions about what is being said, but so slowly can thoughts emerge as coherent that they risk

FIGURE ST.1: One of Lee's notebooks. Author's own image.

being lost even before they have begun. Whatever intuitions and impressions I am grasping at, simply do not matter. It takes time to make a thought matter.

This is where my notebook comes into the picture. It takes time to write down an idea, and for me, the time that it takes is what makes it useful. Momentarily, I can tune out of the speaker's rhythm and negotiate a new tempo with the page. It takes time to write down an idea and we can therefore understand it as a process, but it is also spatialized and we can therefore understand it as a product. In fact, the writing wavers indeterminately between process and product to the extent that any distinction between the two would be artificial. It is both the doing and the being of thought.

So, it is with and through the time–space of my notebook that my intuitions and impressions come to matter. They make differences *in* matter (the physical matter of the pen, paper, and ink) and they make differences *that* matter (differences that have value). It is through the articulation of thought via the written word (along with whatever the thought loses or gains in the process and product) that I am able to listen to myself. And what I am listening for is coherence.

If I am lucky, what emerges is a coherence between what the speaker has said, my impressions of what has been said, what is written down, and some possible future in which the thought can be made useful. Often what emerges does not make sense of these connections. Sometimes what emerges makes no sense at all. What is important though, whether the writing makes sense or not, is that I have had the time and the space to listen.

1

Investigating the Illicit:
The Material Traces of Britain's
Early Trade in Obscene 8mm Films

Oliver Carter

Introduction

Until the year 2000, it was a criminal offence to distribute hardcore pornography in Britain. Despite this, a thriving under-the-counter economy existed, producing and distributing a range of illicit materials via the bookshops of Soho and mail-order businesses, as well as exporting to Western Europe and North America. One of the most in-demand artefacts in the 1960s and early 1970s were hardcore pornographic 8mm films. These were known amongst the trade as 'rollers' because of how the reels 'rolled' when played through a projector. With their low production costs, entrepreneurs were willing to risk fines and possible imprisonment for high profits. Before 1972, this economy was underwritten by an alliance between pornographers and the Metropolitan Police's Obscene Publications Squad. 'The Dirty Squad', as they were colloquially known, were as entrepreneurial as the pornographers. In the 1950s, they introduced an informal 'licensing system' for pornography entrepreneurs, enabling them to do business and profit from their practices by taking regular bribes (Cox et al. 1977; Tomkinson 1982). Because of this, much of the trade became concentrated to Soho, London.

Following a crackdown on the illicit trade in 1972 and the police corruption that surrounded it, the production and distribution of rollers in Britain increasingly dwindled, as imports from Scandinavia took over. Today, rollers serve as artefacts of this forgotten economy of media production that emerged in the permissive era of the 1960s, when discourses of sex and sexuality suddenly became prominent in British popular culture (Mort 2010). Many of these materials have been lost to time, ending up in a landfill after being found in the loft of a dead relative or simply discarded as a piece of valueless ephemera. They predominately reside in personal collections and occasionally appear on auction sites such as eBay. Researching this once illicit enterprise is therefore challenging, with few formal archives to draw on; a common issue faced when studying pornography's history (Williams 1989; Dean et al. 2014). While informal online archives exist, such as *Vintage Erotica*, offering digital downloads of these orphaned films (Church 2016: 37), their remediation as digital files ignores their characteristics as physical material objects. Haptically engaging with the 8mm film itself can offer hints to their clandestine origins. For instance, markings on the film might indicate how they were developed and printed. Sometimes it is even possible to roughly locate and date a roller by identifying its film stock (Bolt-Wellens 2021). Furthermore, their packaging shows how they were distributed, occasionally containing handwritten prices. In this chapter, I draw on an object-based analysis of one specific roller titled *Chez M. Pirgeon* alongside ethnohistorical research to demonstrate how the material properties of British 8mm hardcore pornography reveal more about how these illicit artefacts were likely produced, distributed, and consumed. I suggest that such an approach is productive when attempting to uncover hidden enterprise cultures and the origins of clandestinely produced media materials.

Pornographic materials

The concept of materiality ideally lends itself to studying the history of pornography. As Elena Gorfinkel (2019: 9) recognizes,

> the texts and objects that go under the banner of adult film and media are continually inscribed by material processes: historically marked as obscene; subject to censorship, regulation, redistricting, zoning; proscribed by formats and obsolete platforms as well as drivers of new technological modes.

Particular interest has been placed on the textual distinctiveness of pornographic films. For instance, when discussing the bootleg histories of American home video, Lucas Hilderbrand (2009) notes how both hardcore and softcore pornography was regularly bootlegged and illicitly distributed amongst informal networks. He argues that traces of such illicit practices are apparent in the image of the bootlegged porn videos, as the degeneration of an analogue leaves its visual mark in varying ways and becomes evidence of the video's 'inherent vice'. Therefore, such materials are easily identifiable due to these imperfections. Similarly, in his exploration of the remediation of vintage pornographic films, David Church (2016) posits that materiality plays a vital part in their enduring appeal. He shows how material processes inform not only how adult films move from initial release to concealment are censored and preserved but also their eventual rediscovery via boutique home video releases.

Debates around porn's materiality extend to different forms of distribution. For example, in their analysis of two independent print magazines – a queer feminist porn magazine named *Ménage à trois* from Finland and the 'sexual curiosity' magazine *Phile* from Toronto, Canada – Daniel Cardoso and Susanna Paasonen (2021) consider the significance of these physical artefacts in the context of the increasing immateriality of pornography following the digital turn. They believe that their materiality 'helps anchor and amplify their artistic value and potential while their ethos of production signifies their authenticity' (13). By offering an alternative to the mainstream representation of pornography, *Ménage à trois* and *Phile*'s 'materiality of printed, glossy, pages' ascribe value to diverse sexualities and become key central to their economic survival.

Conversely, Helen Wickstead (2020: 1) gives attention to older examples of illicitly produced British pornographic magazines. Wickstead explores the 'Soho Bible' or 'Soho Typescript', which she describes as 'handmade obscene books produced in the 1950s and 1960s' that were distributed in Soho's bookshops. Taking an archaeological and ethnographic material culture studies approach, Wickstead engages with a sample of Soho Bibles and considers how they were likely produced and circulated amongst Soho's alternative economy of hardcore pornography. She notes how 'material culture studies encourages specialists to pay attention to the idiosyncratic detail of individual examples, comparing these tiny clues with their knowledge of a corpus of objects', noting how a series of pen markings on a number of Soho Bibles added valuable context. Alongside her analysis, Wickstead draws on semi-structured interviews to further understand their illicit origins, speaking with a distributor of Soho Bibles and someone involved in their production.

This chapter aims to build on such debates around pornography's materiality by showing how engaging with one short illicitly produced hardcore film can provide a further understanding of the manufacture and distribution of such materials. It uses ethnohistorical research conducted over seven years. This comprises of 42 primary interviews with those involved in Britain's economy of hardcore pornography production from the 1960s to 2000s alongside archival research, including newspaper and magazine articles, legal documents, and artefacts produced by pornographers. I draw on this here to contextualize my interaction with a film titled *Chez M. Pirgeon*, interrogating its material properties. I begin by recounting how this film came into my ownership via a collector, illustrating how rollers currently circulate and were once distributed. Through examination of the film, I then consider how it was likely processed and printed onto 8mm by its producer. Finally, I discuss digitizing *Chez M. Pirgeon* and analyze the resulting digital file to reveal further evidence of its production. The chapter concludes by placing *Chez M. Pirgeon* alongside other rollers that were likely produced by the same film-maker, as I consider how material approaches to historical pornographic artefacts might help reveal traces of clandestine trade.

A smell of illicitness

The smell of dampness permeated from the box housing a number of rollers. This odour was now all too familiar. It had come to be indexical of the places where these films were likely stored. Rather than being openly displayed on a bookshelf or in ideal archival conditions, the musty scent suggests that it had been hidden from view, somewhere discreet; possibly in a draughty loft, a box in a garage, or even a garden shed. The damp smell connotes illicitness. I take each film out of the box. 'Keith', the seller of the film, warned me that they were not presented in their 'original boxes'.[1] He told me that the film was part of a bulk purchase from a dealer who regularly attends film fairs, where 8mm, Super 8, 9.5mm, and 16mm films are traded amongst collectors. According to 'Keith', rollers are not openly displayed at such events and are only usually available under the counter:

> the fella I bought these off usually has a plastic shopping bag full of these [rollers]. We call them 'Westerns', so no one knows what they are. You never know what's in one of his bags, but that's part of the fun.
>
> ('Keith' n.d.)

Considering that rollers were sold in such clandestine circumstances in the 1960s and 1970s, normally in the back rooms of Soho bookshops, it seems ironic that they continue to be exchanged covertly through such informal trading networks.

After viewing his recent purchases, 'Keith' had decided to sell some of them. He prefers films that are complete, in good condition, boxed, and appeal to him on a personal level, particularly his nostalgia for the 1960s and 1970s. On my second meeting with 'Keith', he recalled a screening of rollers at his factory workplace in the early 1970s, where his manager would project the films to the predominately male staff. Such informal showings were common throughout the 1960s and 1970s, with some dating back to the 1940s.[2] The moralistic British tabloid press termed them 'blue movie shows', and numerous articles report on the findings of investigative journalists who infiltrated these spaces. Thomas Waugh (2001: 280) speaks of the 'homosocial' spaces where stag films – an American colloquial term for rollers – were shown. In a British context, these would be factories, public houses, private dwellings, and even the police station, as was revealed in an anti-corruption investigation into the Metropolitan Police's Obscene Publications Squad (Tomkinson 1982). Drawing on his own experience of participating in a group viewing of a stag film, Waugh (2001: 280) mentions how spectators re-enacted 'some of the basic structural dynamics of the patriarchy, namely, the male exchange of women, in this case the exchange in fantasies and images of women'.

Evidently, the factory screening was a formative experience for 'Keith'. It seems that his collecting of rollers is a sort of nostalgic practice. He often remarks on the how dress and styles of the performers hark back to his younger years. Knowing that I was writing a book about rollers (Carter 2023), 'Keith' contacted me to see if I would be interested in buying his unwanted films. As Peter Alilunas (2016: 29) notes, scholars of adult film rely on costly collectors' networks to build their own corpus due to a lack of formal archives. The film I held in my hand – *Chez M. Pirgeon* – arrived with four others. On examination, all appeared to be examples of unbranded rollers. More often than not, these turn out to be orphaned films, having no indication of a producer or a distributor. Such rollers usually originate from the very early 1960s; a period when British pornographers began to make hardcore films, eventually producing 'the majority – and the best – of the foreign stag material available in the American commercial market' by the late 1960s (Knight and Alpert 1967: 186). This is reinforced by Joseph Slade (2000: 120), who observes that British producers 'outpaced' American stag makers at the start of the 1960s.

I take *Chez M. Pirgeon* out of its makeshift container and ponder how it might have been originally packaged. Was its box lost over the course of 60 years, or did it have no box or branding? If it was the latter, it is plausible that this film was produced in the early 1960s when rollers were released without branding to avoid associating them with a specific producer. As this was a criminal enterprise, outing oneself as a maker of hardcore pornography would have been unwise. Evan 'Big Jeff' Phillips is regarded as the first person to brand rollers, introducing the label 'Climax' – also known as Climax Films and Climax Original – in 1966. In a police interview, fellow roller maker Martin Granby described the impact Phillips's decision to brand had on the economy, changing the way pornographers chose to package their films:

> At first, it was sufficient for me to just have the spool with the film on it, but very shortly after Jeff Phillips came on the scene, he was a very big-time operator, and he marketed his films in boxes with proper titles. I, of necessity, had to compete with him and box and title my films.[3]
>
> (Granby n.d.)

Phillips opted for a more distinctive alternative. Rather than a generic cardboard box, either blank or with a photograph of a scene from the film glued to its front, Climax boxes had an orange and off-white colour scheme, with the branding at the top of the box. Underneath was a glued on photograph, with the title of the film Letraset onto it. More information about the film is printed below, with the text 'black and white' on the left-hand side and the format and length of the film on the right. When issuing films in colour, Phillips chose a green-coloured box. The use of brightly coloured packaging was likely done to make Climax's rollers stand out amongst others in the backrooms of Soho's bookshops, making them distinctive and easily identifiable.

My intuition tells me that *Chez M. Pirgeon* is from the early 1960s and was released unbranded. Such films had small print runs – often no more than 50 – due to the difficulties of processing and printing. Therefore, it is remarkable that many of these films have survived. I question how this film might have travelled. Was it originally purchased from a Soho Bookshop or through mail-order? How did it end up in the carrier bag 'Keith' bought at the film fair? A piece of paper with the words '*Chez Madam*' is loose in the container, scribbled by 'Keith' to help him identify this unbranded roller. I take the film out of its scratched, plastic makeshift container, inspecting the reel for any obvious sign of damage or repair. I also smell the film to see if there is a scent of vinegar, which can signify chemical deterioration. This easily spreads to other films, so it is critical to determine whether the film is 'safe' to store. Fortunately, the only odour here is the all too familiar musty scent of illicitness. My attention now turns to physically examining the film to determine if there are indications of how it was processed and printed.

Processing and printing

The Gallic-sounding title *Chez M. Pirgeon* likely disguises its British origins, associating itself with France, which made many pornographic films (Tachou 2013) that were regularly smuggled into Britain. Like most rollers I have seen, *Chez M. Pirgeon* is around 200 feet in length, black and white, and printed on standard 8mm film. A once-popular small-gauge film format for amateur filmmaking enthusiasts from 1932 onwards, 8mm film was also used to commercially release films for viewing in the home (McKee 1978: 105). I put on my white cotton gloves to touch the film, preventing any grease from my fingers marking the film. I have no formal training in handling film, acquiring skills along the way and being guided by experienced collectors and filmmakers. My white cloth-covered index finger and thumb take the end of the film and gently unravel the first few inches so that I can identify the film stock and see if any unique markings might offer further signs of its origin. The brand 'Ilfords' is clearly printed, meaning that the film stock originated from Ilfords, a high-street photography and film retailer. With a branch in Soho, Ilfords was often the favoured outlet for roller makers, such as Mike Freeman who confirms this in his self-published autobiography *I Pornographer* (2011), as does Evan Phillips in a police interview following his arrest.[4] Therefore, *Chez M. Pirgeon* was likely produced, or at least printed, in Britain.

Holding the film next to a light, I see a handwritten title card naming the film and observe that it is well worn, with each scratch, mark, and line being a trace of previous screenings and possibly poor handling by its owners. Unlike digital film, analogue film degrades every time it is screened. An inexperienced handler, and a cheap projector, may add to the damage. It seems increasingly likely that the film was printed in the early 1960s using informal means. Commercial and amateur 8mm films were typically processed in film laboratories. With the distribution of hardcore pornography in Britain being prohibited under the Obscene Publications Act 1959, using formal film laboratories to process rollers was risky; an attentive lab technician might spot the naked bodies and inform the police. Many labs opened 24 hours, and some roller makers, like Evan Phillips, found an amenable technician who worked nights to process their films, paying extra money for the trouble. Others set up their own informal laboratories. In an interview, Mike Freeman recalled how he initially struggled to develop his 8mm films, unable to get the correct mixture of chemicals.[5]

Others sought the services of informal film laboratories known as 'garage labs'. One early roller maker named 'Derek' told me how he used a garage lab in the back of a London shoe shop to process and print his films.[6] Here, a semi-professional device known as a Todd Tank developed the films. Working in a darkroom with safe lighting, the film – usually 16mm as most rollers were shot on this format, then reduced to 8mm for distribution – would be wound onto a spiral drum sitting in a chemical bath. Rotating the drum, either by hand via the attached handle or an electric motor, the film dipped into the developing chemicals for a designated amount of time. After that, the chemicals were replaced with water to rinse the film. If reversal film was being used, a hardening solution was required, followed by a water rinse. Then, it was time for bleaching solution, a further rinse, and another exposure to white light. An additional run through developing fluid was necessary, followed by a rinse, fixing solution, and a final six water rinses. While on the drum, the film would be left to dry before being wound and ready for printing. R. H. Bomback (1956) states that this precise and lengthy process took at least 60 minutes, depending on the film's length.

Such amateur techniques were not without fault and involved trial and error, with the developer having to learn from their mistakes to avoid repeating them. According to Bomback, the following faults were likely:

- picture too light or too dark (development too long or too short);
- yellow stain (bleaching not fully completed);
- blisters or recirculation (solutions not at the right temperature);
- bleaching too slow (incorrect solution);
- streaky picture (drum rotation too slow);

- drying spots (film not dried properly);
- buckling of film (film stretched during processing or too much heat used to dry the film);
- negative density wrong (film underexposed).

Faults like these are often present in the prints of some rollers, with the imperfections being transferred from the developed negative, revealing the types of processes used. For instance, a decent-quality print suggests a professionally processed roller. This is evident in later titles, implying that a professional processing machine may have been used, possibly via an 'out of hours' service at a formal film laboratory. Specialist shops and the classified sections of amateur film magazines, such as *8mm Magazine* and *Amateur Cinema World*, sold processing equipment like the Todd Tank. Alternatively, they could be handmade, as instructions given in the 13 April 1961 issue of *Amateur Cine World* show.

After developing the negative, a contact printer was needed to duplicate the films. These could also be purchased through mail-order companies or be homemade. Another option was to buy a semi-professional device. In an interview, Freeman told of how he imported two Uhler-branded optical printers from the United States, costing $950 each; a considerable expense in the late 1960s. The Uhler enabled a contact print to be made from the camera negative, positive, or inter-negative. The two films would be sandwiched together and run through the device, the master printing onto the film. With most rollers being shot on 16 mm and printed on 8mm for wider distribution, optical reduction was necessary. An Uhler-type device was beneficial as it could optically reduce 16mm film to 8mm for printing or, as was more common, reduce 16mm to dual 8mm. This would then be split into single 8mm for distribution, saving money and accelerating the duplication process. Imperfect devices like the Uhler were convenient solutions to the limitations of processing and printing rollers. Retired film laboratory technician Brian Pritchard (2019, 2021) described them as 'fast', but they 'did not give the finest quality'.[7] For example, the film could slip during the duplication process, creating an imperfect print. Pritchard pointed out that quality probably meant little to people producing rollers; they were likely more concerned about profit and supplying a demand for hardcore pornography. Like processing faults, printing errors can also be identified, especially when viewing rollers.

Digitizing and viewing

I am eager to view *Chez M. Pirgeon* to see whether it might give further indication of how it was made, but before I do, the film must be cleaned and inspected for damage. Film cleaning is a controversial subject amongst film enthusiasts. Posts on online fora recommend various solutions – some professional, some non-professional – through to suggesting that film should not be cleaned if the owner is too precious about causing further damage to the film. I have two approaches: using a clean cotton cloth with a minimal application of either de-ionized water – recommended by an archivist from the British Film Institute – or a professional solution sold by a film laboratory based in the Netherlands. The latter option is preferred as it evaporates quickly, shortening the drying time. I attach the film and an empty reel to the arms of an 8mm editor, holding the cotton cloth gently around the film and using the arms of the editor to wind it through. Every few feet, I stop and examine the cloth to check for any accumulated debris or grit that might scratch the film as it winds through. If the cloth is too dirty, I use a new section to avoid further grime getting on the film. It is slow, careful work. As my gloved fingers hold the cloth against the film, I also attentively study it for any potential damage that could hinder the scanning process. For this, I rely heavily on the sense of touch, waiting to feel any imperfections, such as broken sprockets, edits, burns, and breaks. I keep note of any damage so that it can be repaired, although I am conscious that any film physically cut out is gone forever, further reminding me of the precarity of this material. Fortunately, *Chez M. Pirgeon* is in surprisingly good condition for its age.

Now digitizing can begin, using a basic high-definition film scanner. Scanning is preferential to viewing through a projector, as it places less stress on the film. Film scanners are specialist pieces of equipment, with semi-professional devices costing around £10,000. Domestic scanners such as mine are much cheaper but less reliable. However, they produce a compressed high-definition digital file where each frame can be closely examined. This is particularly helpful with rollers, as small details in the frame become detectable, presenting further clues. Wearing cotton gloves, I mount *Chez M. Pirgeon* onto the scanner. Once the scanner is turned on, I adjust the frame to capture the full image. Interestingly, the framing of each roller differs, perhaps further evidence of the inconsistencies in processing and printing. Scanning begins, taking approximately two hours for a 200-foot roller. Inconsistencies in the film can result in the scanner stalling, potentially damaging its motor. Therefore, the process has to be closely monitored. Fortunately, *Chez M. Pirgeon* scans smoothly with no stops and is automatically saved on the machine's storage card for transfer to a computer.

I load the scan into an editing programme and begin going through the digitized film. *Chez M. Pirgeon* opens with a handwritten title card. Early rollers tended to use such a technique before being replaced with title card systems by 1967, yet another indication of its era. The high-definition scan highlights the softness of the print, implying this may not have been duplicated from the negative, but a lower-generation source. Because of this, it is difficult to make out the title of the film. The hard-written card appears to read '*Chez M. Pirgeon*' (see Figure 1.1). I send a screenshot of the card to a native French speaker, who translates it as *Mr – or Mrs – Pirgeon's House*. The opening scenes of rollers regularly feature print damage, and this is evident in *Chez M. Pirgeon*. Scratches and other imperfections dance across the black-and-white picture, traces of previous owners running the film through a projector. A long shot shows a brunette female sitting on a living room sofa. Also, there looks to be some chemical damage present in the source, as I could not see or feel any imperfections in the print I scanned (see Figure 1.2). Might this be evidence of its clandestine roots and an error in processing, such as a blister resulting from an incorrect chemical solution, or are they drying spots? The brunette female leaves the sofa and the living room to answer the front door.

A blonde female is at the door. In a medium shot, the blonde hands the brunette a card; they both study it. The film cuts to a closeup of the blonde's smiling face, demonstrating that the filmmaker has, at least, some basic understanding of film technique. The camera pans to a close of the brunette, gesturing to the blonde to enter the house. It now cuts to the living room, with a medium shot of the blonde walking into the living room, looking around. The camera follows her as she removes her coat and sits next to the brunette. They begin to look at a series of Soho Postcards. Roller makers often took photographs during production. These would be printed and sold in packs of five as 'Soho Postcards' in Soho's bookshops. Enterprising producers extended their range of

FIGURE 1.1: *Chez M. Pirgeon*'s handwritten title card. Author's personal collection.

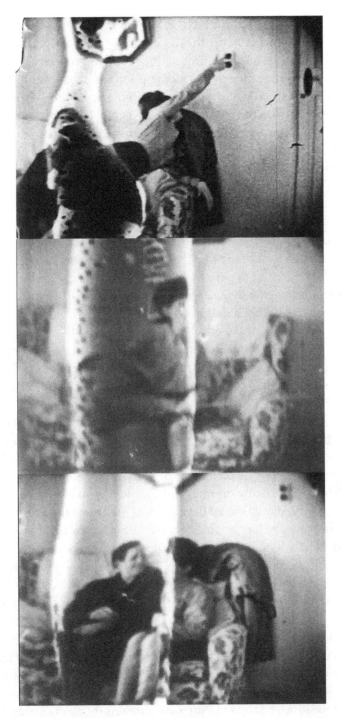

FIGURE 1.2: *Chez M. Pirgeon*'s processing errors? Author's personal collection.

artefacts to make typescripts, known in the trade as 'Soho Bibles' (Wickstead 2020). The film cuts to a closeup, the camera captures the blonde examining the photographs; the softness of the print makes it difficult to make out the content. However, it is clear that they are hardcore photographs. After giving back the photos to the brunette, the film cuts to a medium shot of both women standing up. The brunette lifts up the blonde's skirt, revealing stockings, suspenders, and underwear. The blonde twirls as the brunette inspects her, then leaves the room.

Shortly after, a male and another female wearing a headscarf enter the room. The male hands the brunette what appears to be a payment, which she places in her bra. After two awkward edits, the couple exit the living room, cutting again to a low-angle shot of them walking up the stairs as the man gropes her behind. They kiss and embrace on the landing, and the film cuts back to a medium/long shot of the brunette sitting on the sofa, looking at the Soho Postcards. It cuts to a closeup of her knees, where her hand seems to be teasing herself, and then the camera pans to a closeup of her face. Cutting to a medium/long shot, she answers the living room door to a different male and, again, they move to sit on the couch where he smokes while they look at Soho Postcards. At this point, I begin to wonder whether this is actually a roller, as there has been no 'action'. A 200-foot running timer equates to around 15 minutes at 18 frames per second. Because of this limited running time, roller producers usually had a brief, scene-setting exposition before introducing the sexual act. *Chez M. Pirgeon* differs.

The blonde re-enters the room, and the brunette introduces her to the new male. Once more, they sit on the sofa – the film begins to judder badly – and the brunette hands the male a cane. They stand up, and the male and blonde leave the lounge as the brunette directs them to a particular room. Again, the film cuts to a low-angle shot, showing the man and the blonde walking up the stairs to the bedroom. As they arrive at the landing, there is another cut to a zoomed closeup of their smiling faces before cutting to a medium shot of them inside the room, kissing. Both briefly look at the camera, appearing to take instructions from the filmmaker. The camera watches them strip, focusing closely on the blonde's body. It cuts to them on the bed. She briefly masturbates him, then there are two awkwardly quick edits to a closeup of him giving her oral sex as they move to a 69 position, then another cut to a very brief shot of the man on his back with his legs in the air talking to the blonde. These poor edits might be indicative of an amateur or semi-professional producer. Another cut – the brunette enters the frame. Suddenly, a suited man quickly walks into the shot (see Figure 1.3). Might this be someone involved in the film's production? The brunette joins the couple, giving the man oral sex, and the film cuts to a closeup to capture this moment. Abruptly, it cuts to a medium closeup of the brunette undressing, and the middle-aged, bespectacled,

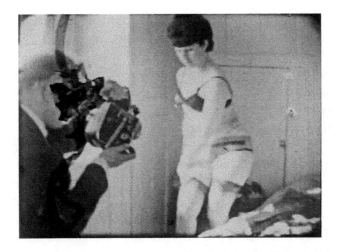

FIGURE 1.3: The mysterious Paillard Bolex operator who makes an accidental appearance in *Chez M. Pirgeon*. Author's personal collection.

suited man enters the frame from the left of the screen, operating what looks to be a Paillard Bolex 16mm camera.

Roller makers opted for this camera. Mike Freeman preferred this device over others, as did Dutch pornographer Willem van Batenburg.[8] According to Barbara Turquier (2016: 156), the Swiss-made Paillard Bolex H16 appealed to 'filmmakers working outside mainstream cinema' who 'chose the Bolex for its robustness, reliability, relative inexpensiveness, and [...] for the range of aesthetic possibilities it allowed'. It offered many advantages over other cameras, being well made and reliable, light, and usable in a range of filming conditions. A turret lens system gave three options that could be easily selected while filming. A drawback was that its hand-wound spring motor could only provide 30 seconds of continuous filming before rewinding. Eventually, Bolex introduced a motor to eradicate this. The camera could only hold 50 or 100 feet of film, allowing four minutes to be captured. As most rollers used 400 feet of 16mm film, several reel changes were necessary. The Bolex and its operator appear in the shot once again. A medium shot shows the brunette lightly caning the blonde woman's rear while she rides the male. The appearance of this mystery camera operator is significant as it suggests that this was a two-camera shoot. But why did the editor choose to leave this footage in and not discard it during editing? Was footage shot by this camera used in *Chez M. Pirgeon*, or was another softer film being made simultaneously? Still, the presence of this second camera operator suggests that roller makers were not lone operators.

After further closeups and medium shots of the performers having sex, the blonde introduces a British-manufactured Pifco electric massager (McAlpine 2012: 150). Both females use it on their bodies. More closeups and fast edits are used, but the image becomes difficult to make out due to sudden overblown contrast; perhaps another printing error? The obligatory cum shot is shown in closeup, with the man ejaculating on the blonde's breasts. Then the massager is used by the blonde to stimulate her clitoris, followed by a medium shot of them laying on the bed. The two women have their legs in the air, while the man sitting in between them holds up a card showing the text '*FIN*', and the film ends. Of the many rollers I have viewed, *Chez M. Pirgeon* is distinctive. It uses the tropes of hardcore pornography, such as closeups and the cum shot, yet it feels that the maker, or makers, of *Chez M. Pirgeon*, are seeking to achieve something akin to the cinematic form. This is evidenced by the innumerable edits and the unnecessarily long exposition, which is uncommon in rollers. On the one hand, it is a messy, disorganized film, but, on the other, there is an attempt to construct a narrative. The story is difficult to decipher, but the brunette is likely M. Pirgeon, the madam of a brothel. She recruits a blonde who has sex with a man; M. Pirgeon later joins. The purpose of the other couple is not clear, but they could be a previous visitor and another sex worker. Also significant is the appearance of Soho Postcards, suggesting that the maker of the film also produced these. This allowed such entrepreneurs to maximize the economic return from one shoot. Performers were usually hired for a set number of hours; therefore, producers looked to make the most of this time to increase their economic return, sometimes making more than one film.

Dating *Chez M. Pirgeon* is tricky. Film archivists can date certain film stocks, giving a rough estimate of when the film was distributed (Bolt-Wellens 2021). However, this may not be the same date as the film's production. Some rollers were reprinted later once initial stocks had been exhausted. Evan Phillips's label Climax is an example of this, re-releasing many of their older titles once he moved his enterprise from London to Denmark in 1969–70 and had access to better laboratory facilities. It is also feasible to date a roller using clues obtained in the film. For instance, the dress and hairstyles of the performers, the interior design of the location and cars can offer hints. Items in the frame, such as record albums, newspapers, and magazines, can also be identified via online search engines. I showed the film to Julian Marsh of the Erotic Film Society, who offered the following observation: 'I'm going off the decor – like my grandparents' council house as I remember it from the early to mid-1960s [...]. Still got that post-war utility furniture and decoration rather than the advent of modern style, which takes a hold from 1963 or 1964, I think' (Marsh 2021).[9] It is likely that *Chez M. Pirgeon* is a very early example of a commercially produced British hardcore film originating from the early 1960s.

Conclusion

In this chapter, I have attempted to show how an object-based material culture approach can be beneficial when analyzing illicitly produced media, specifically an 8mm pornographic film titled *Chez M. Pirgeon*. With later branded rollers, it is possible to obtain a wider sample of their output to reach further conclusions on their clandestine births. However, it is trickier with unbranded rollers like *Chez M. Pirgeon* as it can be difficult to identify films from the same maker, and their scarcity makes them hard to obtain. With *Chez M. Pirgeon*, there was an element of serendipity, as I quickly realized that the title card of another roller in the same package – *Lavabora* – had the same style of handwriting and a similar European-sounding title. *Lavabora* features two males and a female having group sex and is confined to one room. Compared with *Chez M. Pirgeon*, the camera is steadier, and the edits are smoother, but the image is equally soft, hinting at similar processing. This time, there is no drawn-out exposition; the performers are already on a sofa, engaging in foreplay. Like *Chez M. Pirgeon*, one of the men ejaculates onto the breasts of the female, perhaps the director's preferred cum shot? *Lavabora* seems to be a later effort from the same maker, or makers, showing an evolution in skill and an attempt to make a tighter film.

FIGURE 1.4: Title cards from *Chez M. Pirgeon*, *Hotel Sexi*, *La Dolce Vita*, and *Lavabora*. Author's personal collection.

By coincidence, I purchased another unbranded roller with a similar handwritten title card several months before. This happened to be in poor condition, having multiple repairs from previous owners, signifying that it was well used. Again, the same distinctive writing appears on a piece of paper stuck to the wall above a bed where a couple sleeps. *Hotel Sexi* is more similar in style to *Lavabora*. It takes place in one location, possibly a bedroom in the same house where *Chez M. Pirgeon* was filmed and, like *Lavabora*, has no elaborate exposition. 'Mrs Pirgeon' appears as the third female, again evidencing the link between the two titles. Once more, the print is soft, possibly a result of poor duplication. The Pifco massager reappears, and, as with the other two films, the male ejaculates on the breasts of the female; evidently the maker's signature trope.

Weeks later, I obtained a roller with the title *La Dolce Vita* from eBay. The listing had several screenshots of the film, including the title card, which showed the now-familiar handwriting style. Evidently made by the same team as the other films discussed in this chapter, *La Dolce Vita* again features 'M. Pirgeon' and the blonde female from *Chez M. Pirgeon*. It has a similar-sounding foreign title, but explicitly references the Italian movie *La Dolce Vita* (Federico Fellini 1960), hinting at an early 1960s production date. The print has greater clarity than the previous titles, lacking softness and showing better contrast, implying improved printing. However, the print is mirrored, suggesting an error in the duplication process with the master being mounted incorrectly. A diagonal black line appears halfway through, revealing yet another mistake during developing or printing. The filmmakers again use one location – a living room – and there is no lengthy exposition. Immediately, five performers – three females and two males – are shown frolicking on a sofa, participating in an orgy. *La Dolce Vita* shows a shift to a cinema verité style, although the edits are more careful than *Chez M. Pirgeon*, and the camera moves steadily and slowly. Contrasting with the other three rollers, kinkier sex acts are shown. One of the female performers has her hands tied with rope, a strap-on dildo makes an appearance, the Pifco massager is again used, and another female performer urinates into a bowl. Breaking routine, two males ejaculate on the backs of the females rather than their breasts.

As Heather Waldroup (2020: 17) observes, artefacts from the past 'tell us things if we are willing to listen (and look, and touch)'. My physical engagement with *Chez M. Pirgeon* and a brief consideration of *Hotel Sexi*, *La Dolce Vita*, and *Lavabora* demonstrates how such orphaned films carry traces of their illicit past. Whether it be an odour, markings on the film or the content itself, an object-based, material culture approach can broaden our understanding of how such marginal media artefacts are produced, distributed, and, though it has not been the primary focus of this chapter, received. However, as with Waldroup's (2020) analysis of erotic photographs and Wickstead's (2020) study of Soho Bibles, there are always 'varying degrees of unknowing' when attempting to decipher such materials, making them 'intriguing puzzles' (Waldroup 2020: 17). For instance, the question of who made these specific films remains unanswerable, although there are likely candidates.

Hotel Sexi and *La Dolce Vita* offer further clues as to when these rollers were made. Both films were printed on 'S Geveart Belgium' stock. According to Camille Bolt-Wellens (2021), Geveart Belgium merged with the film company Agfa in 1964, becoming Agfa-Gevaert. This indicates that S Gevaert Belgium stock was pre-1964, making Julian Marsh's estimate of 1963–64 a reasonable one and firmly placing these in the unbranded period of rollers. Active pornographers during this period were Ivor Cook, 'Skinny' Ken Taylor, Leonard Thorpe, and 'Derek'. 'Derek', a roller producer I briefly interviewed in 2019, claimed to have shot his films on 8mm rather than 16mm, meaning that he can be discounted. It is highly plausible that *Chez M. Pirgeon*, *Hotel Sexi*, *La Dolce Vita*, and *Lavabora* are the work of an unknown filmmaker, someone who was part of a team and honing their craft, but having difficulty processing and printing their films. Yet, *Chez M. Pirgeon* also indicates that the filmmaker produced Soho Postcards. The Kinsey Institute's listing of *Lavabora* implies that they also made Soho Bibles, pointing towards a producer heavily involved in Soho's hardcore pornography economy, creating a range of illicit commodities. This is consistent with Ivor Cook and 'Skinny' Ken Taylor, who were known pornography entrepreneurs in the early 1960s.

While it may not be possible to determine who produced these rollers, I have attempted to show the value of taking an object-based material culture approach to study illicitly produced hardcore pornography. For Gorfinkel (2018: 152), 'such close case studies can open out onto larger questions of the materiality of the film object and the film experience', and also highlight how attention to illicit films is vital to understanding '*cinema* in its totality'. The challenge here is the lack of formal archives preserving rollers, particularly in Britain. The largest collection of rollers can be found at the Kinsey Institute in Indiana, USA, which hold 367 individual titles donated by a private collector (Slade 1984: 161); the British Film Institute hold none. Through the Kinsey Institute's catalogue, Di Lauro and Rabkin's (1976) filmography, the *Adult Loop Database*,[10] access to private collections and my own attempt to construct an archive, I have identified over 1000 hardcore rollers made between the years of 1960 and 1980 in Britain (Carter 2023). I expect that there were more, but many will have been lost to time. Analyzing a larger sample of these objects, particularly from their early, unbranded period, may tell us more about how these films were produced and circulated. Furthermore, examining other illicit pornographic materials from the same period, such as Soho Bibles and Soho Postcards alongside rollers, might likely reveal how these commodities would inter-relate and crossover. Could specific styles or tropes present in these texts unearth more about their faceless producers? Without archives of these illicit materials, we will never know.

ACKNOWLEDGEMENTS
The author would like to thank Brian Pritchard, Julian Marsh, 'Philip Black', and 'Keith' for their contributions to this article.

NOTES
1. Various interviews with 'Keith' conducted on 12 September 2019 and 18 January 2021.
2. An article in the Swedish newspaper *Aftonbladet* (8 August 1937) speaks of 'illegal movie clubs' showing 'smuggled uncensored film'. It tells of how smugglers evade customs, and how audience of such show is made up of the 'curious' or 'perverts' who 'enjoy the disgusting entertainment'. They note how profitable these shows are and how the police are attempting to shut them down. Curiously, the article also alludes to the existence of 'secret studios' making pornographic films in England. It is difficult to determine the content of the films being show in these 'secret cinemas', but the article highlights that this was a longstanding practice in Britain.
3. The National Archives, UK, Director of Public Prosecutions, DPP2/5809, Virgo, Wallace Harold and others: corruption offences between 1 January 1964 and 24 October 1972.
4. See The National Archives, UK, Director of Public Prosecutions, DPP2/5773, Virgo, Wallace Harold and others: corruption offences between 1 January 1964 and 24 October 1972.
5. All information relating to Mike Freeman is taken from interviews conducted between 3 and 6 April 2016, and the first volume of his autobiography (Freeman 2011).
6. 'Derek', interviewed on 22 February 2020.
7. Brian Pritchard, interviewed on 13 December 2019 and 14 April 2021.
8. Willem van Batenburg, interviewed on 13 October 2019.
9. Julian Marsh, interviewed on 24 January 2021.
10. https://adultloopdb.nl/.

REFERENCES
Alilunas, Peter (2016), *Smutty Little Movies: The Creation and Regulation of Adult Video*, California: University of California Press.

Bolt-Wellens, Camille (2021), *Physical Characteristics of Early Films as Aids to Identification*, Bloomington: Indiana University Press.

Bomback, R. H. (1956), *Processing Amateur Movies*, London: Fountain Press.

Cardoso, Daniel and Paasonen, Susanna (2021), 'The value of print, the value of porn', *Porn Studies*, 8:1, pp. 92–106.

Carter, Oliver (2023), *Under the Counter: Britain's Illicit Trade in 8mm Hardcore Pornography*, Bristol: Intellect.

Church, David (2016), *Disposable Passions: Vintage Pornography and the Material Legacies of Adult Cinema*, London: Bloomsbury.

Cox, Barry, Shirley, John, and Short, Martin (1977), *The Fall of Scotland Yard*, Middlesex: Penguin.

Dean, Tim, Ruszczycky, Steven, and Squires, David (2014), *Porn Archives*, Durham: Duke University Press.

Di Lauro, Al and Rabkin, Gerald (1976), *Dirty Movies: An Illustrated History of the Stag Film, 1915–1970*, New York: Random House Value.

Freeman, Michael (2011), *I Pornographer*, Online: Amazon.

Gorfinkel, Elena (2018), 'Microhistories and materiality in adult film history, or the case of erotic salad', *JCMS: Journal of Cinema and Media Studies*, 58:1, pp. 147–52.

Gorfinkel, Elena (2019), 'Editor's introduction: Sex and the materiality of adult media', *Feminist Media Histories*, 5:2, pp. 1–18.

Hilderbrand, Lucas (2009), *Inherent Vice: Bootleg Histories of Videotape and Copyright*, Durham NC: Duke University Press.

Jones, Mark (2007), 'Down the rabbit hole: Permissiveness and paedophilia in the 1960s', in M. Collins (ed.), *The Permissive Society and Its Enemies: Sixties British Culture*, London: Rivers Oram Press, pp. 112–31.

Knight, Arthur and Alpert, Hollis (1967), 'The history of sex in cinema: Part seventeen – The stag film', *Playboy*, November, pp. 154–58, 170–89.

McAlpine, Katherine (2012), 'Domesticating the orgasm: The vibrator as domestic technology', *Ex Historia*, 4, pp. 147–65.

McKee, Gerald (1978), *Film Collecting*, London: The Tantivy Press.

Mort, Frank (2010), *Capital Affairs: London and the Making of the Permissive Society*, London: Yale University Press.

Slade, Joseph (1984), 'Violence in the hardcore pornographic film: A historical survey', *Journal of Communication*, 34:3, pp. 148–63.

Slade, Joseph (2000), *Pornography in America*, Santa Barbara: ABC-Clio.

Tachou, Frédéric (2013), *et le sexe entra sans la modernité: Photographie 'Obscéne' Et Cinéma Pornographique Primitif, Aux Origines D'une Industrie*, Paris: Klincksieck.

Tomkinson, Martin (1982), *The Pornbrokers: The Rise of the Soho Sex Barons*, London: Virgin.

Turquier, Barbara (2016), '"Bolex Artists": Bolex cameras, amateurism, and New York avant-garde film', in G. Fossati and A. Van Den Oeve (eds), *Exposing the Film Apparatus: The Film Archive as a Research Laboratory*, Amsterdam: Amsterdam University Press, pp. 153–62.

Waldroup, Heather (2020), 'The nude in the album: Materiality and erotic narrative', *Visual Resources*, 36:2, pp. 195–214.

Waugh, Thomas (2001), 'Homosociality in the classical American stag film: Off-screen, on-screen', *Sexualities*, 4:3, pp. 275–91.

Wickstead, Helen (2020), 'Soho typescripts: Handmade obscene books in post-war London bookshops', *Porn Studies*, 7:2, pp. 187–211.

Williams, Linda (1989), *Hardcore: Power, Pleasure, and the Frenzy of the Visible*, Berkeley: University of California Press.

Short Take 2

'Press the Start Button'

Harrison Charles

The adventure begins with a young boy, who one day travelled to a far distant land, coming across a new world for him to explore. Thanks to those before him, one person particularly, he found this utopia. He would continue his journey for many days and many nights, finding experiences that would remain with him for many years to come.

That adventurer was me. Whilst I did not find undiscovered islands or paradises, I had indeed found a new world for myself – a world for me to enjoy, to escape into. I was welcomed to this world by my grandmother, who owned an 'old' piece of hardware – the 'Game Boy Color'. Thanks to her, I have been attached to it for around twenty years. Despite not using it herself, it was something she had prepared for any of my visits when I was younger – it became a past-time, a leisure, something I enjoyed when seeing her.

The Game Boy itself (see Figure ST.2) has seen its fair share of battles in its own journey. Bumps, scrapes, drops – it has fought against them all. The compartment

FIGURE ST.2: Harrison's Game Boy. Author's own image.

that seals the batteries powering it has been broken for many years, and I remember when my grandmother and I would tape it over in order to keep it in place. It was simple but effective – and something we had to continuously redo every so often. I imagine the remnants of the original tape still exist somewhere on the object. But it was an activity me and my grandmother did together and not soon after I would rush off to my adventure.

Hours and hours would fly by, then my journey into my new paradise would end, and I would return home, back to my starting position. This was my ritual, for days, for months, for years. It was only a few years ago that I became the personal owner of the Game Boy. My grandmother knew of my attachment and had then let me live out my days exploring into my utopia in my own home, except over time it has been collecting dust on a shelf in my room – sitting there, waiting for my return.

It was only recently that I came across it once again and I realized how significant it was, and is, to me – and yet it still works perfectly. Each time I see it now, nostalgia hits and I am reminded of playing when I was young, but I am more reminded of the familial ties to my grandmother, to a time that is no longer present but still in memory. Soon after, I then discovered I had collected more similar gaming hardware over time, most, if not all, from family members. I have now, in a way, a small but meaningful archive of memories, and thanks to my grandmother's introduction, I know that to relive the pleasure of the adventure and the happiness of the nostalgia, all I have to do is … Press the Start Button.

2

On, Off, and in the Map: Materializing Game Experiences Through Player Cartography

Nick Webber

Introduction

In January 2017, game historian Dan Boggs published a post entitled 'The Oldest Dungeon Maps in D&D History' on his blog, Hidden in Shadows. The post focuses on maps produced by David Megarry *c.*1972, while a player in Dave Arneson's 'Blackmoor' roleplaying game. Bound within 'an old Chemistry notebook', these maps were, so we are told, drawn by Megarry 'from sketches made as his character H. W. Dumbo braved the depths of Blackmoor Dungeon' (Boggs 2017: n.pag.). The Blackmoor game is considered something of a precursor to 1974's Dungeons & Dragons (D&D; Gygax and Arneson 1974), one of the most established roleplaying games (RPGs) in existence and currently played by an estimated 13.7 million people worldwide in its tabletop form alone (Camp 2019). D&D emerged through collaboration between Arneson and co-creator Gary Gygax, after Arneson introduced Gygax to his game. As Boggs (2017: n.pag.) has it, Blackmoor 'sparked the creation' of Dungeons & Dragons.

For Boggs, therefore, Megarry's maps are important historical documents, worthy of close analysis, and of comparison with later versions of Blackmoor maps issued by game publisher Judges Guild in 1977. The language of the blog post acts to further establish this significance – Megarry is described as 'one of the original players in the Blackmoor campaign' (speaking to his authority), Dumbo his '5th created character' (speaking to the depth of his experience), and in a time 'before D&D existed, probably even before Gary Gygax was himself introduced to the game' (Boggs 2017: n.pag.). The post includes a detailed exploration and annotation of the maps, along with some reflection. Through Boggs's work, we can see in these maps what one comment on the post refers to as the 'prehistory' (Melan 2017: n.pag.) of a much-loved game.

In this chapter, however, I will argue that maps produced by players have a much broader significance in relation to game history and memory. Seeing the Blackmoor maps as important simply because they are old, or because they are artefacts or evidence of a teleological process which ended in Dungeons & Dragons, is to underplay their cultural significance as both part of and remnants of game experiences. While acknowledging the aura (Benjamin 1969) of Megarry's maps, and the connection to a particular time and space so important in their construction here as historical documents, we must also recognize that versions of this aura and connection might be seen in all such maps – even when not associated with a 'moment' in the history of a major international franchise, or with someone who knew its creators.

The expectation that players produce maps as they play is encoded in several generations of D&D rules: 'one player must keep track of the expedition's trek' (Gygax 1978: 106); 'one or more of the characters should be making maps, but one player must make the actual map' (Allston 1991: 5); 'someone should keep a map of the places you explore so that you know where you've been' (Tweet et al. 2003: 166). Mapping as a practice is thus embedded in D&D play but this is not a phenomenon unique to that game. Similar expectations can be seen elsewhere, for example, in game books like the Fighting Fantasy series ('make notes and draw a map as you explore' – Jackson and Livingstone 1982: 17), in Ryuutama (りゅうたま: Okada 2007), where mapping is a core mechanic of the unfolding journey, and in *The Quiet Year* (Alder 2013), described explicitly as a 'map game'. Even where games do not incorporate map-making directly into their gameplay, the desire for players to know where they have been (and, indeed, how to get back there), alongside the tendency for games to include labyrinths and mazes amongst their puzzles, has embedded mapping into game communities, both on- and offline. Videogames are littered with mechanisms which seem to demonstrate the assumption that players will have or will make maps to orientate themselves or to address particular challenges: chains of teleporters, locations which alter the direction of travel, false walls which hide the path onward, and floor traps which return players to earlier sections of the game. Even games which provide players with pre-created maps often omit important details in order to preserve a sense of discovery and surprise, leading players to add their own notes and annotations (see Figure 2.1).

Through mapping, therefore, players act to produce practical representations of game environments to orientate themselves, to solve puzzles and respond to challenges, and in many of the most discoverable cases, to aid other players. Yet these maps are not neutral documents, but instead subjective interpretations of

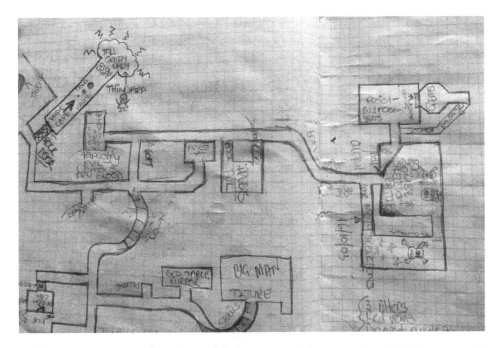

FIGURE 2.1: A player map from a Dungeons & Dragons adventure. From author's personal collection.

game spaces informed by player experiences. Each player map, physical or digital and however 'ordinary', captures – *records* – a moment of experience through what is both an act of creation and an act of witnessing, offering a specific narrative of an experience in time and space. In what follows, then, I will draw upon a range of physical and digital maps, along with resources connected with a variety of games, including rulebooks, archives, blogs, and the games themselves. I will situate these maps within discussions of materiality, agency, colonialism, and story, emerging from studies of material culture and anthropology, geography, literature, and games. In doing so, I will explore what narratives and what pasts such maps can and do record, and how they offer accounts of game experiences.

Materialities, tactility, and agency

At the centre of this exploration is the idea of materiality, or rather *materialities*. Maps of all kinds, not only those drawn by game players, are embedded within a series of relationships which relate to and produce a range of materialities. Megarry's maps have a fairly obvious materiality, or perhaps physicality, about them which has much in common with that of character sheets, something I have discussed elsewhere (Webber 2019). This is visible in the images of the maps included in Boggs's post: scanned and cropped, they convey an incomplete and organic cartography – an unpredictable work in progress – alongside something of the material qualities of these gaming remnants. Freehand pencil on squared paper, with scribbled annotations and evidence of deletions. Corridors that end in question marks, or which seem to break across the book's fold. Some pages yellowing with age. Staining and discolouration at the edges, where sheets had been either taped into the book or taped together to extend Megarry's attempts to capture Blackmoor's sprawl.

Yet the electronic mediation of these maps immediately suggests that their materiality is not limited to physicality. Drawing on dictionary definitions of 'material', Paul Leonardi (2010: n.pag.) identifies three kinds of materiality (the quality of being material), summarized as 'matter', 'practical instantiation' and 'significance'. All of these materialities can apply to maps in one form or another. For Leonardi, concerned with digital materiality, it is the latter two material qualities which are most immediately significant, in developing discussion beyond the idea that materiality bears a necessary relationship to physicality. Building on the work of psychologist James Gibson (1986), he uses the idea of affordances 'to ask whether physical matter really matters at all' (Leonardi 2010: n.pag.), highlighting the importance of ideas of use in relation to the physicality of many objects, tools in particular. For digital objects, 'what makes them "material" is that they provide capabilities that afford or constrain action'; consequently, we 'lose little by focusing on contexts in which there is no physical matter' (Leonardi 2010: n.pag.).

Yet this attempt to set physicality aside is unnecessary, and ironically serves to accord an unwarranted primacy to physical materiality. This is not to suggest that we should not sometimes focus beyond the physical when thinking about materiality, but that we should not dismiss physicality to do so. Writing about maps, Catherine Palmer and Jo-Anne Lester (2013: 237) make explicit the interconnectedness of the physical and digital here, observing that 'the fact that maps can be accessed by digital means such as the Internet, mobile phones and tablets does not take away their essential *materiality* as part and parcel of the material world' (original emphasis). Maps, then, as representations and/or mediations of places or spaces inherit something of the physicality of the location so mediated. In the West at least, and increasingly since the Enlightenment, maps are also understood principally as tools rather than, say, art (Rowland 2014: 195), returning us to ideas of use and affordance. We might also think of maps, either physical or digital, as affording a particular kind of *tactility* which supports their use, visibly reflected 'in the signs of wear that maps accumulate through interaction with their users; from misfolded maps to obliterated "You are here" symbols on street maps, rubbed off by countless fingers over time' (Kent 2019: 2).

Tactility, again, is an idea which invites us to presume a physical form, in its association with the sense of touch, and the idea that to be tactile is to be touch-*able*. Yet tactility, like materiality, can stretch beyond the physical, and the importance of interaction in creating those 'signs of wear' can help think this through. Alexander Kent (2019: 2) focuses on the importance of physical engagement 'whether we are flicking a "slippy map" on a glass screen or feeling the page of a paper atlas'; an equation which reflects the fact that our use of and engagement with digital maps is often mediated by interfaces which account for physical norms, and which we employ in physical ways. We push or pull at the map on the screen before us, resting our fingers, our mouse pointer, on locations of significance. So, tactility across these two forms suggests an invitation, or possibility, of touch – broadly understood: an invitation *to* push, *to* pull, *to* linger. Materiality, then, is what is produced through that touch, when a material is pushed against or lingered on: grain and texture, and the possibilities of the material itself.

Taking account of Leonardi's three forms of materiality, though, as we move beyond the physicality of matter we must account for materiality as 'practical instantiation' and as 'significance'. In both cases, further context benefits our analysis. The former concerns the practical, rather than theoretical, dimension of something – 'the practical instantiation of a theoretical idea' (Leonardi 2010: n.pag). The latter is concerned with matter as a verb – to matter, mattering. What does tactility look like for these materialities? What are we invited to push against, and with what? In the first instance, a practical materialization of theory offers an application of an idea. The tactility offered is intellectual, a critical engagement through which we push against an idea given form. In the second instance, we touch a mattering that contains concepts of investment, of importance, and of attachment. Here, perhaps, the tactility offered is that of an affective engagement with something meaningful, something that matters.

The materialities produced in these processes of touching might thus be characterized as physical, intellectual and/or emotional. When approaching our player maps, we must be mindful not only of these different dimensions of materiality and the ways in which the maps might afford different kinds of tactility, but also our relationship to them. Daniel Miller's (1987) theorization of materiality connects to discussions around objectification, constructing materiality as a 'quality of relationship rather than of things' (Pels 1998: 99–100), a theory that encodes 'an understanding of the assumptions about subjects and objects, and the relations between them' (Borgerson 2005: 440). Although, as Miller (2005: 14) observes, it is perfectly possible in philosophy to dissolve the dualism of separate objects and subjects, the distinction between them reflects the way that people think about the world around them. Thus, if we are to understand relationships between people and things, we must 'return to the vulgarity of our relativism and our empathy with the world [...] to talk and write in terms of subjects, objects and social relations' (Miller 2005: 45).

Understanding the materiality of maps as a quality of a subject–object relationship has two implications, however. As Palmer and Lester (2013: 3, 7) explain, maps mediate in a variety of ways: they mediate the movement of people between places and the connection between people, place and history, but they also mediate space more generally, typically through representation. In this respect, they enact the subjectivity of their creators, for example through their 'silences' (Yan 2007: 7), with the result that they objectify the spaces and places that they represent. Maps, then, are implicated in a network of material relationships, as objects themselves and as mechanisms of further objectification.

This complexity and layering of objectivity (and thus of materiality) is also reflected in the ways in which maps exercise what Latour (1996) would consider agency, through their capacity to constrain action, an issue also raised by Miller (2001) in respect of material culture. Some scholars use the idea of 'cultural techniques' (*Kulturtechniken*) to define this 'agency of media and things' (Vismann 2013: 83), focusing on the ways in which they 'supply their own rules of execution' (Young 2015: n.pag.):

> we do not choose how to open or close a door [...]. We must act according to the rules it sets out for us: push or pull, open or close. A door has agency in the sense that it structures what is possible for praxis.

This approach also attends, and connects, our conception of media to, the 'ontological and aesthetic operations that process distinctions (and the blurring of distinctions) which are basic to the sense production of any specific culture' (Siegert 2011: 14) – for example, inside and outside, matter and form or, as already suggested, subject and object (Young 2015: n.pag.). In terms of the agency of media, then, cultural techniques are seen 'to describe what media do, what they produce, and what kinds of actions they prompt' (Vismann 2013: 83).

Considerations of agency are widespread in the literature on (video)games and are often based on Janet Murray's interpretation of agency as 'the satisfying power to take meaningful action and see the results of our decisions and choices' (Murray 1997: 126). Drawing on Foucault, Rowan Tulloch (2014) has argued that agency in games is itself produced in relationship: it is not, as we might initially assume, about working in opposition to the rules or structure of the game, but rather about relationships with and between the structures of power which 'produce the possibility of agency' (2014: 345). Under this approach, conceptions of constraint are set aside – structures of power can be understood simply to afford different types of engagement, allowing particular types of agency in turn. Returning to tactility, as an affordance which invokes a sense of both action and constraint – pushing *against* – we should perhaps understand materiality as the result of a specifically tactile form of agency, produced in relationship between subjects and objects. Consequently, the narratives, pasts and experiences captured and revealed by player maps are conditioned and afforded (and thus constrained) by the relationships that produce their materiality.

Colonialism

The idea that maps objectify spaces and places has further significance here, given the longstanding association between maps and power; as Kent (2019: 2) has it 'the physical act of holding a map reinforces a sense of ownership and possession'. While a major function of maps is orientation in a range of contexts, both in games and otherwise, Sara Ahmed (2006: 113) reminds us that 'to orientate oneself by facing a direction is to participate in a longer history in which certain "directions" are "given to" certain places: they become the East, the West, and so on'. The subjectivity of these representations is then the performance of control, depicting and describing the world in a way which is suitable to the maps' creators, and presenting power relations as they see them. This is a practice of mastering space, in which maps are cultural technologies that serve as spaces of representation (Siegert 2011: 13). As Cornelia Vismann (2013: 84) observes, 'someone advances to the position of legal owner [...] by drawing a line, marking one's territory – ownership does not exist prior to that act'. Here, then, drawing a line is a cultural technique not just of property and ownership, but sovereignty itself (Young 2015: n.pag.). It is significant that Benedict Anderson (2006: 163–64) saw the map, alongside the census and the museum, as a core institution of power in the imagination of the colonial state (see Figure 2.2).

Of course, the colonial overtones of maps have not gone unremarked in studies of games, and/nor have the more generally colonialist qualities of many games which have maps and map-making at their heart (see, e.g., Lammes 2010; Lammes and de Smale 2018; Mukherjee 2017, 2018). Much of the attention of postcolonial scholarship on games has been directed at historical game series like *Sid Meier's Civilization* (1991–2016) or *Age of Empires* (1997–2020), and while reflecting on how these games encode certain colonialist assumptions, this scholarship has also identified how they create a space in which such assumptions can be challenged. Here player actions and the personalization of these experiences can produce alternate histories, and consequently maps which represent personal power struggles

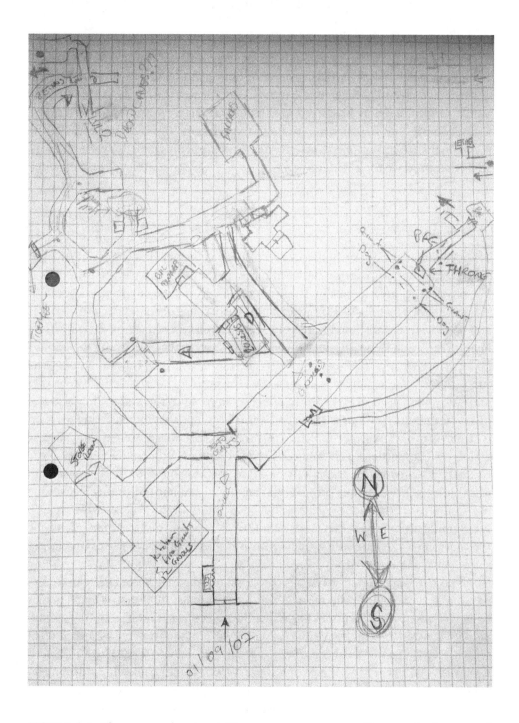

FIGURE 2.2: Player map showing rudimentary compass rose. From author's personal collection.

rather than simply reproducing and continuing colonialism (Lammes 2010: 4), along with outcomes which may reverse historic colonial relations, albeit still within the framework of a 'colonial game' (Mukherjee 2018: 517). These modes of play persist beyond historical games, of course, echoing movements in literature and other representative forms, which responded to the 'end of geography' and the disappearance of *terra incognita* from maps of the world by creating imaginary spaces in which the discoverer's fantasy, fantasies of acquisition and adventure stories could be played out in new imperial geographies (see Phillips 1997: 6–7; Rieder 2008: 31–40; Fuchs et al. 2018: 1477, 1481).

Looking at (early) RPGs like Dungeons & Dragons, these issues are pronounced and compounded by the approaches to gameplay which are assumed. As already observed, there is an expectation that players make maps, and this activity takes place alongside other aspects of play which reinforce colonial expectations within the game and which will be familiar from a range of other games as well. There is investigation and discovery of 'dangerous and forbidding areas' (Tweet et al. 2003: 164) which are then mapped, described, and often named by players, like European geographers filling in 'the hazy outlines on their sea charts and maps with names and symbols' (Phillips 1997: 6). The inhabitants of those areas are othered, and monstrous characteristics attributed to them ('a "monster," technically, is any creature that is not a player character' [Allston 1991: 152]), part of a collection of ways in which, as Antero Garcia (2017: 240–41) argues, 'racism is *built* into the D&D system'. Combat takes place against these 'monsters', and spoils are collected. Such loot, or 'treasure' is 'normally found in the lairs of monsters' (Allston 1991: 224), and 'these rewards might be ancient treasures that [player characters] have unearthed, the hoards of the villains they have conquered, or pay from a patron' (Tweet et al. 2003: 167). As Fuchs (2018: 1482) and colleagues suggest, in western fantasy RPGs, 'in order to make the unknown both known and knowable, the player character has to explore, appraise, and assess the environment, along with everything and everyone contained therein', a process of searching for exploitable resources, taking possession through imperial acts of mapping and naming, and the establishment of nodes of imperial control such as camps and trading posts.

The use of such nodes to push back the 'fog of war' now commonplace in video games reminds us that this constellation of problems is not, of course, exclusive to D&D, to tabletop games or to games which use hand-drawn maps. Fog of war serves to make the practice of searching for resources more meaningful, offers a mechanic to stage the 'discovery' of the previously discovered (such as natural wonders in *Civilization* – see Ford 2016) and allows for the 'remapping of the game space according to one's in-game affordances' (Mukherjee 2018: 508). Having been subject to adventure, then, these now-revealed video game spaces are no longer the site of the kinds of acts of representative erasure discussed by

Yan (2006: 7, 19, 23–26), in which unknown lands are populated with mermaids, cannibals, and monsters rather than polities. Now, their 'silences' convey power, not only through visual, cartographic absences but also, as Sabine Harrer (2018: 7–8) suggests of *Resident Evil V*, through a more conventional meaning of silence as the absence of sound, an absence of activity which signifies domination.

Maps and stories

It is impossible to disentangle our player-made maps from the context of their play – as is clear in the case of D&D, cartography should be understood as part of the play experience. The colonial overtones of these maps produce a particular kind of materiality, an intellectual and emotional quality to players' relationships with their ideological material. However, this is not the only quality of player-map relationships, nor is it necessarily the principal one. In *The Quiet Year* (Alder 2013), players draw a map as the game unfolds, but the focus of this map is their own community and its immediate environs: it reflects the events of the game, but without any expectation of the acquisitive exploration that characterizes D&D. Equally, while the map of a game of Ryuutama (Okada 2007) chronicles a journey of exploration, it is the journey of ordinary people, not conquering heroes. Each of these games begins with a blank map, evoking the *terrae incognitae* or outline maps so often taken as the inspiration for adventure stories, 'malleable spaces', 'in which anything seems possible and adventure seems inevitable' (Phillips 1997: 3). At their inception, then, these maps represent spaces of uncertainty and of potential, in which stories can be told.

Yet to engage with these maps after the game has ended is to understand them not as the grounds of future opportunities, but rather as the remnants of gameplay: the outcomes of choices and experiences which have already taken place. The limitations of these maps – their edges, their silences – thus circumscribe the stories which they tell; which they *can* tell. While spaces and absences on such maps might once have held the promise of further adventure and excitement, when subject to reflection and when understood as past, they speak of adventures which *did not* happen, stories which *were not* told. Here, perhaps, two forms of materiality sit in tension: engagement with the structure of the map presents an intellectual potential, in the knowledge of the possibilities the absence represents; but also an emotional recognition of the possibilities since lost. Blank spaces on player maps, therefore, are both cartographical and experiential silences. So, while other, more 'complete' maps may exist (e.g., game masters' or developers' maps), giving answer to our intellectual pressure, they are unable to provide quite the same deep, affective texture as players' own maps.

This is of particular significance in respect of video game maps, which are often shared widely as part of walkthroughs and other attempts to assist the broader player community. In this context, it is relatively simple to discover online multiple maps of the same game locations, each of slightly different aspect but all representing a tightly defined and programmed space. In some instances, archives draw such maps together, offering a variety of representational strategies, aesthetic approaches, and emphases. Perhaps the most notable is the Play Generated Map and Document Archive (PlaGMaDA 2015), created by artist Timothy Hutchings and held at The Strong National Museum of Play in Rochester, New York, and unfortunately inaccessible online at the time of writing (although a few images of maps from PlaGMaDa [2015] can be seen on the archive's homepage, and on Bittanti 2012). Elsewhere, game journalists and bloggers collate small collections of maps from those that have been made available (see, e.g., Abels 2008; Kuchera 2014a, 2014b).

The *EverQuest Map Preserve* (Prutz 2020), a database of maps of the online RPG *EverQuest* (Verant Interactive and 989 Studios 1999), collects twenty different maps of the adventure location 'Blackburrow'. These are labelled in a mixture of English and Japanese, and prioritize significantly different information: the spawn locations of specific creatures alternate with information about traps and descriptive/community names for parts of the zone ('elite ledge', 'green room'), all set against attempts to capture the extensive complexities of Blackburrow's winding tunnels. Commonalities are also interesting and the consistent labelling of a pit trap near the entrance ('Hollow Tree with Pit', 'Pitfall', 'Pit!'), even on a map predominantly labelled in Japanese, seems to speak to a desire to record, but also to prevent, a significant shared experience. In some instances, maps can be seen to be appropriated and reused – relabelled or altered, sometimes crediting the original author (e.g., a practice visible for at least two of the thirteen maps of the 'Plane of Fear').

Relatively few of these *EverQuest* maps were drawn on paper, but some evidently were – an approach to mapping a precise, digital space mirrored for other video games, for example, older 'grid' games like *Phantasy Star* (1987; Crawl 2007) or the original *Bard's Tale* series (1985–88; Klohan 2016). Increasingly, doubtless as a result of the prevalence of drawing apps and tablets, maps have been produced in a digital form – something demonstrated in the *EverQuest* archive, and which has also been afforded within certain games. The *Etrian Odyssey* series (2007–18) is notable for using the Nintendo DS/3DS touchscreen to make mapping part of gameplay, for example, to complete specific quests. One map-maker's approach during a 2013 replay of the *Final Fantasy* game series (1987–2020) offers a good demonstration of this shift in practice from paper to screen. She moves from pencil sketch maps of the Crystal Tower in *Final*

Fantasy III (1990; Auronlu 2013a) to iPad-based sketch maps of Giruvegan in *Final Fantasy XII* (2006; Auronlu 2013b), which she then polishes into a more finished form (Auronlu 2013c). Her comments on her Giruvegan sketch indicate that this is part of a longer development of her practice – 'I've mapped Giruvegan once before, but it was a messy sprawl across a few notepads'. As noted above, these interactions seem to reproduce many of the physical dimensions of our relationship with maps, suggesting that a consistent form of physical materiality is maintained between the remnants of play in the 1970s and in the 2010s (see Figure 2.3).

Importantly, again, Auronlu's maps include personally specific interventions in these mapped and remapped spaces. Her attempts to capture Sabin's 'epic journey' in *Final Fantasy VI* result in a traced copy of the game map bearing a winding red line (Auronlu 2013a) – her specific interpretation of this aspect of the story. Much like other video game maps, then, this map articulates a story – a narrative – through a general act of reproduction or repetition (of commonly held cartographic information) with a series of individualized interventions as the journey is traced. The idea that maps can tell stories through comparison is not, of course, new: not only does Boggs take this approach to understanding Megarry's maps, as I note above, but this is also the process at the heart of an established genre of cartographic work – the historical atlas. Charting the transformations of (predominantly) political and territorial relationships over time, these atlases offer a historical narrative through raw comparison, of successive representations of the same bounded space, with editorial interventions to attract our attention to particular features. The narratives so produced are of complex, messy interactions, of time and of change, reminding us that maps do not need to be blank to represent malleable spaces where adventures might happen.

Comparative storytelling can also function in another mode, of course – through the sense of a map as a living, developing document which changes as a story is told. The majority of player maps we might encounter are 'complete', in the sense that their development has ended and their stories concluded. In some instances, however, maps are captured during, or throughout, the process of a game, telling a story over time. An example can be seen in the campaign diary of the twenty-year-old D&D game Adventures in the World of Wearth (Morris 2003), where the player map for each game session has been preserved online, alongside a text record of game events. The visual narrative provided by the maps is supplemented by the text, allowing us to better understand both. The slow accretion of story demonstrated in the gradually developing map adds to our sense of its materiality: the map not only spatializes the narrative for us, moving our sense of this tale beyond textual abstraction but also provides a sense of granularity, or

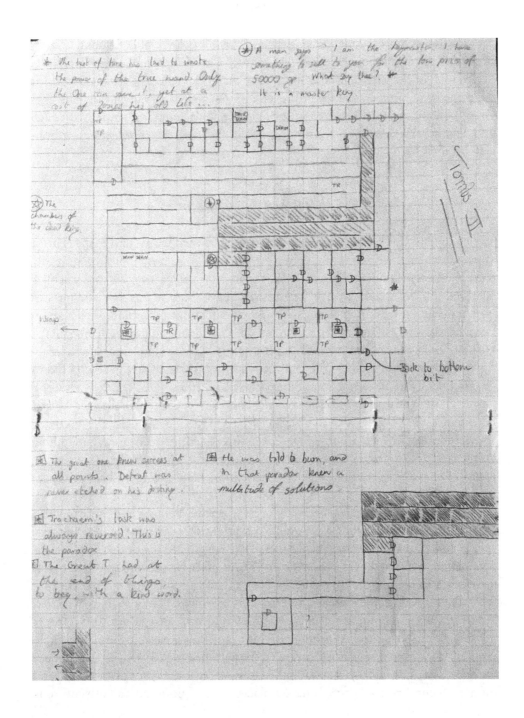

FIGURE 2.3: Player map of a level from *Bard's Tale II: The Destiny Knight*. From author's personal collection.

perhaps sedimentation: time passing through visible growth of layer upon layer of cartographic production. In this respect, much like photographs, the developing 'snapshots' of the map spatialize both time and experience. Maps produced for the game Ryuutama can be seen to reach a similar outcome but through a somewhat different process. Here, map space is explicitly temporal space, with each grid square representing an amount of time in the journey as well as a geographical distance.

What does it mean to map stories?

The complementary nature of the relationship between words and maps is most apparent when player maps are, or at least try to be, in some manner recognizably representative of an imagined world. However, some player maps can be extremely abstract, and reflections on RPG design discuss ideas of maps as flowcharts or 'pointcrawls' (Anne 2018: n.pag.), 'a way of depicting space that maps a set of known locations as "nodes" that are connected by a limited number of "paths"'. Hitherto, my analysis has focused on objects which match a set of aesthetic criteria we expect to see in maps, in that they attempt to articulate, in some kind of geographically accurate manner, the spatial dimensions and characteristics of a place. These kinds of maps serve specific gameplay purposes, as blogger Merric Blackman (2021) highlights: visualization, first and foremost but also the discovery of 'secret areas', which are most effectively identified through precise mapping. Pointcrawl or flowchart maps do away with this kind of geographical specificity, instead focusing on a series of places or locations, and the paths between them (see Figure 2.4).

Writing on the connections between western medieval maps and those in video games, Thomas Rowland (2014) draws our attention to the distinction between spaces and places, following Yi-Fu Tuan (1977) in conceiving of them as interdependent and yet different in character. For Tuan, space is open and free, and places are constrained and defined, 'centers of felt value' with identity and aura (1977: 3–7). For Rowland, reflecting on the travel networks in games such as *World of Warcraft* (Blizzard Entertainment 2004) and *Guild Wars* (ArenaNet 2005), spaces are something to be travelled *through* (or over) and thus are lacking in virtual experience. Places, conversely, are locations to be travelled *to* (2014: 190). Here space is about time, as it is in Ryuutama; but Ryuutama's game experience concentrates on movement through space, *between* places, and exploration and adventure in the blank spaces of the map.

Rowland moves on (2014: 191–200) to explore linear, non-geographical video game maps, and their relationship to (for him a reintroduction of; 2014:

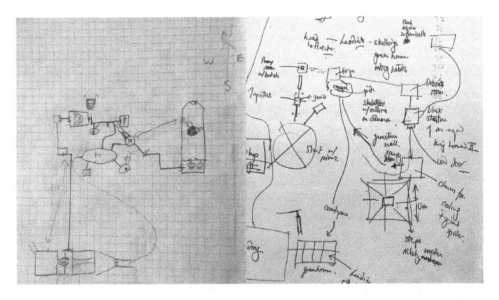

FIGURE 2.4: Two examples of players' pointcrawl maps. From author's personal collection.

190) medieval styles of mapping, particularly *mappaemundi* ('maps of the world'). Medieval maps reject blank spaces, incorporating nothing beyond the limits of the circle of the world, and do not seek to act as accurate geographical representations, instead concerning themselves with locations/places, with detail and information (usually text), and with the ordering of a narrative. Both medieval and video game maps serve as a 'virtual space in which we can view the sequence (both chronologically and geographically) of events via markers (sometimes as dots, icons, or written text), a space which is to be read not left to right, but holistically, circularly and diegetically' (Rowland 2014: 196–97). This narrative information, charting a pathway between different significant places and events, facilitated imagined journeys, spiritual itineraries which offered a form of pilgrimage for those who could not otherwise undertake one.

Nodal maps – flowcharts and pointcrawls included – thus present a process of emplotment (White 1973: 12), a narrative constructed around a sequence of meaningful events. Interconnections remain paths of the possible, but may render the process of movement between events itself uninteresting. Maps in this form abstract the relationship to space and indeed duration in favour of a concentration on significance and sequence, on the events which offer narrative outcomes. And while these maps echo everyday geographical maps much less directly, they still present physical, intellectual and emotional forms of materiality, in some ways offering greater tactility through their uncluttered abstraction, and concentration of affective modes of meaning-making around events. This is reminiscent of Bernard Siegert's (2011: 16) observation that the interaction between the materiality of a map and the medium of its representation can ultimately deterritorialize that representation.

Although Rowland (2014: 200) argues that it is particularly video games that have prompted a return to seeing maps as narrative spaces in the medieval fashion, this is only partially true, and requires us to hold a relatively narrow perspective on where maps might be found. Moving away from both video games and tabletop games, we can find widespread use of nodal maps by players undertaking game books – for example, the *Fighting Fantasy* and *Destiny Quest* series (in essence, more complex Choose Your Own Adventure books). Structured around a series of numbered entries that focus on events leading to decision points and minimize discussion of travel, these books concentrate on the narrative experience and often pay relatively little attention to the coherence of the space which they purport to represent. In one blogger's case, this prompts shifts between cartographical and nodal mapping styles, according to which is most suitable for the information presented:

> Some books are easy to map, because they are logically laid out in geographical terms [...]. Others, though, present something more of a challenge, either because their geographical layout is not logical (e.g. turning left and right ultimately lead you to the same place), they are not geographically structured (so that the focus is on what you do, and how and when you do it), or their structure is so complex that simple forms of representation just don't cut it.
>
> (Paltogue 2013: n.pag)

The relatively limited space of these books permits, even encourages, players to produce maps which represent less a specific play experience and more a mapping of all of the narrative possibilities of a book. These normally include multiple failure/end points which would not come to light on a strictly experience-based map, rendering them akin to video game walkthroughs. And as already indicated, video games make widespread use of nodal maps – not only in terms of the representation of narrative through the non-geographic progress maps which Rowland identifies but also in terms of the very structure of the games themselves. In *Radiant Historia: Perfect Chronology* (Atlas and Headlock 2017), the nodal map at the game's heart is represented as part of gameplay, through two parallel timelines within which the player characters move in a decidedly non-linear fashion, jumping forwards, backwards and between events in an attempt to produce the 'true history'. This mechanism is implemented to an even greater extent in the full representation of the narrative map or story tree provided to players of *Detroit: Become Human* (Quantic Dream 2018). Here, it is possible to identify clearly where further narrative possibilities exist and, should they choose to, players can explore additional nodes through repeated plays.

Of course, these are not player maps, but there is an extent to which they have a similar function, in identifying which segments of the game have been experienced. Indeed, the open representation of narrative maps in video games, paired with the increasing tendency for tabletop RPGs like D&D to be played *on* a map provided by the gamemaster, has resulted in some longstanding players bewailing the loss of mapping as a practice (Rehm 2019), even as others cheer its disappearance (DM David 2016). However, innovations in online tabletop play, an area of particular focus in recent years, have seen the introduction of dynamic lighting mechanics which black out areas on the tabletop map as player characters pass through them, encouraging some to take up mapping once again (Chris C. 2014).

Conclusion: Maps, memories, and materiality

The nostalgia of some players for pen and paper mapping in particular is a reminder that the materiality and meaningfulness of these maps goes beyond their capacity to represent and record stories. This can be further explored with reference to Megarry's maps. While many player maps can be found in more or less formal archives such as PlaGMaDa (2015), the organic nature, relative age and lengthy preservation of Megarry's ephemeral documents evoke the personal, informal archive (see, e.g., Kibby 2009; Ashmore et al. 2012), as a repository of meaningful objects and things which illuminates an individual life. Such illumination occurs not only in private, everyday terms but also in more public, shared contexts: professional life, for example, or, in this case, gaming. Commentators on posts about maps (and, relatedly, character sheets; see Webber 2019) discuss retaining (or losing) their own maps in a manner which attests to their meaningfulness, and their (physical and affective) materiality: 'I still have all of mine saved in a box of treasured possessions. Is there a name for this kind of perversion?' (Tom 2009: n.pag.); 'i [sic] had tons of maps drawn out on graph paper most of them are in the game case/box which sadly i [sic] no longer have' (SomaXD 2014: n.pag.).

The importance of such atypical archival material – of 'objects, ephemera, memorabilia and *tactile "stuff"*' (Mills 2013: 704, emphasis added) – lies in 'the memories associated with them, and the personal experience invested in the event, and recalled through their contents' (Ashmore et al. 2012: 87). This is demonstrated by a comment from Boggs on his blog post:

> I asked Dave [Megarry] about the mapping process and here is what he said [...] 'The basic scenario is Arneson telling us, "10 feet, 20 feet, room 20 × 20 with an up staircase in southeast corner, down staircase in northwest corner, a passage on the north wall and east wall and an ugly troll standing in the middle of the room. What are you going to do?" [...] We would be scrambling like mad to figure out a strategy. We would have been drawing the map by hand on loose graph paper [...]. For Dumbo, I would transfer the loose map into the chemistry notebook later'.
>
> (DHBoggs 2017: n.pag.)

Here, maps can be seen not only to record but also to prompt memories of game experiences, both general and specific, for their creator. In this respect, they serve almost as a form of external memory: as game journalist Ben Kuchera (2014a) suggests, 'hand-drawn video game maps are physical memories [...]. We're mapping our memories as much as the landscape'. And while this attests to the relationship between maps and the memory of game experiences, the existence of Mapstalgia, a collection of 'video game maps drawn from memory' (Millard 2014: n.pag.), indicates that this relationship is not entirely one way. Player maps are, then, mnemonic objects, objects around and through which memories are formed, articulated and remembered. Furthermore, in the idiosyncrasies of their form, they have the potential to prompt memories amongst other players as well. Such prompts might be understood to operate at two levels of recognition: first, that of more general understandings of the relationship between maps and gameplay; and second, that of a specific recognition of an affecting game experience – of a scenario, for example, or of a conversation in an imaginary place. This in turn suggests that these maps may tell stories which are not only individual but also collective in character, recognizable and legible by others with similar experiences (see Figure 2.5).

Player maps, therefore, are enmeshed within and contribute to relationships of meaning; and these relationships result from the maps' material qualities, and the tactilities they afford. In general terms, this insight is already established in material culture studies, as discussed above. Yet these maps present specific affordances which help to further nuance our understanding of how these relationships function, and which seem to speak to broader issues arising around the materiality of media, especially when put to mnemonic purposes. Discussions of player maps often attach importance to the idea of the hand-drawn map; not necessarily a pencil and paper map, this, but a map produced through direct physical agency, in engagement with the tactility of a surface, be that paper or

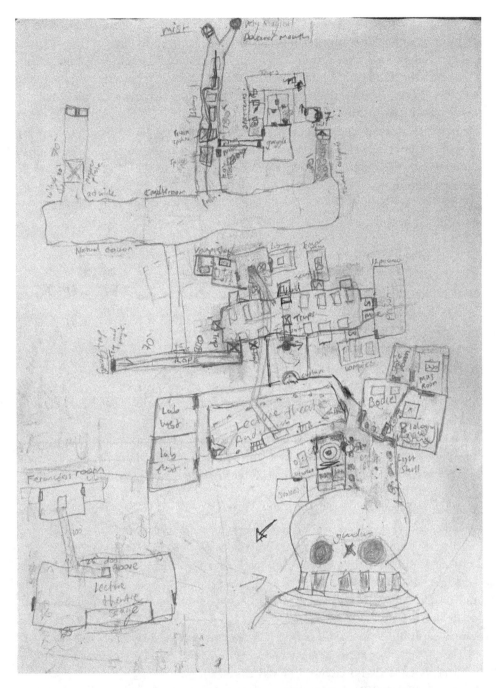

FIGURE 2.5: Map of the Advanced Dungeons & Dragons adventure 'Tomb of Horrors'. Maps such as this may provoke memories for others, who may have played the same published scenario or simply produced similar records of their game experiences. From author's personal collection.

screen. Such a map serves in the first instance to record, but also to orientate, to capture imagination and set it into a form. In so doing, it also captures experience through its notation, its gradual development and its absences, and creates a lasting affective bond which can be returned to later to prompt – to evoke – memory. In this respect, the materiality of player maps invites us to think further about our relationship with other kinds of mediation, the outcomes of other creative practices through which we exploit the affordances of a form to capture deeply personal experiences: the selfie, for example, or the diary. For the value in these maps – their meaning, their auratic character and their nature as record – *is* their materiality, the product of the relationships between them and the players who make them, who use them, and who archive them, either formally or informally, for posterity.

REFERENCES

Abels, Nathan (2008), 'Hand drawn vintage video game maps', *Minutiae*, 1 May, http://nathanabels.blogspot.com/2008/04/hand-drawn-vintage-video-game-maps.html. Accessed 15 May 2021.

Ahmed, Sara (2006), *Queer Phenomenology: Orientations, Objects, Others*, Durham NC: Duke University Press.

Alder, Avery (2013), *The Quiet Year*, n.p.: Buried Without Ceremony.

Allston, Aaron (1991), *Rules Cyclopedia (Dungeons & Dragons Game)*, Lake Geneva, Cambridge: TSR, Inc.

Anderson, Benedict (2006), *Imagined Communities*, rev. ed., London: Verso.

Anne (2018), 'Sub-hex crawling mechanics – Part 1, pointcrawling', DIY & Dragons, 28 February, https://diyanddragons.blogspot.com/2018/02/sub-hex-crawling-mechanics-part-1.html. Accessed 14 May 2021.

ArenaNet (2005), *Guild Wars*, Pangyo: NCSOFT.

Ashmore, Paul, Craggs, Ruth, and Neate, Hannah (2012), 'Working-with: Talking and sorting in personal archives', *Journal of Historical Geography*, 38, pp. 81–89.

Atlus and Headlock (2017), *Radiant Historia: Perfect Chronology*, Setagaya, Tokyo, Irvine: Atlus/Höfen: Deep Silver.

Auronlu (2013a), 'Maps', Let's Play *Final Fantasy*, http://finalfantasy.istad.org/maps/. Accessed 15 May 2021.

Auronlu (2013b), 'Giruvegan – Map of the great crystal levels 1-5 (WIP)', Mages Do It With Flare, 8 November, https://auronlu.tumblr.com/post/66359750057/giruvegan-map-of-the-great-crystal-levels-1-5. Accessed 15 May 2021.

Auronlu (2013c), 'FFXII: My map of the great crystal', Let's Play *Final Fantasy*, 16 November, http://finalfantasy.istad.org/2013/11/ffxii-giruvegan-map-of-the-great-crystal/. Accessed 15 May 2021.

Benjamin, Walter (1969), 'The work of art in the age of mechanical reproduction' (ed. H. Arendt, trans. Harry Zohn), *Illuminations*, New York: Schocken Books, pp. 1–26.

Bittanti, Matteo (2012), 'Project: "The Play Generated Map & Document Archive" (PlagMaDa)', *Gamescenes: Art in the Age of Videogames*, 26 September, https://www.gamescenes.org/2012/09/book-the-play-generated-map-document-archive-plagmada.html. Accessed 15 May 2021.

Blackman, Merric (2021), 'The map and the mapper', Merric's Musings: Reviews and Play Advice for Dungeons and Dragons, 1 May, https://merricb.com/2021/05/01/the-map-and-the-mapper/. Accessed 14 May 2021.

Blizzard Entertainment (2004), *World of Warcraft*, Irvine: Blizzard Entertainment.

Boggs, D. H. (2017), 'The oldest dungeon maps in D&D history', Hidden in Shadows, January, http://boggswood.blogspot.com/2017/01/the-oldest-dungeon-maps-in-d-history.html. Accessed 8 April 2021.

Camp, Paul (2019), 'How many D&D players are there worldwide?', Dungeon Vault, 3 March, https://dungeonvault.com/how-many-dnd-players-are-there-worldwide/. Accessed 9 April 2021.

Chris C. (2014), 'Hand-drawn mapping during online play', Old School D&D and Other Gaming Pursuits, 9 November, http://clashofspearonshield.blogspot.com/2014/11/old-school-mapping-during-online-play.html. Accessed 14 May 2021.

Crawl (2007), 'Phantasy star maps', Crawl's Review Site!, http://crawl.flyingomelette.com/notes/phantasystar.html. Accessed 11 May 2021.

DHBoggs (2017), 'Comment: The oldest Dungeon maps in *D&D history*', Hidden in Shadows, 18 January, http://boggswood.blogspot.com/2017/01/the-oldest-dungeon-maps-in-d-history.html?showComment=1484742030458#c8437291013680665520. Accessed 8 April 2021.

DM David (2016), 'Mapping – Or not-fun things that Dungeons & Dragons players learned to skip, Part 1', DM David, 11 May, https://dmdavid.com/tag/mapping-or-not-fun-things-that-dungeons-dragons-players-abandoned-part-1/. Accessed 14 May 2021.

Ford, Dom (2016), '"eXplore, eXpand, eXploit, eXterminate": Affective writing of postcolonial history and education in civilization V', *Game Studies*, 16:2, http://gamestudies.org/1602/articles/ford. Accessed 27 April 2021.

Fuchs, Michael, Erat, Vanessa, and Rabitsch, Stefan (2018), 'Playing serial imperialists: The failed promises of bioware's video game adventures', *The Journal of Popular Culture*, 51:6, pp. 1476–99.

Garcia, Antero (2017), 'Privilege, power, and Dungeons & Dragons: How systems shape racial and gender identities in tabletop role-playing games', *Mind, Culture and Activity*, 24:3, pp. 232–46.

Gibson, James (1986), *The Ecological Approach to Visual Perception*, Hillsdale: Lawrence Earlbaum.

Gygax, Gary (1978), *Official Advanced Dungeons & Dragons Players Handbook*, Lake Geneva: TSR, Inc.

Gygax, Gary and Arneson, Dave (1974), *Dungeons and Dragons*, Lake Geneva: TSR, Inc.

Jackson, Steve and Livingstone, Ian (1982), *The Warlock of Firetop Mountain*, Harmondsworth: Puffin Books.

Kent, Alexander J. (2019), 'Maps, materiality and tactile aesthetics', *The Cartographic Journal*, 56:1, pp. 1–3.

Kibby, Marjorie (2009), 'COLLECT YOURSELF: Negotiating personal music archives', *Information, Communication & Society*, 12:3, pp. 428–43.

Klohan (2016), '*Bard's Tale I: Tales of the Unknown*: Hand-drawn color maps by Klohan', *Old Games.sk*, https://www.oldgames.sk/en/game/bards-tale-1-tales-of-the-unknown/download/9364/. Accessed 11 May 2021.

Kuchera, Ben (2014a), 'Hand-drawn video game maps are physical memories, so let's see yours', *Polygon*, 23 May, https://www.polygon.com/2014/5/23/5745002/zelda-maps-gaming. Accessed 15 May 2021.

Kuchera, Ben (2014b), 'We mapped our past: Our readers share their favorite hand-drawn video game maps', *Polygon*, 7 June, https://www.polygon.com/2014/6/7/5773534/we-mapped-our-past-our-readers-share-their-favorite-hand-drawn-video. Accessed 15 May 2021.

Lammes, Sybille (2010), 'Postcolonial playgrounds: Games as postcolonial cultures', *Eludamos: Journal for Computer Game Culture*, 4:1, pp. 1–6.

Lammes, Sybille and de Smale, Stephanie (2018), 'Hybridity, reflexivity and mapping: A collaborative ethnography of postcolonial gameplay', *Open Library of Humanities*, 4:1: 19, pp. 1–31.

Latour, Bruno (1996), 'On interobjectivity', *Mind, Culture and Activity*, 3:4, pp. 228–45.

Leonardi, Paul M. (2010), 'Digital materiality? How artifacts without matter, matter', First Monday, 15:6, https://firstmonday.org/ojs/index.php/fm/article/download/3036/2567. Accessed 11 April 2021.

Melan (2017), 'Comment: The oldest Dungeon maps in D&D history', Hidden in Shadows, 17 January, https://boggswood.blogspot.com/2017/01/the-oldest-dungeon-maps-in-d-history.html?showComment=1484642225202#c3049374713371157275. Accessed 8 April 2021.

Millard, Josh (2014), 'Mapstalgia: Video game maps drawn from memory', https://mapstalgia.tumblr.com/. Accessed 15 May 2021.

Miller, Daniel (2001), 'Possessions', in D. Miller (ed.), *Home Possessions, Oxford*: Berg, pp. 107–21.

Miller, Daniel (2005), 'Materiality: An introduction', in D. Miller (ed.), *Materiality*, Durham: Duke University Press, pp. 1–50.

Mills, Sarah (2013), 'Cultural–historical geographies of the archive: Fragments, objects and ghosts', *Geography Compass*, 7:10, pp. 701–13.

Morris, James (2003), 'Campaign diary for 3080 Y.E.', Adventures in the World of Wearth, 18 January, https://www.angelfire.com/rpg/wearth/campaign_calendar.htm. Accessed 14 May 2021.

Mukherjee, Souvik (2017), *Videogames and Postcolonialism: Empire Plays Back*, London: Palgrave Macmillan.

Mukherjee, Souvik (2018), 'Playing subaltern: Video games and postcolonialism', *Games and Culture*, 13:5, pp. 504–20.

Murray, Janet (1997), *Hamlet on the Holodeck*, Cambridge: The MIT Press.

Okada, Atsuhiro (2007), りゅうたま *(Ryuutama)*, Shinjuku: Jive Ltd.

Palmer, Catherine and Lester, Jo-Anne (2013), 'Maps, mapping and materiality: Navigating London', in J. Lester and C. Scarles (eds), *Mediating the Tourist Experience. From Brochures to Virtual Encounters*, Farnham: Ashgate, pp. 237–54.

Paltogue (2013), 'Fighting fantasy SVGs', The World of Fighting Fantasy, 27 November, http://worldoffightingfantasy.blogspot.com/2013/11/fighting-fantasy-svgs.html. Accessed 14 May 2021.

Phillips, Richard (1997), *Mapping Men and Empire: Geographies of Adventure*, London, New York: Routledge.

PlaGMaDa (2015), 'The play generated map & document archive', http://plagmada.org/Home.html. Accessed 15 May 2021.

Prutz, Steve (2020), '*EverQuest* map preserve', 19 March, https://www.steveprutz.com/eq/. Accessed 10 May 2020.

Quantic Dream (2018), *Detroit: Become Human*, San Mateo: Sony Interactive Entertainment.

Rehm, Scott (2019), 'Lost player skills: Mapping', The Angry GM: RPG Advice with Attitude, 29 November, https://theangrygm.com/lost-player-skills-mapping/. Accessed 14 May 2021.

Rieder, John (2008), *Colonialism and the Emergence of Science Fiction*, Middletown: Wesleyan University Press.

Rowland, Thomas (2014), 'We will travel by map: Maps as narrative spaces in video games and medieval texts', in D. T. Kline (ed.), *Digital Gaming Re-imagines the Middle Ages*, London, New York: Routledge, pp. 189–201.

Siegert, Bernard (2011), 'The map *is* the territory', *Radical Philosophy*, 169, pp. 13–16.

SomaXD (2014), 'Comment: Hand-drawn video game maps are physical memories, so let's see yours', *Polygon*, 23 May, https://www.polygon.com/2014/5/23/5745002/zelda-maps-gaming#235924677. Accessed 15 May 2021.

Tom (2009), 'Comment: Hand drawn vintage video game maps', *Minutiae*, 10 December, http://nathanabels.blogspot.com/2008/04/hand-drawn-vintage-video-game-maps.html?showComment=1260485738112#c3817054880747462065. Accessed 15 May 2021.

Tulloch, Rowan (2014), 'The construction of play: Rules, restrictions, and the repressive hypothesis', *Games and Culture*, 9:5, pp. 335–50.

Tweet, Jonathan, Cook, Monte, and Williams, Skip (2003), *Dungeons and Dragons Player's Handbook: Core Rulebook I v.3.5*, Renton: Wizards of the Coast.

Verant Interactive and 989 Studios (1999), *EverQuest*, San Diego: Sony Online Entertainment.

Vismann, Cornelia (2013), 'Cultural techniques and sovereignty', *Theory, Culture & Society*, 30:6, pp. 83–93.

Webber, Nick (2019), 'Table talk: Archives of role-playing's personal pasts', *Analog Game Studies*, 2019 Role-Playing Game Summit special issue, https://analoggamestudies.org/2019/12/archives-of-role-playings-personal-pasts/. Accessed 8 April 2021.

Young, Liam Cole (2015), 'Cultural techniques and logistical media: Tuning German and Anglo-American media studies', *M/C Journal*, 18:2, https://doi.org/10.5204/mcj.961.

Short Take 3

Making Order Out of Chaos

Hilary Weston Jones

I have carried this little bit of solar-powered plastic around with me for the last 29 years (see Figure ST.3). It has sat beside me at every freelance job, worked

FIGURE ST.3: Hilary's calculator. Author's own image.

long hours, and is now semi-retired. It draws me back to the pre-online and digital world, to the long stressful hours trying to balance the editorial, creative, and logistical demands of television production. It reminds me of my failures and my successes.

During my TV career, I managed budgets of hundreds of thousands of pounds and sometimes into the millions. Yet I had failed Maths O'Level.

Maths at school did not make any sense to me. Why would I ever need to understand those squiggles and rules? I was creative. I read. I wanted to do an English Literature degree.

Maths was dead to me.

Yet, in my TV career, budget management was one of my favourite parts of the job. For years I grappled with why this should be, given my dark relationship with numbers and percentages in the past. It was only when I started to teach as a guest lecturer at Birmingham City University that I was forced to analyze this. How could I make this world of rates, estimates, and quotes sound sexy? Why would any student want to spend a day researching the cost of hiring a submarine, working out what kit you needed to film on a boat in the North Sea in February, or how to feed a crew of 40 at midnight on a Saturday in Piccadilly Gardens Manchester?

During these ponderings I realized that what I did and what I loved doing was *making order out of chaos*. The chaos is a drama script, a series proposal or even just a paragraph idea for a documentary. I took this chaos, with all its unanswered questions, possibilities, and challenges, and turned it into a single figure. I then spent months negotiating my way through a production to stick to that figure. This was my order. And my calculator was there along the way, spilling out its numbers and keeping everything on track.

It has survived the battleground of production. Vodka spilt on it after an arduous night shoot turns into an impromptu office party. It has survived many hands grabbing it to make their own calculations, my eyes warily watching its progress and return. It has even survived the era of Microsoft Excel and mobile phone calculator apps. It is quick and portable; it can attend meetings, locations, and classrooms. Over our friendship, it has never crashed and the sunlight has never let its battery die.

So my calculator, still slightly vodka sticky (like a scratch on vinyl) brings back happy, busy memories of my television career. More importantly, it reminds me of my 15-year-old struggles and how the chalk and talk of my Maths O'Level teaching failed to make the subject relevant to me. And how I want to learn from those lessons to ensure that I can be a better teacher.

3

The Solid State of Radio

Sam Coley

Introduction

The idea for this chapter grew from my attachment to a radio which has been with me since the age of 6. My parents bought it at Kai Tak Airport's Duty-Free shop in Hong Kong, and it remains the best gift I have ever received. The radio is only 10 cm tall and has a commando-style design in military khaki. Although it looks like something from the Armed Forces, I doubt it would have lasted long on the front line. It stopped working decades ago, but I still keep it as a memory of childhood and a reminder of my early obsession with radio. Songs I still cherish today were first heard through the tiny speaker and it is fair to say that my ongoing interest in broadcasting started with this transistor. It is a radio cliché, but I used to sleep with it under my pillow; drifting off to the sounds of 3ZB and Radio Avon 1260, the AM stations which used to broadcast in Christchurch, New Zealand, where I grew up. My first, albeit limited, understanding of radio presenting, production and programming began with this radio and, due to its influence, I have been working in the radio industry throughout my adult life.

As I grew older, and possibly more sentimental, I began to question the significance of this small green box and pondered why, amongst all the other paraphernalia of youth, this particular artefact has remained with me. The bond which can form between a listener and the medium of radio has been thoroughly explored in past studies. Robert McLeish (2005) and Michael Keith (2007) refer to the sense of friendship which exists between a radio presenter and their audience, while David Lloyd (2015: 4) describes the medium as a 'compelling companion'. However, there are far fewer investigations that explore the connection an owner may feel towards their radio as a physical artefact. While Andreas Fickers (2012) focuses on the tuning dial as a mediating interface, this study considers nostalgic associations felt towards the object of a radio. Any affection for a collection of diodes and circuits will usually require, in the first instance, some form of emotional attachment to the medium itself. Yet, I suggest a transference can take place between the affecting qualities of radio broadcasting and the artefact itself. It is the regard for the physical materiality of radio that I explore in the following three sections.

My methodology uses concepts of material culture to bring a new perspective to the field of radio studies. I explore the changing role of radio in contemporary culture and society by drawing together radio scholarship, design theory and the study of consumer behaviour. In addition, I consider several design case studies and utilize aspects of autoethnographic investigation by using personal experience to better understand concepts of nostalgia and attachment. I begin by examining notions of intimacy that are shared between the listener and the medium. This is necessary, as an initial connection to the medium itself can help in building a lasting attachment to the object of a radio. I draw on Jo Tacchi's (1998: 25–26) ethnographic research to show how the sound of radio can be an important part of a home's material culture, contributing to the creation of domestic environments and providing 'a texture in which everyday life can take place'. This section considers radio's ability to generate strong emotional responses; an attribute that is central in building lasting bonds between the medium and its listeners. Sound has the ability to create a psychological space for the listener, drawing on memory and nostalgia (Lefebvre 2000). However, while the sounds generated by a radio can bring back certain nostalgic recollections, its physical form can equally inspire connective memories with the past. The primary connection felt towards radio is auditory in nature, yet I suggest this bond can subsequently be extended towards the object of a radio. A radio may also serve as a reminder of place or time, as a memento of a previous owner, or be held in regard solely for its aesthetic value, thereby holding meaning outside of its purpose as audio device. However, this chapter is more focused on relationships that form over time between a functioning radio and its listener. I explore the relationship I have with my aforementioned childhood radio as a personal case study and consider the Sony CRF-150 as an example of how listeners may forge deep connections with radio as a material object.

In the coming section, I discuss key moments in radio design history and show how certain technical innovations have impacted on the domestic use of the medium. I explore how changes in radio's form have altered listener interactions with stations as well as the user's haptic relationship with radio. I then consider contemporary radio design by assessing manufacturers use of retro-styling to attract customers, while still offering the latest technologies. This approach aligns with Eleonora Cattaneo and Carolina Guerini's (2012: 685) definition of retro products as being 'a combination of old-fashioned forms with the most advanced functions'. Michele Hilmes (2013: 43) states that contemporary radio has reached a 'transformative new materiality' enabled by the advent of digital platforms which have increased accessibility and widened the scope of content to a global scale; 'radio has not only survived but revived both as a creative medium and as a shared cultural experience'. While this may be true for the medium, the materiality of radio as a physical object has not fared as well. I discuss whether the digital revolution has rendered the concept of a stand-alone radio all but redundant. I investigate how manufacturers have responded to the emergence of increasing sophisticated audio technologies by disguising innovation within the forms of earlier radio designs, and question whether this trend risks the materiality of radio becoming an anachronistic novelty. Finally, I conclude by looking ahead to the possible future of radio as a physical object, recognizing the sentimentality of radio as an object and suggesting that the ongoing development of radio as a medium may be leading to its obsolescence as a mass market device.

The intimacy of radio

This opening section considers the personal relationship that can form between the object of a radio and its owner. However, I begin by exploring the emotional connection that joins the listener to the medium itself. As indicated, the foundation of this attachment is intrinsically auditory. Once a radio has been switched on and the desired station and volume have been selected, the link between the listener and the materiality of a radio is, for the most part, invisible. A listener may occasionally glance at their radio to check the time, confirm a frequency, or, in the case of digital radio (DAB), check the song title or artist of the track being played. Yet, physical relationships with radio essentially take place inside the listener's head, in the delicate interaction of sound waves and vibrating eardrums. We hear a radio in the same way we hear any other sound and, if the signal is sufficiently good enough, the brain does not differentiate between a person speaking to us in the same room, or via a speaker. It is this 'illusion of presence' which makes a voice on the radio 'memorable and convincing' (Kuffert 2009: 306). While a physical radio may be a small and insignificant object, the sound and meaning it produces can literally fill a room. Daniel Miller (1998: 7) makes the important distinction between the materiality of a radio which is switched on, and one which is switched off. We tend to feel a connection to the sound an operational radio produces, not with the object of a radio.

The affection felt towards radio may stem from its ability to offer companionship or a convenient diversion from day-to-day anxieties. Simply put, radio entertains us and helps us relax (McLeish 2005). The medium also provides a sense of human connection, which subsequently creates a feeling of closeness. In CBC Chairman Davidson Dunton's 1946 address to listeners, he likened radio to a close friend who 'comes to talk to you, or play to you, in your living room' (Kuffert 2009: 306). This notion of intimacy is referred to by Lou Orfanella (1998: 53) as radio's 'special power [...] a one-to-one connection that no other medium can match'. For this reason, when a station changes its format or a long-term presenter moves on, it can be especially traumatic for some listeners, who may miss the comfort of a familiar voice.

In the field of social psychology, intimacy is closely related to concepts of privacy (Luca 2016). According to Raymond Betts (2004: 16), the radio was the 'first electronic device to enter the intimate space of the individual', sitting proudly in the living room before assuming 'a more discreet position on the bedroom table'. One of radio's defining strengths is this ability to share our private spaces, an attribute which helps build rapport with audiences. Until the rise of laptop and mobile phone technologies, radio's adaptability to follow the listener from room to room, and then beyond the home, was unparalleled by other electronic media. A memorable radio advert, produced by the UK's Radio Advertising Bureau in 1994, played on this virtue with a riddle-like conceit that teased listeners to imagine who was sharing their most intimate moments:

> You have a bath with them [...]. You undress in front of them [...]. You fall asleep next to them [...]. You turn them on first thing in the morning [...]. A lot of people make love to them [...]. They're with you in your car, your office and your bedroom [...]. People love listening to their radio's everywhere.
>
> (RAB radio advert, UK, 2004)

The work of Fredrik Stiernstedt (2014) showed how radio personalities often emphasize ordinariness and authenticity. Stiernstedt found that styles of presenta-tion were often informal and direct, while the subject matter they discussed, such as day-to-day trivialities and personal anecdotes, reflected the common banalities of everyday life. This approach is a deliberate technique to help radio's sonic presence blend into a family environment. As a result of this shared intimacy, listeners tend to place a great deal of trust in the medium (McLeish 2005). As radio broadcasts have actively sought to fit seamlessly within domestic environments, the physical materiality of radio has been similarly discreet, or at times proudly obvious in its design; I discuss this further in the following section.

There can be many reasons why a certain radio might find its way into a home. It may have been a gift or handed down through generations. If the owner purchased it, their decision could be based on purely aesthetic grounds or maybe a particu-lar model offered certain unique features? Perhaps it was a persuasive salesperson or marketing campaign that influenced the choice. Regardless of how a radio may arrive, the materiality of its shape and sound can quickly establish itself within the day-to-day routines of a house. Tacchi (2003: 281) shows how radio integrates easily within everyday life, 'forming an important part of domestic environments, or soundscapes'. As Simon Frith (2002: 41) observes, radio altered the use of domestic spaces, 'blurring the boundary between the public and the private, idealizing the family hearth as the site of ease and entertainment, establishing the rhythm of everydayness'. This can be seen in the way radio manufacturers often advertised a new model as an additional member of the family, as if it was a participant in the day-to-day routine of a well-run, happy household, as illustrated in Figure 3.1.

A key factor in radio's ability to connect with audiences stems from its use of emotion. Since its inception, broadcasters have exploited the medium's potential to create strong feelings in listeners, in the hope this will add to a station's TSL (time spent listening). This use of emotion can be heard in the good-natured humour of a Breakfast show, or in the exhilaration felt from hearing a favourite song at full volume. Although 'Shock Jocks' may cause outrage and talkback/news stations might deliberately put argumentative callers to air, playing devil's advocate to prompt a reaction, most broadcasters seek to build a friendly rapport with their

FIGURE 3.1: Cover of Danish Philips radio catalogue, 1959. Courtesy of the Royal Philips/Philips Company Archives.

audiences. The industry has traditionally been entertainment driven and keen not to unduly offend, for fear of 'tune out', or possible litigation. Generations of radio programmers have sought to hold audiences by 'eliminating or minimizing objectionable elements' (MacFarland 2011: 13). Listeners tend to agree with the views of the presenters they let into their homes, valuing the judgement and taste they express.

Radio is closely interwoven within the history of popular music and has been an important method to disseminate the work of musicians (Brabazon 2012). Music-formatted stations are able to harness the strong feelings a listener may have for certain songs or musical genres. Jeanette Bicknell (2009: 45) refers to music's ability trigger emotions within a listener, leaving them 'overwhelmed or overpowered by music, reduced to tears, and experiencing chills or shivers and other bodily sensations'. It is, therefore, unsurprising that a listener may form a bond with the station that provides a convenient gateway to the music they love. Tacchi's (2003) study of nostalgia in the consumption of radio explores the regard a listener may have for certain radio stations and formats. In one particular case study, a listener's connection to the station 'Classic Gold' is described as being nostalgic, 'reaching back across time and across memories, bringing something into the present, to take her into the future' (283). While this revealing study considered the materiality and presence of radio's sound, the physicality of radio as an object is not addressed. It is the connection between a listener and their radio as a tangible artefact which underpins this chapter. I suggest that it is possible for a relationship to form with the materiality of a particular radio, which is distinct from the regard which may be felt toward the programming it transmits.

Weston Baxter et al. (2015) discuss the range of relationships which may develop between a person and an object, such as the sense of psychological ownership held over a particular item. Individuals can often develop intimate relationships with objects which surround them and may feel that the target of this ownership is 'theirs' (Pierce et al. 2001). This is certainly true in the instance of my childhood radio and helps explain my ongoing attachment to it. It was the first radio I ever owned and one of my first possessions that was not a toy. In some instances, the emotional connection felt towards the medium may become so profound that it becomes imbued within the object of a radio. Personal associations with the medium, or past owners, can be projected into a radio. It then becomes a totem for memory, regardless of whether the radio is operational or not. This is certainly the case with my own radio, which stopped working decades ago.

While researching this chapter, I became curious about the origins of my old radio and wondered whether it could be repaired. The years had almost worn away its brand name, but I still could barely detect the words 'Eastronic' on a shiny silver label in the top left corner. This company began 1955 and still exists today as 'the largest hi-tech distributor in Israel'.[1] However, the business never actually manufactured radios. I spoke to a company representative in Tel Aviv, who explained how they would commission the design and assembly of electronics from Chinese manufacturers, which were then sold under the Eastronic brand. I then visited Audio Technical Services, a small family company in Erdington, North Birmingham, which incidentally started trading around the same time my radio was built. The company often repairs old valve and transistor radios of sentimental value, so they were not especially surprised by my enquiry, although the technician was somewhat surprised at how small the radio was. He explained the radio's origins and confirmed its economical production in Hong Kong. The configuration of the electronics followed the standard Chinese layout from the late 1960s to mid 1970s, with 6 germanium PNP and silicon NPN transistors and an 8-ohm, 0.25-watt speaker.

This model was originally designed for the British market, as the tuner was set to the British Medium Wave bandwidth, ranging from 1600 Hz to 500 Hz, which was also compatible in my home country of New Zealand. The initial diagnoses noted several possible failings; the ferrite rod aerial could have broken coils, the tuning of the trim pots might be permanently damaged, it may need a new transformer, or most likely, the problem was with the battery terminals. I asked whether it was likely it would ever work again and although the technician was non-committal ('it's a bit of a fiddle'), he seemed optimistic. I took the opportunity to ask whether customers ever discussed their relationship to the radios they bought in for repairs:

> [With] most of the old stuff there's always a story. It was given to them from their parents who have now died, so they want some connection. A lot of people mention that it was the first thing they brought with their first wage package. That's happened a surprising amount of time [...]. The amount of times people will tell you the story behind the unit, and I'm standing there for ten minutes and I'm saying 'Could you actually tell me why you came in?' While it's very interesting – I don't really care – I just want to know what's wrong with it. And it happens a lot.[2]
>
> (Tandy 2020: n.pag.)

Lester Tandy, an electronics repair man for the company, specifically mentioned Sony 'World Radios', such as the Sony CRF-150 (see Figure 3.2), as an example of the types of radios which were often brought in for repairs:

> They were hard to repair. But people were always willing to spend the money to get them repaired. [They were] like a member of the family (and) they always seemed to be really, really happy to have them fixed. When you couldn't repair them, they were visibly upset really – which is quite strange.
>
> (Tandy 2020: n.pag.)

FIGURE 3.2: The Sony CRF-150, Surplus Tech Mart. Author's personal collection.

These radios tended to be owned by 'elderly ex-service men or people working aboard in foreign countries' and seemed to hold an especially deep significance for the owners, which went beyond their basic functionality. The CRF-150, now discontinued, was a 13-band receiver that covered longwave (150–400 kHz), medium wave and ten shortwave bands. These units could therefore receive transcontinental broadcasts and were ideal for receiving the BBC World Service, which Tandy referred to as 'a British voice you could get anywhere in the world […]. It's what got them through' (Tandy 2020: n.pag.).

It is easy to imagine the importance of a radio like this to someone a long way from home, in exotic or even dangerous surroundings. The radio provided a portal back to familiar voices and sounds. Radio reassures and comforts through the medium's ability to provide companionship (Lloyd 2015). When listening to a favoured station, the displaced owner is once again part of the community they left behind. The protective front cover of the Sony CRF-150 and CRF-160 even came with a built-in world map and a time zone conversion wheel to help the listener orientate themself. Although these broken radios no longer functioned, and it would have been cheaper and more convenient to simply purchase a new one, the owners felt compelled to have the radio repaired and returned to working condition. Helping, in a sense, with the convalescence of an old friend. Baxter et al. (2015: 11) describe how the investment of time and money required to maintain objects can increase a sense of ownership. By 'caring' for a radio – fixing it, rather than replacing it – this bond is strengthened. In my own case, I was not particularly concerned about the functionality of my Eastronic radio, or whether it could be repaired. Its material presence was enough, as it served its purpose as a tangible reminder of the past, and not as a working radio. Having discussed the emotional connection a listener may feel towards both the medium and the physical materiality of radio, I now begin to focus on the evolution of radio's actual form.

Radio design history

Roger Silverstone and Leslie Haddon (1996) point to the mutual relationship which exists between technical and aesthetic innovation in radio design. Similarly, there is symbiotic connection between the changing shape of radio and listeners use of the medium. This section historicizes key stages in radio design and reflects on how these changes have ultimately altered interactions with the medium. The Bauhaus priority of technical functionality (Leitner 2011) comes to mind when considering the aesthetics of radio design, which tend to obey the famous dictum *form follows function*. In many instances, a radio's form does little more than present the essentials; a housing for components and a power source, aerial, tuning dial, speaker, volume control and an on/off switch (and possibly a headphone socket). Decorative elements can vary, but radio's core components have been reconstituted and repackaged by manufacturers for well over a century. Yet, despite the relative simplicity of its appearance and functionality, radio has attributes that belie its visible materiality. As Valerie Geller (2012: 3) notes, the outward form of a typical radio does not convey the true strength of the medium: 'sitting on a shelf, in your bag or in a car dashboard, it's merely a box full of wires and silicon chips'. It may have a modest appearance but, in Geller's opinion, radio is 'clearly one of the most ingenious devices ever created'.

Adrian Forty's (1986) *Objects of Desire*, which interrogates the relationship between society and product design, features a section on radio design as a specific case study. Forty identifies three distinct periods in the history of radio design, beginning with the classification of the wireless as a technical object. During this early-stage, manufacturers and consumers were more interested in the scientific properties of radio and had little concern with its physical appearance. The magic which powered this new technology was not concealed with components such as wires, diodes, capacitors and resistors all clearly visible. However, the shape of radio became more self-conscious as it reached adolescence. As Fickers (2012) points out, the introduction of the tuning dial transformed radio from an electrical device to an item of domestic furniture and was a crucial moment in human–machine interaction. The ease of turning a dial freed radio from being the preserve of 'tinkerers or hobbyists' and finally enabled it to become a truly mass medium

(411). The pace of technological innovation in radio design began to slow around the same time as the medium became more accessible to the public (Silverstone and Haddon 1996). As a result, manufacturers in the late 1920s had fewer innovations to offer potential customers and it became increasingly difficult to differentiate their products from the competition. Appearance began to take on a far greater significance, and radio entered its second design stage. According to Silverstone and Haddon (1996: 47), when new technologies reach the stage of mass consumption, they need to be designed as domestic objects in order to mediate the 'the tension between the familiar and the strange, desire and unease, which all new technologies respectively embody and stimulate'. Manufacturers addressed this tension by producing radios with a more subdued, harmonious appearance, to better fit within the décor of a home. Radio no longer drew attention to itself and became a hidden medium. Concealing radio within cabinets helped the medium's integration into domestic settings. As Kate Lacey (2000: 285) notes, loudspeakers were often designed to blend with the fabric and furnishings of a home to give 'the illusion of an equipment-free reproduction of reality'. By taking on the forms of furniture, this 'unfamiliar medium' was assimilated into everyday life (Forty 1986: 202).

Radio's final design stage emerged when the medium was accepted as a familiar technology. According to Forty (1986), the UK company Ekco ushered in a new era of technological futurism with the production of the AD65 in 1934. This model, manufactured from Bakelite, represented a radical departure from radio as furniture with its combination of 'technical sophistication' and 'futurist imagery' (205). Ekco quickly recognized the potential of Bakelite and employed leading architectural designers to exploit this new material (Geddes and Bussey 1991). Other manufacturers soon followed and during the 1930s, the materials used to house radios began to favour new synthetic materials, eschewing decorative woods like walnut, mahogany, and oak. With the emergence of industrial plastics such as Plaskon and Catalin, manufacturers introduced a range of models in bold new colours. Now radios were designed to stand out, rather than merge into their domestic surroundings. By adopting a futuristic approach to materials and design, radio once again became a conspicuous object of modern technology. Tuning dials were more prominent and design aesthetics took on cleaner, more progressive forms. In Alison Stone's (2016) assessment of aesthetic pleasure, an object's form can bring enjoyment for its own sake, regardless of practical considerations. As collectors will attest, this is especially true for the Art Deco styled radios of the 1930s, which remain beautiful aesthetic objects in their own right, regardless of their functionality. According to Angeliki Gazi and Tiziano Bonini (2018: 116), radios became status symbols, with the manufacturing of new designs 'refined enough to occupy the central stage in the kitchens and the living rooms of the houses of the middle class'. The creation of the transistor in the late 1940s marked another important turning point in radio design. Manufacturers were now able to shrink receivers down to a size which could fit more discreetly within the home as well as allowing for greater mobility (Keith 2007). Suddenly freed from living rooms and kitchens, radio listening became a far more personal, individual experience during the 1950s.

It is worth noting that Forty's (1986) history of radio design was written in the mid 1980s and does not consider the dramatic innovations brought on by the digital revolution. Amongst these changes was the transformation of haptic connections that take place when operating a radio. There has always been some form of haptic relationship between the listener and the transmissions of radio stations. Buttons are pressed on and off, and volume sliders and dials are turned up and down. An aerial may need to be moved around, or a tuning knob adjusted, sometimes with delicate precision, to find a strong and clear reception on a radio's bandwidth. However, the advent of online radio, instantly accessible by an array of technological devices, has all but done away with the need for these types of physical interactions. Today, a swipe or tap is a far more common form of user interface. Michele Hilmes (2013: 44) refers to contemporary radio as being a 'screen medium', accessed through mobile and static screens, which relies on tactile 'visual and textual' interfaces. The work of Gazi and Bonini (2018) develops this idea further, stating that mobile devices connected to the internet have essentially remediated the materiality of radio listening.

Early radio's inability to interact with audiences and receive instant feedback was once seen as a weakness of the medium. While Martin Shingler and Cindy Wieringa (1998) referred to radio as a one-way system communication, Andrew Ingram and Mark Barber (2005: 161) note how the medium has often sought participation from listeners in the form of competitions, promotions, phone-ins, dedications, and helplines, claiming, 'rarely an hour goes by without the presenter inviting the listener to phone, text, e-mail their thoughts on a particular topic of conversation, or to enter a competition'. These forms of interactions can be useful as a means of reflecting the audience back at itself, thereby creating a stronger sense of community and ultimately strengthening the listener's bond to the station. Although Chris Priestman (2002: 8) believes that some radio listeners may feel compelled to complain 'or, even more rarely, praise' something they have heard, he believes that many solicited audience interactions are of little real value. However, since the arrival of digital listening, audience interactions with radio presenters and stations have become more immediate and even monetizable. As Gazi and Bonini (2018: 117) point out, listening to radio via smartphones and tablets, and communicating with stations through text messages, Twitter, WhatsApp, Facebook, etc. are 'forms of interaction with radio personalities and radio content' which have become largely mediated by screen technologies.

Although technical innovation has not done away with radio, the concept of owning a radio to only receive radio broadcasts is becoming increasingly obsolete. In 2018, the United Kingdom reached the milestone of having over 50 per cent of all radio listening taking place on digital platforms.[3] This was the continuation of a trend which had been rapidly growing since 2011 and continues to. The UK's 'Q1' 2020 figure for digital listening share stood at 58.6 per cent.[4] DAB, DAB+, and HD radio have all valiantly tried to move linear radio forward into a new era and succeeded in convincing many consumers to upgrade their old analogue radios. However, many academics and industry experts were sceptical about the long-term viability of these technologies (Goddard 2010). Marko Ala-Fossi (2010) labelled DAB as outdated and inefficient, while Guy Starkey (2008) similarly saw the platform as an old remnant from the previous century, which has been super-seded. There is also the issue of DAB not being globally accepted, with Japan and America notably not adopting the technology.[5]

While audiences may still enjoy traditional radio and loyally tune into their favourite station, they no longer need a radio to do so. The ownership of a radio has increasingly become an act of nostalgia; the possession of a retro *'objet d'art'* that primarily reflects the owner's sense of style, rather than serving as an audio device. Manufacturers appear to be responding to customer demand from a demo-graphic that seeks comfort in shapes they may recall from their past, either in the form of radios they once owned or were seen in the homes of older relatives. I explore this concept further in the following section, which considers the trend towards retro-styled designs in the manufacturing of contemporary radio. I show how the design aesthetics of the past have been used as a veneer to disguise new radio and audio technology, such as Bluetooth streaming, DAB, and smart speaker functionality, amongst other innovations.

Retro-futurism

Having discussed various stages in radio's design history, I now focus on how manufacturers responded to the arrival of new audio technologies by integrating them within radio's form. I am particularly interested in what Laurence Fort-Rioche and Claire-Lise Ackermann (2013: 495) call the retro-phenomenon in design, otherwise referred to as 'retro-revival', 'vintage-revival', or 'retro-boom'. This section presents four case studies as examples of contemporary models that intentionally reference the supposed 'Golden Age' of radio for design inspi-ration. As highlighted earlier, radio has always been an earlier adopter of new audio technologies. Manufacturers have excelled at integrating the latest innovations within new models, often creating new forms of listening in the process. Clock radios are a good example of how seemingly disparate technologies can be combined to offer additional functionality within the shell of a radio. The cabinets described in the previous section often housed both a radio and a turntable side by side, sharing amplification and speaker system. Placing these two technologies within a single unit known as a radiogram was technically simple to achieve. Yet, Keith Geddes and Gordon Bussey (1991: 109) saw the merging as being 'commercially and socially significant', with radiograms becoming important status symbols in the 1930s. Years later, three-in-one systems enjoyed popularity, adding the audio cassette to the more established combination of turntable and radio. This process of integration reduced radio's prominence yet allowed it to interact more easily with new technologies.

Another example of 'technology-mashing' came in 1966, when Philips unveiled the Radiorecorder RQ-231 – the first portable radio to incorporate both an FM/AM radio and a cassette recorder (see Figure 3.3). This innovation gave the world an entirely new form of portable music player and allowed radio broadcasts to be easily and affordably captured via one domestic product. In doing so, it offered an early form of time-shift/on-demand radio. The medium could be conveniently captured and reheard at the listener's discretion. Readers of a certain age may recall patiently listening to a chart countdown, waiting to 'download' a favourite song by releasing the pause function on a similar model of radio cassette player. This represented a big step forward for the medium, as a potential competitor had been co-opted and successfully integrated within radio's traditional form. As

FIGURE 3.3: Philips Radiorecorder, 1966. Courtesy of the Royal Philips/Philips Company Archives.

these radio-recorders grew in size and loudness, they eventually became the boom-boxes or ghetto blasters, which found international popularity as 'one of the great consumer products of the 1970s and 1980s' (Millard 2000: 451). Conversely, the audio cassette had its revenge in 1981, when radio was incorporated within the Akai PM-01 to become the first 'Walkman' style cassette player to include an FM receiver.

Although audio cassettes and subsequently the compact disc could happily co-exist alongside traditional radio, the internet posed a more existential challenge to the materiality of radio as a physical object. The internet itself was not the problem. In fact, radio responded well to the challenge. As Rufus McEwan (2010: 7) notes, the arrival of internet radio succeeded in joining two separate technologies together 'with such intimacy that they appear inseparable'. The medium was well suited to adapt to new online technologies and, as a result, listeners could access a world of content at convenient times that best suited their lifestyle. Mark Barber, a planning director of the UK's Radio Advertising Bureau (RAB), observed how radio became part of a much wider audio ecology, which included on-demand audio and streamed music. This meant audiences had more options than ever: 'You can get almost anything, anywhere, at any time' (RAB 2015: 2).

Now, the medium could be heard via laptops and tablets, mobile phones, Freeview and satellite receivers, and such like. Radio no longer required a radio. Not only were programmes more accessible thanks to a range of new platforms but, according to Michele Hilmes (2013: 44), listeners had the added benefit of being able to access radio archives which reached as 'far back as the first golden age of network broadcasting'. Content itself also evolved into new forms of audio. While some might argue that podcasting is wholly distinct from radio, I tend to agree with Hugh Chignell's (2009: 2) belief that creating distinctions between them is splitting hairs: 'no medium can be defined by the technology of its delivery: a podcast remains radio because of the way it is produced'. Similarly, I suggest that contemporary radios, which may feature Bluetooth technology, DAB, iPhone inputs, ports for memory sticks, for instance, are still, intrinsically, radios. Nevertheless, the need for a traditional radio as a specific household object risked being superseded by ubiquitous WiFi and Bluetooth speakers, which can connect to a range of audio platforms and possibilities. At this point in radio's design history, manufacturers responded by creating stand-alone radios which provided AM/FM functionality alongside other new audio technologies.

Manufacturers from the 1950s onwards constantly tried to make radios which looked like 'they were breaking the frontiers of science' (Forty 1986: 205). Yet, once audio technologies reached new levels of hi-tech sophistication, many manufacturers retreated to the designs of yesteryear for inspiration. Fort-Rioche and Ackermann (2013) cite the Roberts Radio company as an example of repetition in retro-product design; the reproduction of a product from the past, but which incorporates new technology. A 1950s style Roberts DAB radio may feature new audio innovations, but its design 'is nothing more than the replication of the design of the original portable transistor radio Roberts R200' (497). The new model merely imitates the form of an anterior version, rather than improving on it. They refer to this retro-marketing as an example of playing the heritage card. For newer manufacturers without an established track-record of models to draw direct inspiration from their models take on more notional concepts of early radio design.

Greadio, a company whose motto is 'unique and retro design', had its trademark registered in 2018. This business, owned by the Zhuhai Ge Ge Lan Technology Co., has little design heritage to draw on, and therefore their range of radios features generic concepts of what a vintage radio might supposedly look like. The Greadio GR919C advertises 'retro classic aesthetics' which combine new digital audio technologies with a '1950s retro vibe ... We can feel like back into the golden age of music in 1950s, enjoying a soothing moment in today's busy life'.[6] There is no direct design parallel for this model, yet it arguably succeeds in looking suitably retro in its styling. Fort-Rioche and Ackermann (2013) classify this type of product as belonging to the neo-retro category of retro-products, which offer the consumer newness, but does not mislead them. The product, which incorporates the latest technologies, is 'inspired from past visual codes' and then reinterprets them (498).

The Steepletone company has a longer radio design history, dating back to the early 1970s, and stresses its motivation is 'innovation and not imitation' by offering a 'modern twist on old classics'.[7] The marketing of its NR880 LXA radio does not attempt to convince younger consumers of its benefits. Instead, it is promoted as a gateway device for older generations who might be intimidated by new technologies: 'if you know someone who might find futuristic tech a little scary, then just disguise it in the old style!'[8] This radio has a 'vintage feel' which features a 'handmade Classic Wooden case finished in an Oak veneer in the style of a war time radio'. The Steepletone is noteworthy for the inclusion of Amazon Alexa Dot Gen3 functionality, allowing users to access content using voice control technology. This product is clearly targeted at an older demographic, as it purports to be 'the perfect gift for Mum, Dad, Granny or Grandad or that special Anniversary or retirement gift'.

As Figure 3.4 illustrates, the Auna Belle Epoque 1906 provides another useful example of neo-retro-product design. Auna, a German company founded in 2007, markets this radio as a 'a musical bridge between the past and the future'.[9] Within the unit's retro-styled housing is a multitude of new audio technologies. Along with an analogue frequency band (with manual station search), it offers a DAB+ receiver, a CD drive that also reads MP3s, Bluetooth functionality, and a

FIGURE 3.4: Belle Epoque 1906 DAB Retro Stereo System, Auna. Courtesy of the Berlin Brands Group.

USB interface which allows for recording. Aside from its discreet digital screen, you could be mistaken for thinking the Belle Epoque 1906 was a well-preserved model from the 1920s. The product description notes how its design follows the 'visual tradition of its older brothers from the past. [...] The shapely curved case emphasises the charming nostalgic approach, as do the authentic details such as the fabric speaker cover'. Although a tangible product is essentially the same for everyone, its intangible qualities and meanings are different for the individual (Hirschman 1980). In the instance of radio, a listener's personal memories and associations will inform their preference for a certain period of design, be it Art Deco, Sixties Mod-Revival, or Retro-Eighties, etc. The case studies provided here demonstrate how manufacturers have drawn on various nostalgic associations of the past to market new audio technologies alongside traditional radio. Each of these units provides a sonic gateway to endless hours of audio content yet could conceivably never be used to listen to an actual radio broadcast.

According to Forty (1986: 200), customers once saw radio as holding the promise of an optimistic future and as a symbol of scientific progress 'putting them in touch with changes that they were told that technology would bring in all areas of life'. Technological futurism in radio design moved the listener's attention away from the difficulties they might face in everyday life, offering instead the promise of a better, uncomplicated future (Silverstone and Haddon 1996). It could be argued that present-day radio consumers may be influenced by a sense of techno-pessimism, which has replaced these earlier hopes for the future. A global sense of dissatisfaction was noted in a 2019 study from the Pew Research Centre, which identified a general feeling of pessimism towards income inequality, governance and job opportunities across the 34 countries surveyed.[10] As Cattaneo and Guerini (2012: 683) state, consumer 'anxiety for the future and the pace of innovation' is a key reason why consumers yearn for the stability and security of the past. A sense of disillusionment with the present state of the world could conceivably be a factor for those who find reassurance in objects which represent the imagined safety of yesteryear.

Andy Gutowski (2006), the creative director of a US marketing and design firm, calls retro-branding 'one of the most effective and lucrative marketing strategies of the past 10 years', as companies are able to 'cut through the clutter of modern life and transport consumers back to a simpler time'.[11] Appealing to customers who yearn for the good old days would seem to be a key motivator in manufacturers adoption of retro-designs. Or, perhaps, in the absence of creativity and innovation, a company simply falls back on designs from the past because they look like a radio is supposed look. The trend to recycle earlier forms suggests that radio manufacturing is at risk of becoming a sentimental cul-de-sac. Nevertheless, harnessing nostalgia, often viewed as a consumer's preference for goods and experiences from the past (Holbrook 1993), would appear to be good for business. Cattaneo and Guerini's (2012) research shows how customers are inclined to purchase retro brands over newer options. However, while there is an inclination towards brands with nostalgic associations, purchasers still have a desire for updated product features. Similarly, Stacey Menzel Baker and Patricia Kennedy (1994) refer to consumers having a sentimental yearning for products of the past and suggest that nostalgia is a useful selling tool, especially in hard economic times.

Radio is hardly a new technology. As it continues to age, there is perhaps an opportunity to add an additional category to Forty's (1986) three radio design classifications. This fourth stage could move beyond technological futurism to reflect manufacturers referencing of past radio designs, while still offering the latest innovations. I suggest the term retrofuturism can be applied to this new era of radio design. Sharon Sharp (2011: 25) refers to this movement as a 'distanced interest in past visions of the future', which draws on early representations of technical progress to form a sense of nostalgia for an idealized future that never arrived. By celebrating the heyday of radio, manufacturers remind users of the medium's innate strengths, at a time when traditional radio arguably faces its biggest challenges. The rise of streaming music services, podcasting and the attraction of social media, along with a myriad of other portable online activities, now vie for the listener's attention and have eroded radio's status as the pre-eminent electronic medium. Radio has a long design history to draw from, and manufacturers seem only too willing to exploit this heritage to maintain relevance and sales figures.

MEDIA MATERIALITIES

Conclusions

Over the course of this chapter, I have considered tensions which exist between radio as a seemingly ephemeral concept and radio as a concrete, material artefact. I showed how the shape and function of radio has constantly evolved, instep with the pace of technical innovation and the changing habits of radio listeners. However, while the form of radio as an object has transformed, the medium itself is largely unchanged. It remains a sound heard by an audience. Viewers are required to look at a television, focusing their attention on the object as they consume its content, yet this is clearly not the case with radio. The nostalgic concept of a family sitting round the radio listening to shows together is fast reaching the end of living memory. A radio's physical purpose is to exist as a conduit. Aside from the merits of fidelity and ease of use, etc., a radio has little bearing on the owners' enjoyment of content. This is perhaps just as well. As a teacher of radio production skills, I note that many students have never actually owned a traditional, stand-alone radio; their listening is wholly digital. For me, it is somewhat sobering to think that many young people have never even touched a radio and fail to recognize what one is. I am required to pass around my old Eastronic, as a relic of radio's once physical form. Indeed, many people today have never actively heard the medium, except as a secondary experience through visits to grandparents, standing in supermarket aisles, or being stuck in a car with aging parents. This may seem pessimistic, but it is the reality of radio's changing status an electronic medium.

Readers will no doubt be anxious to learn whether my precious Eastronic was able to be resurrected (see Figure 3.5). The repairer diagnosed the problem, ordered the required parts and carried out the necessary repairs. It was a strange moment to switch it on again, after decades of silence. There was a wash of static noise as I turned the tuning dial in search of a signal. Ultimately, I could only find four AM stations and the reception was poor. However, the fact that this technology still functioned after almost half a century struck me as impressive. While I have attempted to explain sentimental attachment to objects of the past and specifically the bond that may exist between a listener and their radio set, I recognize that these forms of connection are ultimately a trick of nostalgia. Radio does not exist in the wire coils and magnets which produce pressure waves, it exists inside our heads when these signals are converted into meaning.

Forty (1986: 203) questioned the housing of radio within cabinets, calling it a convenient design decision but 'not true to its nature'. But what exactly is the true form of radio's nature? As an auditory medium, does the future of radio even require a physical artefact? With the arrival of voice assisted 'smart speakers', such as Siri, Google Assistant, and Amazon's Alexa, a user can now control all of radio's functionality through spoken word commands. Perhaps this is the

FIGURE 3.5: The author's Eastronic portable radio. Author's own image.

future of radio's materiality; to be absorbed into the convenience of wireless speaker systems, which provide an output for multitudes of audio technologies and platforms. Gazi and Bonini (2018: 109–10) describe radio listening as an 'intangible and unworldly practice'. It would seem appropriate if the medium finally transcended the need for any physical form and became a truly invisible medium, as Peter Lewis and Jerry Booth (1989) once described it. The 'wireless' may yet become 'radioless'.

NOTES
1. https://www.easx.co.il/pages_e/221.aspx.
2. Interview with Lester Tandy, 27 August 2020.
3. https://www.rajar.co.uk/docs/news/RAJAR_DataRelease_InfographicQ12018.pdf.
4. https://www.rajar.co.uk/content.php?page=news.
5. https://www.worlddab.org/public_document/file/1048/Global_Summary_24.09.18.pdf.
6. https://www.amazon.co.uk/Bluetooth-Greadio-Fashioned-Enhancement-Connection-Walnut/dp/B07R3J2KVH.
7. https://www.steepletone.co.uk/about-us.

8. https://www.steepletone.co.uk/radios.
9. https://www.auna-multimedia.co.uk/Home-Audio/Stereo-Systems-Mini-HiFi-Systems/ Stereo-System-with-CD-Players/Belle-Epoque-1906-DAB-Retro-Stereo-System-Bluetooth- CD-USB-MP3-FM-CD-Player-Bluetooth-DAB-Radio.html?gclid=CjwKCAjwqIiFBhA- HEiwANg9szloEYnKzpzDdeFNwM97BE0LN7VDOLyl_v0KLk_UM7HpzxRJqq- T1OBoC9bQQAvD_BwE.
10. https://www.pewresearch.org/fact-tank/2020/08/06/many-around-the-world-were-pessi- mistic-about-inequality-even-before-pandemic/.
11. https://www.packagingstrategies.com/articles/92333-finding-comfort-in-the-past.

REFERENCES

Ala-Fossi, Marko (2010), 'The technological landscape of radio', in B. O'Neill, M. Ala-Fossi, P. Jauert, S. Lax, L. Nyre, and H. Shaw (eds), *Digital Radio in Europe: Technologies, Indus- tries and Cultures*, Bristol: Intellect, pp. 43–65.

Baker, Stacey Menzel and Kennedy, Patricia (1994*)*, 'Death by nostalgia: A diagnosis of context-specific cases', *Advances in Consumer Research*, 21, pp. 169–74.

Baxter, Weston, Aurisicchio, Marco, and Childs, Peter (2015), 'A psychological ownership approach to designing object attachment', *Journal of Engineering Design*, 26:4&6, pp. 140–56.

Betts, Raymond (2004), *A History of Pop Culture*, New York, London: Routledge.

Bicknell, Jeanette (2009), *Why Music Moves Us*, London: Palgrave Macmillan.

Brabazon, Tara (2012), *Popular Music: Topics, Trends and Trajectories*, London: Sage.

Cattaneo, Eleonora and Guerini, Carolina (2012), 'Assessing the revival potential of brands from the past: How relevant is nostalgia in retro branding strategies?', *Journal of Brand Management*, 19, pp. 680–87.

Chignell, Hugh (2009), *Key Concepts in Radio Studies*, Los Angeles, London: Sage.

Fickers, Andreas (2012), 'Visibly audible. The radio dial as mediating interface', in T. Pinch and K. Bijsterveld (eds), *The Oxford Handbook of Sound Studies*, Oxford: Oxford University Press, pp. 411–39.

Fort-Rioche, Laurence and Ackermann, Claire-Lise (2013), 'Consumer innovativeness, perceived innovation and attitude towards "neo-retro"-product design', *European Journal of Inno- vation Management*, 16:4, pp. 495–516.

Forty, Adrian (1986), *Objects of Desire: Design and Society Since 1750*, London: Thames and Hudson.

Frith, Simon (2002), 'Music and everyday life', *Critical Quarterly*, 44:1, pp. 35–48.

Gazi, Angeliki and Bonini, Tiziano (2018), '"Haptically Mediated" radio listening and its commodification: The remediation of radio through digital mobile devices', *Journal of Radio & Audio Media*, 25:1, pp. 109–25.

Geddes, Keith and Bussey, Gordon (1991), *The Setmakers: A History of the Radio and Televi- sion Industry*, London: Brema.

Geller, Valerie (2012), *Beyond Powerful Radio: A Communicator's Guide to The Internet Age. News, Talk, Information and Personality*, Burlington: Focal Press.

Goddard, Grant (2010), *DAB Digital Radio: Licensed to Fail*, London: Radio Books.

Guffey, Elizabeth (2006), *Retro: The Culture of Revival*, London: Reaktion Books.

Hilmes, Michele (2013), 'The new materiality of radio: Sound on screens', in M. Hilmes and J. Loviglio (eds), *Radio's New Wave*, New York: Routledge, pp. 43–61.

Hirsch, Alan R. (1992), 'Nostalgia: A neuropsychiatric understanding', *ACR North American Advances*, 19, pp. 390–95.

Holbrook, Morris B. (1993), 'On the new nostalgia: "These foolish things" and echoes of the dear departed past', in R. B. Browne and R. Ambrosetti (eds), *Continuities in Popular Culture: The Present in the Past and the Past in the Present and Future*, Bowling Green: Bowling Green State University Press, pp. 74–120.

Ingram, Andrew and Barber, Mark (2005), *An Advertiser's Guide to Better Radio Advertising: Tune in to the Power of the Brand Conversation Medium*, Chichester: John Wiley.

Jameson, Frederic (1991), *Postmodernism, or, The Cultural Logic of Late Capitalism*, Durham: Duke University Press.

Keith, Michael (2007), *The Radio Station*, London: Focal Press.

Kuffert, Len (2009), 'What do you expect of this friend?', *Media History*, 15:3, pp. 303–19.

Lacey, Kate (2000), 'Towards a periodization of listening: Radio and modern life', *International Journal of Cultural Studies*, 3:2, pp. 279–88.

Lefebvre, Henri (2000), *La Production de L'espace*, 4th ed., Paris: Editions Anthropos.

Leitner, Birgit (2011), 'Ernst Cassirer and (?) the Bauhaus: The question of functional aesthetics', *European Society for Aesthetics*, 3, pp. 167–209.

Lewis, Peter M. and Booth, Jerry (1989), *The Invisible Medium*, London: Macmillan.

Lewis, Peter M. (2000), 'Private passion, public neglect: The cultural status of radio', *International Journal of Cultural Studies*, 3:2, pp. 160–67.

Lloyd, David (2015), *How to Make Great Radio: Techniques and Tips for Today's Broadcasters and Producers*, London: Biteback Publishing.

Luca, Cecilia (2015), 'Affordances of intimacy: The extended self in human–environment interaction', in O. Kutz, S. Borgo, and M. Bhatt (eds), *Shapes Third Interdisciplinary Workshop SHAPES 3.0 – The Shape of Things 2015 Co-located with CONTEXT 2015*, Larnaca, Cyprus, 2 November, pp. 67–73, http://ceur-ws.org/Vol-1616/paper6.pdf. Accessed 21 April 2023.

MacFarland, David (1997), *Future Radio Programming Strategies: Cultivating Listenership in the Digital Age*, Mahwah: Lawrence Erlbaum Associates.

McEwan, Rufus (2010), 'Radio on the Internet, opportunities for new public spheres', *Journal of New Zealand*, 11:1, pp. 24–38.

McLeish, Robert (2005), *Radio Production*, London: Focal Press.

Millard, Andre (2000), 'Cassette tape', in T. Pendergast and S. Pendergast (eds), *St. James Encyclopedia of Popular Culture*, Detroit: St. James Press, pp. 451–52.

Miller, Daniel (1998), 'Material cultures', in D. Miller (ed.), *Material Cultures. Why Some Things Matter*, London: UCL Press, pp. 3–21.

Orfanella, Lou (1998), 'Radio: The intimate medium', *The English Journal*, 87:1, pp. 53–55.

Pierce, Jon, Kostova, Tatiana, and Dirks, Kurt (2001), 'Toward a theory of psychological ownership in organizations', *Academy of Management Review*, 26:2 pp. 298–310.

Priestman, Chris (2002), *Web Radio: Radio Production for Internet Streaming*, Oxford: Focal Press.

Radio Advertising Bureau (2015), *Audio Now; How a New Era of Listening is Helping the Advertiser Be Heard*, Industry Publication, London: RAB.

Shingler, Martin and Wieringa, Cindy (1998), *On Air: Methods and Meanings of Radio*, London: Arnold.

Sharp, Sharon (2011), 'Nostalgia for the future: Retrofuturism in Enterprise', *Science Fiction Film and Television*, 4:1, pp. 25–40.

Silverstone, Roger and Haddon, Leslie (1996), 'Design and the domestication of information and communication technologies: Technical change and everyday life', in R. Silverstone and R. Mansell (eds), *Communication by Design: The Politics of Information and Communication Technologies*, Oxford: Oxford University Press, pp. 44–74.

Starkey, Guy (2008), 'The quiet revolution: DAB and the switchover to digital radio in the United Kingdom', *Zer*, 13:25, pp. 163–78.

Stiernstedt, Fredrik (2014), 'The political economy of the radio personality', *Journal of Radio & Audio Media*, 21:2, pp. 290–306.

Stone, Alison (2016), *The Value of Popular Music: An Approach from Post-Kantian Aesthetics*, London: Palgrave Macmillan.

Tacchi, Jo (1998), 'Radio Texture: Between self and others', in D. Miller (ed.), *Material Cultures. Why Some Things Matter*, Chicago: University of Chicago Press, pp. 25–46.

Tacchi, Jo (2003), 'Nostalgia and radio sound', in M. Bull and L. Back (eds), *The Auditory Culture Reader*, Oxford: Berg, pp. 281–95.

Short Take 4

Materialities of Television History

E. Charlotte Stevens

In 2018 and 2019, I was lucky enough to access fanzine collections in Ontario and Texas. In both, I focused on a subset of zines that published 'letters of comment' (LOCs), known as letterzines, focusing on a sample from the late 1970s and early 1980s. The LOCs are not only about the programmes that the letter-writers are watching but also about how, where, and when this watching happens. In terms of materiality, these letterzines account for historical relationships with television in at least three directions:

- Reflecting on working with paper documents and their digital copies.
- In one case, the complementary collections overlapped, and the handwritten annotations on archived pieces differ.
- Material conditions of watching television are part of fans' accounts of being an audience.

This piece expands and reflects on these directions.

As material objects, I encountered these documents as physical artefacts and in their digitized versions. In Ontario, I worked through uncatalogued paper zines, pausing to note the texture, colour, and form as I took thousands of photos for future study. The material in Texas was supplied as pdf and tiff files, without getting hands-on. I'm mindful of my different approach to working with zines in both forms: the practice of reading and reviewing documents by flipping through physical pages (having sat on a plane to get there) differs from reading text in an image file at my leisure on a laptop, which differs again from being able to search through OCR'd pages in a pdf.

Each zine is a unique object, and this is emphasized with handwritten notes that individualize these 'mass' printed materials. For example, in the two collections, there are a pair of copies of the same zine issue, one postmarked June 1976, the other postmarked July 1976, with handwritten notes on the final page. One is

91

evidently a personal reply to a previous query; the other apologizes to the recipient for the delay in mailing the zine. These each give the individual object an anchoring in someone's life, making them more than just printed matter. They are not only periodicals but they are also used as notepaper.

The zines are a forum for television talk, with the letters themselves capturing historical accounts of television viewing. This is not merely what fans thought about storyworlds but includes the practice and experience of being a television audience. Offhand comments around the shows themselves show how media consumption is integrated into daily life and the material conditions thereof. For example, one LOC writer in 1975 describes keeping a Nielsen diary but points out its design does not capture that their schedule was atypical, or any qualitative response to what they watched, and that they had to fight with their antenna to get a decent colour picture of a syndicated *Star Trek* episode. However, in these comments and peripheral details in between plot and character chat, we get something of the texture, colour, and form of the material realities of pre-digital television.

The author subsequently developed this reflection into two articles (see Stevens 2020, 2021).

REFERENCES

Stevens, E. Charlotte (2020), '"Researching *Starsky and Hutch* is exquisite torture": Letters about television in 1980s media fanzines', *Alphaville*, 20, pp. 213–19.

Stevens, E. Charlotte (2021), 'Historical binge-watching: Marathon viewing on videotape', in M. Jenner (ed.), *Binge-Watching and Contemporary Television Studies*, Edinburgh: Edinburgh University Press, pp. 23–39.

SECTION 2

FORMAT

Introduction

Having considered the significance of form to our changing understanding of media materialities, this second section of the book moves on to notions of format, specifically the functions, uses, and social meanings of form within a given context. Questions of format have long been central to the ways in which we discuss and understand a broad range of media, with the term often used interchangeably with 'medium' as a way of indicating a particular unit of media consumption – be it compact disc or reel-to-reel, VHS or Blu-ray, minidisk or MP4.

In the context of this section, however, we seek to explore the complexities of format and its interconnections with wider notions of practice and cultural meaning. As Jonathan Sterne (2012: 8) observes, the notion of format is not as simple as merely describing a medium. For him, format is 'what specifies the protocols by which a medium will operate'. It demands a sense of specificity in the way that we think and talk about categories of media, and that we consider them not just as purely technological, but in relation to what people *do* with those media in order to create and understand their meaning.

In an ever-changing media landscape, such agility in our conception of format is essential to our understanding of the changing meanings of existing formats, and their influence and impact upon the ways in which new formats of media consumption are conceived and consumed. The chapters in this section, illustrated and supported by a range of short takes and reflections, invite us to reflect upon the changing relationships between media formats, social meanings, and cultural practice.

Philip Young's introductory article deals with many of these matters, recalling how his compact disc containing a recording of a David Bowie concert was damaged following the flooding of his home. Young's piece highlights the precarity and fragility of physical formats. Next is Iain A. Taylor's chapter, which explores independent recordings of artists distributing music on the assumed obsolete cassette tape format. Drawing on interviews with bands and their fans, Taylor investigates the relationship between digital and analogue technologies, arguing that it is a hybrid cultural artefact which appeals to music fans. Continuing with the music theme is Chris Mapp, who offers a short reflection on a free patch lead that came into his possession in 1994. Although Mapp rarely uses this cable, it travels with him as a reminder of why he became a musician.

Tensions between the digital and analogue are discussed by Christian Moerken, whose chapter looks at the cultural value of the physical book in the digital age. Using research into the German book market, Moerken argues that the physical book's material properties are central to its continuing popularity, especially during the COVID-19 pandemic. Dima Saber's material reflection also addresses the pandemic, questioning the material realities of her lockdown in rural Wales and its connection to the experiences of her family in Beirut. Moving back to video games, Regina Seiwald also explores the relationship between physical and digital materiality by addressing the paratextual elements of video games. For Seiwald, the physical and digital paratextual elements are fundamental to understanding the materiality of video games. Karen Patel closes this section by briefly considering how a materiality approach calls into question the skills and expertise of makers and the context in which they operate.

REFERENCE

Sterne, Jonathan (2012), *MP3: The Meaning of a Format*, Durham: Duke University Press.

Short Take 5

Only Dancing. Again

Philip Young

Cracked Actor (Live Los Angeles' 74) is a favourite among the 70?, 80?, 90?, David Bowie's CDs I 'own'. Favourite in a way, but by no means the most played. It doesn't include many of my favourite songs. In truth, I have very seldom played the actual CD, pictured in Figure ST.5.

You see, I am not a naturally tidy person. But I do take great care of books – you cannot tell which I have read and which I have not. (Unless I have spilt wine on them. Then you can.) My CDs, likewise, are pristine, especially the deluxe, bonus track, and special limited edition packaging ones which I am so easily lured into buying. (Yes, it is 2023 and I buy CDs.) But this *Cracked Actor* is not in pristine condition. You don't have to look carefully to see that the sleeve is warped, twisted, chipped, stripped, sticky, and deformed.

Collateral dampness. One night a canal paid a visit to my ground-floor flat. I lost hundreds of CDs. But the music is still there. They are playable. And I have most of the tracks saved digitally.

But I lost them.

So why *Cracked Actor*? It is a recording that captures a moment of transition, halfway through the gruelling American tour during which Bowie mutated from Diamond Dog to (plastic) soul singer. The metamorphosis, the changing of costume, of persona, the shedding of roles, was documented by Alan Yentob for a 1975 BBC documentary which I taped, microphone in front of the TV, and watched by my horrified father. (If he had seen my make-up experiments ...) Bowie in the back of a limousine (twenty-feet long?), a near corpse sustained by milk and cocaine. I was captivated as seen before but shocked to learn Ziggy was now a soul singer. Teenage rebel me didn't do soul. It took me a couple of years to remember President Nixon and become a *Young American*.[1]

There was an official release, the *David Live* double album (1974). It is not great. But in 2005, with a dial-up modem and great patience, I downloaded *Portrait In Flesh* (1996), a bootleg of the Philly Dogs show that is (or isn't) drawn

FIGURE ST.5: The author's copy of David Bowie's *Cracked Actor* CD. Author's own image.

from an illicit recording pirated as *Strange Fascination*. I burnt the mp3s onto a CD, made a cover, and I played it a lot. It turned me on.

In 2018, Parlophone released a Tony Visconti remix of the *Fascination* tapes as *Cracked Actor*. The sound is considerably better, but David's bizarre, regrettable (?) intros as a Puerto Rican street hustler are gone: 'Is-a goin' alright? Is a wantee rocknrollee now?', 'Everyone walk around. No fall down'. It features 'John, I'm Only Dancing (Again)' (1975) and that tender song about terrible behaviour, 'It's Gonna Be Me' (1975). If you don't know these tracks, and can't debate *Leon*, don't talk Bowie with me.

So my artefact is a flood-damaged version of a cleaned-up version of a less-than-authentic album that most people have never heard of, one that I will not use the insurance money to replace. Crack baby crack. Show me you're real.

NOTE

1. *Young Americans* was released in 1975.

4

Between Analogue and Digital: The Cassette Tape as Hybrid Artefact

Iain A. Taylor

Introduction

For many, the cassette tape is something of a lost format. In the prevailing decades, since sales of the format peaked in 1988 at 73 million units (BBC 2005: online), the cassette fell into relative obscurity in the western world, superseded in functionality by the compact disc and the digital file, and lacking the aesthetic and tactile staying power of the (recently reinvigorated) vinyl record. However, in recent years, the cassette tape format has seen a modest, but notable, cultural and commercial resurgence (see Taylor 2021). According to British Phonographic Industry figures, 156,542 cassettes were sold in the United Kingdom in 2020, the highest figure since 2003 and an increase of 94.7 per cent on 2019 sales (BPI 2021: online). This was driven by a number of big-name acts such as Lady Gaga, Dua Lipa, and The 1975 opting to release on cassette; evidence, from the recorded music industry's perspective, of 'the fan appeal of music in tangible formats as a complement to streaming' (BPI 2021: online).

While this spike in mainstream appeal, and subsequent media attention, suggests a sudden and perhaps unexpected reinvigoration of the format, interest in the cassette tape as a desirable medium of popular music consumption has been developing steadily over recent years, particularly within niche, underground, and do-it-yourself (DIY) circles of popular music culture (Curran 2016). This can be attributed to, at least in part, the increasingly inextricable relationship between the materiality of the cassette as a physical artefact and its proximity to a wider system of digital technologies and cultures (Düster 2020). This chapter explores the question of why this otherwise seemingly redundant format might be experiencing a new lease of cultural life, and what role an increasingly digitalized landscape of production and consumption might play in the format's reinvigoration, and shifting material meanings.

The cassette tape's shift from being a format in-and-of itself to being a 'tangible compliment to streaming' arguably reflects a shift in the cultures and practices that surround it. Traditionally, the consumer relationship with music formats like the cassette was predominantly a functional one; they were understood primarily in relation to their function as a music playing device – something to be listened to, and to be used. Below this surface pragmatism, however, has developed a more complex, symbolic relationship that exists between music fans and the materiality of formats as *things* – artefacts that act as 'objectified forms of psychic energy' (Csikszentmihalyi and Rochberg-Halton 1981: 175). Such artefacts, on the one hand, act as a site of identity construction, and as a focal point for the generation of meaning or under-standing of reality through that object. They are imbued with meanings which are inscribed upon them by music fans, forming part of an 'object-biography' concerned with constructing and comprehending notions of the self (Taylor 2019). On the other hand, these objects, by virtue of their own materiality, also play an active role in shaping such processes of objectification, pointing beyond themselves to the wider social processes through which meaning is produced and understood (Pottage 2012).

In its original cultural incarnation, the immediately apparent value of the cassette was largely a pragmatic one – a use value relationship based on the relative convenience of the format – stemming from the format's capacity for 'user-programming' (McCourt 2005: 250). In this framing, the cassette tape's capacity for user copying, recording, and re-recording dominated discussions of the meaning and value of the format (see Foster and Marshall 2015), and distin-guished it from other formats of music consumption, such as the vinyl record, in which the track-listing (and indeed the content) of the record was firm and fixed. Yet, the cassette tape as a format has also – in part retrospectively – acquired a wider symbolic meaning, derived from to its association with DIY and mixtape cultures which were actively shaped by the newfound capacity that cassettes offered music fans to copy, curate, and share music (see Moore 2005).

In the cassette's current re-emergence, these relationships have become frag-mented. With the act of listening increasingly migrating to digital channels, and the cassette becoming redefined as 'a compliment to streaming', what was once primarily a utilitarian object defined by its use value as a means of storing and playing recorded music is redefined as primarily symbolic in nature. As Margie Borschke (2017) notes, this technological and cultural shift has considerable impli-cations for producers, distributors, and consumers of culture. Moreover, it also has implications for 'the uses and meanings of systems of representation and media formats themselves; that is, their rhetorical use' (2017: 6). That is to say that the meaning of older, analogue formats becomes increasingly defined in relation to newer, digitalized ones, and as such possess different meanings and 'cultural possibilities' than they did in previous decades (6). As technologies of music production and consumption evolve and adapt, so to must their socio-cultural meanings. The cassette tape, when considered in this manner, represents a useful illustration of such shifting socio-cultural meanings of analogue artefacts in increasingly digitalized arenas of music production and consumption.

To that end, in this chapter, I draw upon a range of semi-structured interviews with artists, label owners, and fans from Scotland's independent music scene, in order to argue that the cassette tape represents a useful example of what might be understood as a 'hybrid artefact' – one in which the meanings, and socio-cultural implications, of that artefact are constructed and understood as somewhere between analogue and digital in form, and between pragmatism and symbolism in their socio-cultural use and meanings. From there, I speculate on the wider significance that this hybridity of format might have for discussions of the changing materiality of media more broadly.

Music, format, and hybridity

In spite of recorded music's relatively short history, the forms and formats which constitute it are in a constant state of flux, with each new form shaping both our interactions with, and perceptions of, the meanings and value of music. A common observation amongst scholars exploring the relationship between music, culture, and technology (for instance, Taylor 2001; Katz 2010) is that while the technologies which shape music production and consumption evolve rapidly, the deep-rooted cultural meanings which inform our engagements with such technologies are often slower to evolve and adapt. Music's materiality has been engrained in culture over the past hundred years, with the meanings stemming from that materiality intimately entangled with the wider meanings of popular music (Taylor 2019). With each new technological development, and each subsequent format of music consumption, there has been a seemingly irresistible move towards digital digitalized forms and formats, and a perceived sense of digital intangibility – a reversion back to music's 'age-old transience' which 'transforms a moment then disappears like a troubadour leaving town' (Pareles in McCourt 2005: 50), or perhaps a fulfilment, at least in part, of David Kusek and Gerd Leonhard's (2005: 3) prophetic claim that 'music will become like water: ubiquitous and free flowing'. However, as irresistible as it may seem, it must be acknowledged that this process of digitalization is never linear, and that increasingly, the lines which separate established categories of formats are becoming blurred. Jonathan Sterne's work on what he calls 'format theory' is particularly useful in helping conceive of, and articulate, what is meant when talking about 'format' in this sense:

> Format denotes a whole range of decisions that affect the look, feel, experience, and workings of a medium. It also names a set of rules according to which a technology can operate. In an analogue device, the format is usually a particular utilization of a mechanism. An old record player may play back a variety of formats such as LP, 45, 78, while a tape deck might only take compact cassettes. In a digital device, a format tells the operating system whether a given file is for a word processor, a web browser, a music playback program, or something else. Even though this may seem trivial, it can open out to a broader politics, as an administrative issue across platforms.
>
> (Sterne 2012: 7–8)

For Sterne, format is important as a concept is because it allows for distinction between the technologies which give form to particular ways of interacting with media, and consideration of the ways in which they are *used*. It is what 'specifies the protocols by which a medium will operate' (Sterne 2012) and as such, offers an ontological frame through which the meanings of that format can be understood and applied. It demands a sense of specificity in the way that we think and talk about categories of things and that we consider them not just as purely technological, but in relation to what people *do* with that technology:

> If there were a single imperative of format theory, it would be to focus on the stuff beneath, beyond, and behind the boxes our media come in, whether we are talking about portable MP3 players, film projectors, television sets, parcels, mobile phones, or computers.
>
> (Sterne 2012: 11)

This is a fundamental point in understanding the role of format in the context of music and culture. There is a compelling case that in the face of ever-increasing digitalization of music and culture, the very physicality of older, pre-digital formats takes on new significance in the context of this digitalization. Digital music, and the growing prevalence of access over ownership as the predominant mode through which we engage with music, inevitably demands a reconsideration, and perhaps a redefinition of our relationship with analogue, material music formats. There is an argument, however, that the opposite is also true – that our understanding of music in relation to material culture also informs and impacts upon the relationships that we form with digitalized, cloud-based music. The digitalization of music reveals itself, quite paradoxically, as a 'process in which the reconfiguration of the relationship between materiality and culture leads to a renewed role played by material objects in people's life and activities' (Magaudda 2011: 16).

This move to new technological forms, then, is often accompanied by 'unanticipated cultural consequences in the form of persistence and resurgence of the old stuff that somehow withstood the pressure of the new', or in forms of 'hybrid arrangements between old and new', each with its own 'dynamic of cross-fertilization' (Bartmanski and Woodward 2015: 165). Such a hybridity of meaning, arguably, can be observed in the changing consumption practices of recorded music. The vast majority of new releases on vinyl, for instance, have also come with a digital download code for some time, with platforms such as Amazon providing a digital copy as standard with all online sales (Baldwin 2013). It is also notable that research by carried out in 2016 by Independent Communications and Marketing Unlimited suggested that out of the people surveyed who purchased music on vinyl in March of that year, 48 per cent admitted to not having actually played the records that they bought (Savage 2016). For many who currently purchase vinyl, it could be argued that the physical record and the sleeve that houses it are only part of the experience. The digital component of the record is a fundamental part of the way that it is understood, engaged with, and valued and, if the above figures are to be believed, is perhaps an even more fundamental part to the way that purchases on this format are listened to and used. The value attached to the physical artefact, therefore, has been redefined and adapted as a result of technological and cultural interventions in the relationships that we as individuals form with it.

Hybridity and materiality

> I think some of [the people involved in the indie and punk scene] are going out and buying tape players. I would say that it's fifty-fifty [between people who listen to the tapes they purchase and those who only listen to downloads]. But you get the download code and it looks cool.
>
> ('James' 2014)

It is notable, then, that a key theme emerging from this investigation into cassette culture was a significant disconnect between the music cassette as music format and the music cassette as a cultural artefact in the eyes of the majority of participants. Across 23 interviews, it became increasingly apparent that the number of people actually *listening* to music cassettes was very low, a point which mirrors the figures cited above in relation to the number of people who purchase, but do not actually play, vinyl records. While 'James', an indie-punk musician and cassette proponent in his mid twenties, put the figure at around half-and-half, other participants put it even lower, with one cassette label owner, telling me 'I'll be honest, I know two people who regularly buy from me who actually own a cassette player' (2014).

Instead, as 'James' suggested, many of the people purchasing the music which is being sold in cassette format are *listening* to that music digitally, either via the digital download code accompanying the physical cassette or through online streaming platforms such as Bandcamp, as opposed to playing the cassette tapes themselves. This merging of formats, technologies, and cultural experience – the analogue physicality of the cassette tape, and the digitalized, cloud-based nature of streaming and digital downloads – effectively recreates the cassette tape as a hybrid artefact. It cannot be understood in its current cultural context without considering how these two technologies and formats function together to create meaning in relation to the cassette as an artefact. While physically, and technologically indistinguishable from pre-digital iterations of the format, the meaning and value of the cassette tape is now increasingly defined by its hybridity, through its pairing with digital music technologies, and, as a result, redefining users' relationships the materiality of the cassette tape as format and artefact.

The significance of the cassette tape's materiality was a recurring theme across interviews, and many conversations with participants focused on their relationship to the physicality of artefacts like cassettes. There was a sense that a significant part of the cassette tape's appeal was closely intertwined with its existence as an artefact, the physical presence of the format itself, and by extension, its degree of distinction or difference from other more digitalized forms of music consumption. There was broad consensus amongst participants that their enjoyment of the format, and the reason that they chose to purchase music on cassette, was linked in some way to the materiality of the cassette as *thing*, in the sense of Mihaly Csikszentmihalyi and Eugene Rochberg-Halton's (1981) use of the term, and the materiality of the cassette tape as an artefact: 'I like having things. They're all kind of becoming a bit defunct now, but I just like having something. That's my hobby, music is my hobby, and that's how I spend my money' ('Ollie' 2014).

For 'Ollie', a punk and hardcore fan in his late teens, it was not always made explicitly clear *why* the physicality of the format was so important. 'It's kind of hard to explain', he remarked, 'I think it's just sort of something to *have*' (2014). While the significance of the format's materiality was not always precisely articulated, there was rarely any ambiguity as to the importance of meaning attached to the physical qualities of the artefact. At a moment in time where music listening continues to become increasingly digitalized and cloud-based, there was a sense that the physicality of formats like vinyl records and tapes, once a taken-for-granted quality of any recorded music format, began to take on new significance. For many participants, the sense of the cassette tape's materiality was understood and articulated as being intimately linked to its difference from more familiar physical formats, such as the CD and the vinyl record, as well as in relation to the perceived non-physical nature of other, digitalized formats. As a result, the meaning of the cassette tape, in this context, is defined and articulated as part of a wider system of music formats, and in relation to their collective social and cultural meanings, defined in part by tensions between old and new formats, and the redefinition of meanings in the face of new forms and formats of mediation (Tischleder and Wasserman 2015). This otherness of the cassette is illustrated in the comments of 'Ross', a former cassette-label owner: 'it's not a CD, it's not a record – it's something completely different. Some kids who come to shows and buy things are, like, 15 and had never experienced cassettes in their lives' (2014).

It is noteworthy that, for many of the younger people participating in the independent music scenes explored in this research, the cassette tape was not a nostalgic throwback – cassette tape, in this context, was something experienced simultaneously as both retro connection to a popular past, and a novel, new cultural discovery. There is an interesting juxtaposition here, wherein the CD, essentially a physical manifestation of a digital music format, clearly lacked the same degree of novelty or fascination afforded to vinyl or cassette tapes to many participants. There was a sense that the CD occupied a space of the common, familiar, and every-day, whereas the cassette tape, in particular, possessed a sense of excitement and aura stemming from its broader socio-cultural symbolism as a retro artefact, and its relative novelty of not being as readily and commercially available as vinyl records.

Many participants spoke of the desire to come away from a gig with some*thing*, and with CDs falling out of favour, and vinyl often prohibitively expensive, the cassette offered an interesting material compromise. 'Korin' commented:

> If there's a tape at a show I'd buy it. It's not necessarily my first choice, like, I'll buy vinyl if I can, but I like buying tape because you get a download code, and I think a lot of bands sound great on tape. Tape's cool, it's cheap, so aye I buy a tape if I can.
>
> ('Korin' 2014)

The materiality of the cassette tape, and its relative affordability in comparison to vinyl, contributed significantly to its appeal for 'Korin', and others like them. For many, beyond the format's relative affordability, it stuck out in relation to other formats by virtue of its comparative novelty, both to teenagers who were discovering the format for the first time, and to others who had previously listened to music on cassette, and noted the format's re-emergence. Once such person was 'Nessa', a DJ and music enthusiast in her early 30s:

> One thing I've noticed at wee indie gigs around Glasgow is that they'll have a variety of formats for sale, CDs, vinyl, and cassettes [...]. I bought two cassettes actually, part of the reason was I was like 'Oooh, it's a cassette!'
>
> ('Nessa' 2014)

There was often an implicit understanding amongst participants that, for people who were not involved in the independent music scene, this fascination with an obsolete format, particularly one which often went un-played, might be seen as verging on fetish, or at the least, materialistic or shallow. This self-awareness and reflexivity often came across in several conversations, particularly when asked about what it is that motivates participants to buy music on physical formats like cassette when they could access the same music online, in a way which is cheaper and arguably more convenient. It is through these kinds of reflections that the notion of hybridity becomes particularly apparent. At a point in time when so much music is available in a digitalized and cloud-based form, the very need by many participants to articulate the 'physical' nature of these formats highlights an important and essential distinction between what a format *was* and what it now *is*:

> I guess it represents a sort of consumerism, well, not a consumerism, but kind of materialistic because you want to own something, you know? But I know guys who own loads of fucking expensive clothes and they never wear them or only wear them on the odd occasion, so why own them? [...] [With tape, it's] something a bit different, it's a collector's item [...], you're not necessarily going to listen to it, you might buy it and download it, but it's having it.
>
> ('James' 2014)

Certainly, it is possible to frame this pre-occupation with physicality in musical stuff in terms of claims of shallow materialism – an acquisition of objects for their own sake. Indeed, a number of participants, as illustrated by the above quote from 'James', specifically frame their interests in the context of a 'kind of' materialistic consumerism. However, it is this notion of the 'kind-of-material', a sense of *sort-of-but-not-quite* in relation to the physicality of the artefact, which arguably is so important, and often overlooked, in attempts to understand the way that these participants value the materiality of recorded music. So many musical artefacts – be they cassette tapes, vinyl records, or CDs – are no longer *truly* necessary, in terms of use value, to access music. For original adopters of the music cassette, the value of a cassette was an aggregate of its exchange value (what you paid for it/what you could swap it for), its symbolic value (as a statement of taste, identity, and cultural competency), and its use value (primarily as a means of transporting and reproducing music). Yet, for the participants in this research, these values have become disrupted. While the exchange value and symbolic value still reside with the artefact itself, its use value as a means of actually listening to music now resides elsewhere, in the digital otherness of the download code and the cloud. In this sense, the cassette or the vinyl record is no longer a pragmatic tool, rather, it is recreated as a symbolic artefact, primarily (but not exclusively) used in identity construction.

Hybridity and nostalgia

Because hybridity is articulated and understood in relation to the *revaluing* of the cassette tape's materiality, and a change in its meaning from what it *was* to what it *is*, it is perhaps also inevitable that the notion of hybridity is intimately linked with a sense of the history and past cultural meanings of that artefact. To those who experienced its pre-digital incarnations, the cassette tape had (and continues to have) a very particular set of cultural meanings attached to it. There is a sense of nostalgic resonance to the format, often closely linked with the freedom that the format offered for creative user-programming – of creating mixtapes in the way that is romanticized in the likes of Nick Hornby's (1995) novel *High Fidelity*, or Thurston Moore's (2005) art-book *Mixtape: The Art of Cassette Culture*. As a result of the format's strong and enduring cultural resonance, in many of wider conversations on the subject cassette tapes, the question of nostalgia inevitably came up. Nostalgia, in this sense, might be considered in a manner akin to Jannelle Wilson's (2005) notion of 'collective nostalgia'. This form of nostalgia speaks to the way in which an individual might experience a romantic fondness for an idealized moment in the past which they did not experience personally, or a reimagining of a period that they did experience in line with the cultural narratives which describe that period. 'The public culture', Wilson (2005: 31) argues, 'contains powerful symbols of the past. These cultural symbols become more personal, as we, unavoidably, construct our identities from that which is available to us culturally'. In the context of cultural conversations around music and format, this kind of collective nostalgia often manifests itself in a re-emergence of old cultural forms, reinterpreted or re-appropriated in a new way. The re-emergence of the cassette tape as a format is a particularly clear example.

In much of the critical and cultural commentary which engages with these kinds of reappropriations, re-valuings, and *representations* of cultural artefacts, the broad discussion is framed along the lines of Simon Reynolds's (2011) concept of 'Retromania' – of a popular culture which is increasingly fixated with a nostalgic recreation of its own past. For Reynolds, and many others who share his point of view, the re-emergence of seemingly superseded formats such as cassette tapes or vinyl records is just another example of popular culture's unhealthy fascination with its own past, and its nostalgic obsession with the perceived authenticity uncritically afforded to past cultural forms and practices. Writing for the online publication *PopMatters* towards the start of the cassette's re-emergence, Calum Marsh (2009: n.pag.) comments that 'at best, the cassette revival is merely a vacuous fad of no genuine value; but at worst, it's a confused cultural misstep more dangerous than most would admit', something which is imbued with 'a kind of antique novelty' in the face of new digital systems of production and consumption. For Marsh, and many other commentators echoing the sentiment of his piece, the revival of cassettes may be emblematic of wider cultural regression – a churlish, knee-jerk rejection of the possibilities afforded by new, digital means of production and distribution, rooted in a misplaced sense of authenticity, nostalgia and retro hipness.

Many participants indicated an awareness of this form of hipster stereotype relating to the revaluing of cassettes, which most were, unsurprisingly, eager to distance themselves from. When asked about the cassette tape's ties to wider clichés around the hipster character, for instance, one participant, a heavily tattooed hardcore-punk fan in their mid twenties, angrily responded 'Do I look like a fucking hipster to you?' The offense taken at the term, for this participant and many others like them, appeared not to stem from a fear of surface association with a particular sense of style or fashion. Rather, it appeared to stem from a sense that the hipster stereotype describes a kind of cultural participation which is superficial and surface, and importantly, one which belied the depth of the sense of community and participation they saw as inherent to their involvement in the independent music scene. This eagerness not to be defined in accordance with cultural stereotype was often expressed in conjunction with one of the other key themes from the interviews, that of participation in 'the scene' – those 'informal assemblages' of participants in music communities (Peterson and Bennett 2004: 4) from which their socio-cultural meaning is defined and derived. The core importance of a sense of community, and the significance of being *part of something*, was seen as being a key component of participants' relationship with music and culture, and as a substantial factor to the way in which they understood and articulated their own personal sense of identity through their music consumption.

Hybridity and participation

I've got some tapes and records that I hardly ever play, but I think it's sort of a collector's think. One, it supports the band, which is the main thing.

('John' 2015)

The vast majority of participants with whom I spoke to told me that this sense of participation within an independent music culture, and the sense of community derived from it, was one of the main motivating factors, if not *the* motivating factor, in purchasing cassettes. Being seen to support the bands and labels who were producing and performing the kind of music that they wanted to hear and see was a core component of how one participated in the scene. For these participants, purchasing a cassette had the pragmatic value of supporting acts and artists that they admired, as well as a symbolic value of distinguishing them as active contributors compared to others on the peripheries of the scene. It was widely acknowledged that you did not need to purchase the music to access it, that you could stream it for free online, get copies from their friends, or simply download the music illegally. As such, the act of purchasing and owning a certain cassette became a symbolic token of one's involvement in the scene, as someone who does not merely observe or listen, but instead as an active participant in independent music and who actively contributes to the *production* of culture. 'Tape', as one participant remarked to me, 'is for people who care, who put a bit more into music than listening to the radio or watching TV. It's for people who *care*'. For these participants, buying cassette tapes from independent artists and labels was less concerned with the kinds of conspicuous consumption associated with the hipster stereotype and concerned with a desire to contribute, participate, and belong. This is significant, as it illustrates a notable shift in the primary motivation for purchasing cassettes from that of the generation that originally adopted them, transforming the artefact itself from being broadly practical – a means of storing and playing music – to something broadly symbolic – at once a pragmatic way of contributing to the scene, and a symbolic badge of that participation, recognizable to other likeminded participants.

Likewise, for those running the labels producing and distributing the cassettes, the overarching aim appeared to be participation in the wider independent music scene, and supporting bands who produced music which excited them. One cassette enthusiast, and owner of a cassette label, emphasized that their decision to run a label was all about helping the local bands that he listened to, and who were, themselves, seen to be contributing to the local scene: 'the ethos behind it is that I kind of like to help bands that are in that local sort of mind-set, you know?' This sense of locality and community, by its very nature, tends towards small but enthusiastic audiences. Without large enough audiences to take advantage of the kinds of economies of scale needed to secure profitable manufacturing costs on other formats such as vinyl records, the bands and labels producing and releasing music within these scenes operate within very tight margins. While many acts and labels, if asked, would likely prefer to be releasing music on vinyl because of the format's perceived superiority (both sonically and aesthetically), a major appeal of the cassette tape was its convenience to produce, manufacture, and sell, in short runs, and at low cost. As one cassette label owner noted when asked about the appeal of cassette as a format:

> We tend to release on tape because [...] it's cheap to manufacture, it's easy to recoup, and it leaves money left over for the bands to get something [...]. The average run is about 50, yeah. It's a pretty niche market.
>
> ('Ross' 2014)

The cassette tape, then, becomes a convenient compromise – a means servicing music fans' desire for physical forms and formats, but at a low enough cost so as to allow money from the sales to go back to the artists who produce them. As previously noted, the majority of cassette releases within the Scottish independent music scenes explored in this study came with a digital download code, but even if they did not, most participants seemed to agree that they would be able to find and listen to the music online if they so desired. In fact, it was commonplace for some cassette-based labels, after a period of weeks or months from a cassette's original release, to make digital copies of that release available for free anyway.

> If we're selling [cassettes] at a gig, I'd normally just tell people to email the label and I'll manually give them a code, just so they've got one, but they never ever get in touch. I would expect them to, and I always say you can, but nine times out of ten, after two weeks I put everything I release up for free on Bandcamp.
>
> ('Ross' 2014)

In spite of an awareness that the music would eventually find its way online, when asking if this digital altruism impacted upon sales, there was a general that the short runs of cassettes that are being produced and sold generally tend to sell out:

> The first run of [our debut] tape release we got 50 made and sold them in a month, so we got another 50 made [...]. Our most recent we got 60, but the good thing about that is [our current label] makes them, so they just make 30 and sell them and make another 30.
>
> ('John' 2015)

It may seem unusual to purchase music which is available for free, especially on a format that you are unlikely to (or may even lack the necessary equipment to) listen to. However, there was a sense amongst participants, sometimes implicit, sometimes explicitly stated, that the act of buying a cassette – of handing over currency in exchange for an artefact – was not necessarily linked to the actual practice of *listening* to the music being purchased. Instead, it was an act of contributing to, and participating in, the future production of that music as part of a community of music fans and producers. It extended beyond the act of individual listening and into a wider cultural participation in their chosen scene. In this sense, the symbolic value of the cassette as an artefact might be better understood as referring to consumers' use of the symbolic meaning embodied in cultural goods in the construction, sustainment, and expression of their sense of self-identity (Larsen et al. 2010). The decision to purchase the cassette had less to do with its functionality and use value as a music playing device, and instead was intimately tied to the way in which that individual understood and expressed their personal identity as a music fan. However, equally importantly, the practice of purchasing cassettes as an act of participation was, and is, also a means of being *seen* to participate. In this sense, the cassette as an artefact, and the act of purchasing it within that particular context, might be understood as valuable primarily as a symbolic token of participation in that scene – one which signals that involvement to like-minded participants, while also actively contributing to the ongoing cultural production of sustains that scene into the future.

Conclusion

This chapter has argued that increasing digitalization of culture in general has led to a re-approaching of physical music formats such as audio cassettes. Over the past couple of decades, cultural practices associated with music consumption have been increasingly defined (and redefined) in relation to the rapid development and adoption of digital music playing technologies and formats. Yet, as shown through the example of the use of cassettes in Scottish independent music culture, for many individuals and groups within contemporary popular culture, increasing digitalization has also led to the rediscovery and redefinition of artefacts and materialities from previous cultural moments. As Paolo Magaudda (2011) has noted, 'new objects and devices and old ones are not mutually exclusive', with their respective 'material configurations' facilitating the development of a range of listening practices stemming from 'both material activities and symbolic value' (2011: 31). The example of the cassette tape in this chapter offers a useful illustration of the evolving materiality of old technologies redefined in the context of new. Moreover, it highlights the ways in which a sensitivity to the changing materiality of music consumption can offer insight into the complex and evolving value relationships that music fans have with recorded music formats and artefacts. While music listening practices continue to migrate towards digital platforms, this shift in listening practices has, in turn, redefined old and (arguably) broadly redundant formats. It invests these formats with a new-found symbolic value and a newfound materiality which is defined and understood by its degrees of difference to digital forms and formats.

So, what does this changing materiality mean for our relationship with music artefacts? Certainly, there is the risk that by separating our functional relationship with an artefact from the artefact itself, such relations become reduced to a 'fetish-isation of objects for objects' sake; a state of 'alienated attention' (Csikszentmihalyi and Rochberg-Halton 1981: 186) in which these music formats are reduced to attention-getting devices, defined purely by superficiality as opposed to the specific functions or qualities of the formats themselves. However, to describe the relationships with the cassette tape illustrated above as mere fetish would be to take a very narrow conception of the cassette's function in the context in which it is used. Although the cassette is not used primarily as a music playing device, it does not immediately mean that is without function. Through an examination of the changing materiality of a formerly redundant format redefined in relation to new digitalized forms of listening, this chapter has attempted to illustrate some of the ways in which independent music fans negotiate value in a system of culture that is increasingly defined by accelerating digitalization on the one hand, and the rediscovery and redefinition of material things on the other. By viewing artefacts like the cassette not as a materialistic fetish, but rather, as a symbolic thing, linking together sets of digital and physical cultural practices, we can better understand the richness and totality of how these practices as a whole enact meaning and value, without over-privileging, or arbitrarily dismissing one or the other.

REFERENCES

Baldwin, Roberto (2013), 'Now when you buy vinyl from Amazon, you get a digital copy free', *Wired* [online]. Available at: https://www.wired.com/2013/04/amazon-vinyl-to-digital/. Accessed 21 April 2023.

Bartmanski, Dominik and Woodward, Ian (2015), *Vinyl: The Analogue Record in the Digital Age*, London: Bloomsbury.

BBC News (2005), 'Not long left for cassette tapes'. Available at: http://news.bbc.co.uk/1/hi/technology/4099904.stm. Accessed 21 April 2023.

Borschke, Margie (2017), *This is Not a Remix: Piracy, Authenticity & Popular Music*, London: Bloomsbury

BPI (2021), 'Fans turn to music to get through 2020 as a new wave of artists fuels streaming growth'. Available at: https://www.bpi.co.uk/news-analysis/fans-turn-to-music-to-get-through-2020-as-a-new-wave-of-artists-fuels-streaming-growth/. Accessed 21 April 2023.

Curran, Kieran (2016), '"On Tape": Cassette Culture in Edinburgh and Glasgow Now', in R. Purcell and R. Randall (eds) *21st Century Perspectives on Music, Technology, and Culture*, Basingstoke: Palgrave Macmillan, pp. 33–55.

Csikszentmihalyi, Mihaly and Rochberg-Halton, Eugene (1981), *The Meaning of Things: Domestic Symbols and the Self*, Cambridge: Cambridge University Press.

Düster, Benjamin (2020), 'Obsolete technology? The significance of the cassette format', in T. Tofalvy and E. Barna (eds) *Popular Music, Technology, and the Changing Media Ecosystem: From Cassettes to Stream*, London: Palgrave Macmillan.

Foster, Pacey and Marshall, Wayne (2015), 'Tales of the tape: Cassette culture, community radio, and the birth of rap music in Boston', *Creative Industries Journal*, 8:2, pp. 164–76

Hornby, Nick (1995), *High Fidelity*, London: Victor Gollancz.

Katz, Mark (2010), *Capturing Sound: How Technology Has Changed Music*, Berkley: University of California Press.

Kuseck, David and Leonhard, Gerd (2005), *The Future of Music: Manifesto for the Digital Music Revolution*, Boston: Berklee Press.

Larsen, Gretchen, Lawson, Rob, and Todd, Sarah (2010), 'The symbolic consumption of music', *Journal of Marketing Management*, 26:7-8, pp. 671–85.

Magaudda, Paolo (2011), 'When Materiality Bites Back: Digital music consumption practices in the age of dematerialization', *Journal of Consumer Culture*, 11:1, pp. 15–36.

Marsh, Calum (2009), 'Reconsidering the revival of cassette tape culture', *PopMatters* [online]. Available at: https://www.popmatters.com/116282-reconsidering-the-revival-of-cassette-tape-culture-2496127682.html. Accessed 21 April 2023.

McCourt, Tom (2005), 'Collecting music in the digital realm', *Popular Music and Society*, 28:2, pp. 249–52.

Moore, Thurston (2005), *Mixtape: The Art of Cassette Culture*, New York: Universe.

Pottage, Alain (2012), 'The Materiality of What?', *Journal of Law and Society*, 39:1, pp. 167–83

Reynolds, Simon (2011), *Retromania: Pop Culture's Addiction to Its Own Past*, London: Faber and Faber.

Savage, Mark (2016), 'Music streaming boosts sales of vinyl', BBC [online]. Available at: http://www.bbc.co.uk/news/entertainment-arts-36027867. Accessed 29 June 2021.

Sterne, Jonathon (2012), *MP3: The Meaning of a Format*, Durham: Duke University Press.

Taylor, Iain A. (2019), '"Well-worn grooves": Music, materiality and biographical memory', *Popular Music History*, 12:3, pp. 256–74.

Taylor, Iain A. (2021), 'Audio cassettes: Despite being "a bit rubbish", sales have doubled during the pandemic – Here's why', *The Conversation*, https://theconversation.com/audio-cassettes-despite-being-a-bit-rubbish-sales-have-doubled-during-the-pandemic-heres-why-157097. Accessed 21 April 2023.

Taylor, Timothy (2001), *Strange Sounds: Music, Technology & Culture*, London: Routledge.

Tischleder, Babette and Wasserman, Sarah (2015), 'Introduction: Thinking out of sync', in B. Tischleder and S. Wasserman (eds), *Cultures of Obsolescence: History, Materiality, and the Digital Age*, Cham: Springer, pp. 1–17.

Wilson, Jannelle (2005), *Nostalgia: Sanctuary of Meaning*, Lewisburg: Bucknell University Press.

Short Take 6

Patch Lead Possibilities

Chris Mapp

I'm not overly sentimental.

Despite owning sizeable collections of musical equipment, records, bikes, books, and tools, very little is kept unless it is of some practical use. Possessions come and go as they are needed. When it comes to my pedalboard I'm particularly ruthless. If I buy a new pedal I keep its box, not for posterity, but so it will hold more value when I (sometimes quite hastily) decide to sell it on eBay.

Amongst all of the useful sound manglers, wires, cables, and power leads is a patch lead I've owned for nearly 25 years (see Figure ST.6). A patch lead is designed

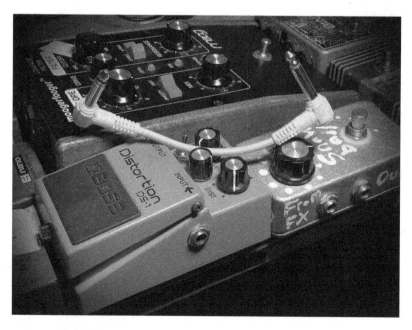

FIGURE ST.6: The author's patch lead. Author's own image.

to carry an audio signal from one device to another. As someone who uses multiple effects pedals simultaneously, I have a lot of patch leads but, unless they are awaiting repair, they are all plumbed into my board. This one remains in my gig bag, unused. The patch lead is made from badly moulded yellow plastic. It measures less than six inches. There is a manufacturing defect at one end and some of the plastic casing has come away. It has always been like this.

It came free with the August 1994 copy of *Guitarist* magazine, sellotaped to the front in a small baggie. The cover featured a grinning Mark Knopfler superimposed onto a collage of multi-coloured Dire Straits album covers. I have never been a guitarist or a fan of Dire Straits, and I don't know if I ever bought the magazine again. The only reason for me to buy it was to get that yellow patch lead.

At the time I didn't own a single effects pedal, let alone multiple pedals that would require a patch lead to chain them together. I had no practical use for it yet, to me, the lead represented a world I aspired to be a part of. This was the sort of thing that 'professional musicians' owned and to a teenage bass player that meant everything.

I could only dream of the wah-wahs, distortions, fuzzes, phasers, octavers, reverbs, delays, and as-yet-unknown-to-me pedals that I could plug my new lead into. The endless possibilities of creating new sounds with my bass were represented by this tiny patch lead. My teenage curiosity led me to scour magazines, album covers, and liner notes to learn more about the world to which I felt I now held the key.

When I eventually began to build my collection of effects pedals, I realized that the lead was of little practical use to me. It's too short to make the connections I need around my current board. Despite this, tucked in my gig bag, it goes everywhere with me. The lead has survived hundreds of gigs, countless house moves, and outlived many other jack leads, patch leads, XLR connectors, and power cables that have come and gone.

It represents possibility.

It reminds me to stay curious.

It reminds me of why I got into this in the first place.

5

'Because It Is Not Digital':
The Cultural Value of the Analogue
Book in the Digital Age

Christian Moerken

Introduction

In the autumn of 2020, the Organization for Economic Co-Operation and Development (OECD) released a study that considered the economic impact of the COVID-19 pandemic on the cultural sector (Travkina et al. 2020). The report highlighted the sector's abrupt drop in revenue, as concerts were cancelled and museums, theatres, and cinemas were forced to close, resulting in reduced earnings and job losses in many countries around the world (Comunian et al. 2020: 112; Jeannotte 2021; Martins et al. 2020: 477). Yet, in Germany, the book industry continued to operate with almost no restrictions, despite many other businesses in the cultural sector being shut down. Bookshops were deemed to be important in ensuring the intellectual wellbeing of the population and remained open. Some criticized this decision. In an article published in *Cicero*, a German national magazine dedicated to political discourse, Marius Müller (2020: n.pag.), the director of one of Bavaria's largest state libraries, expressed his difficulty in understanding the rationale behind keeping physical bookstores open when it seemed both feasible, and potentially more fitting, for individuals to access e-books or purchase books online. Why were analogue books and physical sales outlets preferred over the digital and remote forms of consumption? I will attempt to answer this question by considering how the materiality of the book plays affects its cultural value in the digital age.

At this point, it is essential to explain how I use the term 'materiality' in this chapter, as the distinction between the digital and what is referred to as material is complex. Digitization is often equated with the dematerialization of objects (Magaudda 2011: 15; Smil 2016). Bruno Latour and Adam Lowe (2011) and

Wanda Orlikowski and Susan Scott (2008) suggest that the physical or material and conceptual (immaterial) are phenomena of different orders. For them, the physical or material can be touched and the conceptual (immaterial) cannot. Conversely, Paul Leonardi (2010) argues that the definition of materiality cannot be reduced to whether something can be touched or not. For example, he sees software as not tangible but points out that it still has hard constraints and affordances in much the same way as physical material artefacts do. Leonardi therefore argues that the definition of whether something is material or immaterial should be rather based on the constraints and affordances an object provides. It is these constraints and affordance that Katherine Hayles (2003: 263) refers to when suggesting that the meaning of a work, whether print or electronic, cannot be separated from its physical manifestation. She states that the distinctive physical organization of novels is crucial to how they are read and the purposes they serve. According to Leonardi (2010: n.pag.) and Hayles (2003: 263), there are similar limits and preconditions to the use of media in the digital world as in the non-digital world. This means that a separation of analogue and digital media, as is often brought forward in the discussion of the dematerialization of media, cannot be maintained. For this chapter, however, the discussion of whether the digital has similar material properties as the physical or analogue is of secondary importance. This chapter is primarily concerned with the cultural value of the analogue book and how the difference between haptic and non-haptic, respectively, analogue and digital media, is perceived.

Consumers' perception of material has been an essential aspect of my research into the cultural value of the analogue book in the digital age. Today, sales of compact discs have fallen compared to those of digital music downloads and music streaming (Koh et al. 2019: 25; Rashidi 2020: 127; Wang 2019), while more films and television series are streamed by consumers than are sold on DVD (Whitten 2019; Yu et al. 2017). However, fourteen years after the introduction of the Amazon Kindle, sales of analogue books outnumber those of e-books (Richter 2021), suggesting that most readers still prefer analogue books. Why might this be? To answer this question, I investigated the German book market, one of the largest in Europe, home to the world's biggest book fair – in Frankfurt – and Random House, of the world's biggest publishing group. In 2018, I carried out interviews with publishers, authors, booksellers, as well as focus groups with readers and collectors of books. Speaking to a range of players in the book market made it possible to gain an understanding of how producers and consumers of books valued the material properties of the analogue book.

This research produced three key findings. First, the cultural value of the analogue book depends on its materiality, while its apparent limitations are perceived as an advantage. Second, the analogue book evokes feelings of nostalgia, and this is valued by collectors and authors alike. Publishers and booksellers take advantage of this nostalgia by producing special editions for these target groups. Third, the advancing digitization of media has resulted in the emergence of a group of readers and authors I call the connoisseurs of the book. These protect the analogue book from disappearing by buying more books. Each of these findings highlights the importance and significance of the materiality of the analogue book in the digital age.

Content and format: Research on books in the digital age

Previous research on the book in the digital age has often focused on the processes of mass and large-scale digitization. Scholars have explored different approaches to digitization, for example, in Project Gutenberg, Google Scholar, and Google Books. They have considered Anglo-American dominance in the digitization of libraries, along with copyright issues and the impact that digitization has on a book's structure (Coyle 2006: 641, 2009; Gooding et al. 2013: 629; Nunberg et al. 1996; Richardson 2015). Another focus has been on reading, particularly the ability of readers to concentrate on, and comprehend, digital and analogue texts (Baron 2015; Rosenberg and Simon 2015; Singer et al. 2017: 1007). Most of these scholars take a negative attitude towards the reading of e-books. Sven Birkerts (1994), for example, claims that it means the loss of what he calls 'deep time' where people allow the words of the text to create an understanding of its more profound meaning. He argues that reading large amounts of digital text causes our attention span to decrease. Maryanne Wolf (2008) fears that future generations will become so used to the immediate availability of on-screen information that their attention and inferential and semantic skills will be less developed. Naomi Baron (2015) argues that e-book readers provide too many distractions for readers, seducing them into surfing the internet or watching films, rather than concentrating on texts. The significance of the book as a material object has been of little interest to most of these scholars.

However, other researchers such as Donald McKenzie (2002) and Filipe Carreira da Silva (2015) focus on the variances of a book's form and its importance for understanding meaning. Carreira da Silva (2015) argues that books can be read differently when their appearance is changed. For example, colportage editions of previously published novels can reach a broader readership with their flashy covers and cheaper paperback formats. Anne Mangen (2016: 240) focuses on the emotional reactions of readers to the material forms of texts, showing how participants in her research project perceived texts differently when they were presented in the form of a codex or on loose sheets of paper. Her participants explained that in book form, the content seemed more valuable, and consequently they gave them more attention.

The work of McKenzie (2002), Carreira da Silva (2015), and Mangen (2016: 240) suggests that there is a connection between the materiality of the book and the cultural value ascribed to it. However, the digitization of the book and its relation to the perception of its cultural value has not played a role in their research. The focus of my study has been on how the value of the analogue book is perceived in the digital age when it has a counterpart in the form of the e-book. In what follows, I discuss the main findings of my research, focusing on the limitations of the analogue book, the meaning of analogue nostalgia and the emergence of a group I call the connoisseurs of the book. Finally, I will show that the cultural value of the analogue book in the age of digitization is based, to a large extent, on issues that result from its materiality.

Limitations as an asset: The materiality of the book in the age of digitization

According to Jonathan Westin (2012: 18), the limitations of a form or medium are not necessarily a negative feature. Instead, they operate as a prerequisite for anchoring these in society. Westin (2012: 18: 24) uses the example of a Greek statue in a museum, explaining that visitors are dependent on the museum to tell them what is essential about the statue. The presentational and informational guidance provided for visitors in the form of lighting and signage shows them where to look and what to pay attention to. This provides a framework for visitors' understanding of the statue, putting it into context for them, and preventing them from discovering the statue in other ways. These kinds of restrictions, or 'limitations', are also present in the analogue book. For example, an analogue book cannot be used to surf the internet, listen to music, or watch videos. Unlike digital devices used for reading books, such as tablets, smartphones, laptops, and PCs, they do not enable 'multitasking' (Baron 2015). My research shows that these limitations shape the cultural value that society assigns to the analogue book in the digital age.

Many of the participants I engaged with mentioned that the digital devices used for reading books encouraged distraction. The analogue book, in contrast, offered the user no such opportunity. Many of my participants found this limitation to be an advantage. Bender, an author I interviewed, considered reading an analogue book as 'time out' from a busy life full of time-consuming distractions such as smartphones or computers (Bender 2018).[1] In his view, life had become increasingly digitized. While he felt positive about this process in many other areas of life, reading an analogue book provided a break from this digital world, time that allowed 'for drowning into another character's life and story without distraction' (2018: n.pag.). He compared reading an analogue book to a fancy dinner: 'You get involved in it, and you dedicate your time to it. An analogue book is nothing that is consumed on the go' (2018: n.pag.). In contrast, services such as Netflix and the internet were part of a world of everyday life that expects us to deal with several things at the same time. The world of reading an analogue book kept this restless world out. His comparison to a 'fancy dinner' suggests that the moment of contemplative reading is experienced as unique and valuable, something that one must plan, and for which one must take time.

Another participant, a novelist named Brenner, echoed Bender's view:

> a book [...] in this fast-paced digital age, a book is something that is real. When one opens a book, one holds it in one's hands, one smells it, one can access it page by page [...] one does not have to turn on a computer to access a book, therefore a book is relaxing for me. The book wants me to focus on the story. There are no ads, no sounds, nothing is popping up. It is this limitation that makes reading a book relaxing.[2]
>
> (Bender 2018: n.pag.)

Brenner emphasizes the material properties of the book, such as the feel and smell of the paper. She also notes that the analogue book does not have to be switched on; it can be picked up, opened, and used immediately, without an internet connection or the need for electricity. In Brenner's view, the materiality of the analogue book made it possible to focus entirely on its content; its lack of features becomes an asset.

This preference for the analogue book over the e-book or digital reading device was also expressed by the publishers I spoke to. Hierling, a representative of the publisher Hoffmann und Campe, stated that she found it easier to focus on a physical book as it did not provide any distractions (Hierling 2018).[3] She also saw this from a publisher's perspective, arguing that the book now had increased competition: 'Given all the media that we consume daily, the book has the disadvantage that we cannot multitask while reading a book' (Hierling 2018: n.pag.). This, she felt, would be problematic as 'people want to make the best use of their time [and therefore they multitask] which places the analogue book in a challenging position' (n.pag.). An analogue book requires time and dedication. Just like a fancy dinner, contemplative reading does not fit into a busy everyday life, it needs a special space in which it can take place.

For these participants it is the analogue materiality of the book that makes reading a special activity, requiring focus and concentration. Kuntze, a leading editor of the Random House imprint Blessing, also noted a break in the generational consumption of books, claiming that younger people – he termed them 'digital natives' – would no longer be able to concentrate on longer texts: 'they grew up with cell phones, and neuroscientists say that this generation cannot concentrate for more than a few minutes. They are just not used to reading and comprehending longer texts anymore' (Kuntze 2018: n.pag.).[4] Although this is a sweeping statement that makes a generalized assumption about an unspecified group of young people, perhaps it reveals something about the way publishers think. For instance, it suggests that publishers may not prioritize a young readership and that they carefully consider how this generation reads and concentrates. Kuntze explained that Blessing is more likely to focus on readers who grew up reading analogue books and are willing to spend money on beautifully designed publications. Selling more expensive editions would be a way for Blessing to try to make up for lost sales.

However, most participants did not share Kuntze's negative assessment of younger generations. Henelink, a member of a book club and a primary school teacher, thought that analogue books now fulfilled a particular need in the context of other media such as television, radio, the internet, and audio plays: 'children love stories, and sometimes they watch the stories, sometimes they listen to the stories, and sometimes they read the stories' (Henelink 2018: n.pag.).[5] She explained how her pupils often chose analogue books when they wanted to rest and required time for themselves. She described how the children would take a book and withdraw to a quiet corner to devote themselves to the story. Like Bender, Henelink saw reading an analogue book as a form of 'time out'. In a similar way, Kuntze described what Blessing provided for its readers: 'precisely the opposite [to Netflix and other digital media] [...] it's a digital detox. Our readers are looking for a quiet time without distractions' (Kuntze 2018: n.pag.). The use of the term 'digital detox' presents the analogue book as a kind of counter-medium to the perceived oversupply of the digital. In this way, it becomes a form of cleansing that grounds and calms its readers and helps them focus, whereas digital media is distracting and overwhelming. Hochhuth, an editor at Carlsen publishers, echoed this view: 'the analogue book is a digital detox, and we must market it that way. It is a somewhat anachronistic format to the digital world we live in, but I am convinced that this is the advantage of the book. That is what our customers want' (Hochhuth 2018: n.pag.).[6]

Hochhuth described how Carlsen once tried to introduce an app that could turn children's books into interactive experiences. Many parents rejected the app as they wanted the time of reading a book with their children to be free of screens and digital distractions. Carlsen discontinued the app. Hochhuth concluded by saying that the analogue book has exactly the right format to help people focus in a world full of distractions. The statements of these interviewees echo Westin's (2012: 18) comment on the limitations of cultural objects. The material limitations of the analogue book meant that most of my participants used it when they needed time to focus and withdraw from the digital world. An analogue book unfolds its intended use when it is read. Its 'limitations' – its materiality in the form of paper, cardboard, leather, and other materials – provide one reason for its cultural value in the digital age.

MEDIA MATERIALITIES

Longing for the past: Nostalgia and the materiality of the book

In recent years, a fascination with analogue and vintage digital photography has become apparent (Caoduro 2014; Pickering et al. 2006: 919). Computer gaming communities share, collect, and play retro games or use emulators to create the looks of old computers such as the Commodore C64 (Darnton et al. 2016; Handberg 2015: 165; Suominen 2008: 18). Nostalgia has also been researched in relation to movies (Lee 2018: 55; Sperb 2015) and popular music (Bartmanski et al. 2015; Reynolds 2011). This discourse was similarly communicated by my interviewees and focus group participants, who regularly commented on how the materiality of a physical book evoked feelings of nostalgia. For example, Cramer, a member of a reading group in Augsburg, remembered how her parents read a book of fairy tales by the Brothers Grimm to her when she was a child (Cramer 2018).[7] Cramer still owns this book, noting that it is 'totally worn out; the edges are broken. But I cannot give that book away. That bookmarks the beginning of my love for books' (n.pag.). Although she owns a newer version of the book, Cramer used the old one when reading the tales to her daughter:

> When I grab that old book and open it is as if I read two stories. First, it's the stories in the book, but simultaneously I remember how my parents read to me, which is just like another story. It's just a nice walk down memory lane.
>
> (Cramer 2018: n.pag.)

Here it is the material qualities of Cramer's copy of book that triggers sentiment and nostalgia. Furthermore, Cramer noted that the Grimm Brothers book was one of the few books she owned as a child, raising another issue often mentioned by my participants – scarcity.

Older participants, particularly those born during or shortly after the Second World War, recalled the scarcity of paper and, consequently, the value of books. According to science fiction author vom Scheidt:

> When I was a kid, and I wanted to buy a new book, I had to bring old paper to the bookshop. The money was not enough. The paper I brought would be recycled and turned into a new publication.[8]
>
> (vom Scheidt 2018: n.pag.)

While the practice described by vom Scheidt lasted only for a short time, this experience shaped his perception of the analogue book as scarce and therefore valuable. Participants also acknowledged the durability and timelessness of the analogue book. For example, Lange, an author and a reading and writing group member, recalled the moment she found a German edition of Antoine de Saint-Exupéry's *The Little Prince* (published in 1962) at a doctor's waiting room in Munich:

> Such an old thing and I took it and thought, how amazing that this book survived all these years, it is older than me. It was around six years before I was born, so it is somewhat historical, and I think that books [...] last throughout the times. They have always been there, and they will [...] and one knows that these things will outlive us, and that is a great feeling.[9]
>
> (Lange 2018: n.pag.)

Lange's sentiment was not about the book itself or the story it contained. She did not remember when she read the book for the first time. What struck her was the understanding that this book had been around for so many years, that it was older than she was, and that printed books are durable and special.

Philipp Schweighauser (2020) discussed a first edition of Ezra Pound's *Lustra* (1916), drawing attention to the book's material properties, particularly the font, the relief printing of the title, the quality of the paper, and the cloth-wrapped cover. All these gave the book a certain feel of 'something precious, something worthwhile preserving, something of note' (2020: n.pag.). Schweighauser is fascinated by the fact that the book can still be looked at and leafed through more than 100 years after its publication. Floppy discs and CD-ROMs are no longer usable for most people because their devices have no playback functions for these anymore. In contrast, the content of an analogue book remains accessible, even centuries after its publication. It is not only the book as an object but its function that can last throughout time.

A further issue – the element of design – was mentioned by Haselbach, a director of fiction for the German publishing group, Droemer-Knaur. According to Haselbach, books are regularly designed to evoke nostalgic feelings or memories (Haselback 2018).[10] A bookseller named Haberkorn shared this assessment, recalling the different editions of the children's classic *Heidi* by Swiss author Johanna Spyri (Haberkorn 2018).[11] The books were first published in 1880 and 1881 and are part of Germany's children's book canon. Haberkorn explained that she stocked various editions of the Heidi books in her store because different generations ask for different editions. While grandparents would look for cover designs from the 1950s and 1960s, she told me how parents often sought editions from the 1970s and 1980s. In contrast, children typically preferred digital artwork that is more akin to the style used in Pixar movies and reminded them of computer-animated films. While the story remains the same, Haberkorn's interview suggests that book design can determine which edition each generation will buy.

Participants collectively identified four aspects that indicated the importance of analogue books and their cultural value in the digital age. First, material signs of wear and tear determined its emotional value. Second, the books were assumed to have value because of the material from which they were made. Third, the sense that analogue books continue to exist, even beyond one's own lifetime, added to their significance. Fourth, the reissue of historical editions of books that reminded different generations of readers of their own favourite edition reinforced a view of the analogue book's importance. Against a background of digitization, however, some participants experienced a feeling of fear that the analogue book might disappear, and they were willing to act to ensure that it would be preserved. I discuss this final aspect in the next section.

Saving the book: The connoisseurs of the analogue book

Throughout my research, it became evident that many publishers considered the analogue book to be a medium for a specific group of readers, authors, and booksellers. I have named them 'connoisseurs of the book'. This group cannot be clearly classified according to social class or income and includes authors as well as readers and booksellers. Instead, members are characterized by an intense relationship with the analogue book that goes beyond buying, reading, collecting, or socially engaging with books. It can be observed that connoisseurs are constantly struggling with the digitization of books and the book market and that they try to distance themselves from this.

I found that analogue books serve as a symbol for setting oneself apart from the aspects of digitization that my participants perceive as negative. This symbolic role is underpinned by the cultural value that books have held throughout the centuries, for example, in the religious use of books in antiquity and the Middle Ages (Faulstich 2004: 41; Jochum 1993). Later, books became an item for collection (Erler 2005; Jochum 1993) and, therefore, an object that could be used to express one's cultural capital (Becher 1990; Bourdieu 1984; Manguel 1996), representing education (Rautenberg et al. 2001), membership of the middle or upper class, and belonging in an environment in which the understanding of literature is of importance. The analogue book has become a medium that transfers cultural capital to its users and owners, and this cultural capital is endorsed and promoted by institutions that are perceived as authorities (Bourdieu 1984). One way of reinforcing this distinction has been through the production of luxury editions of works of world literature (Bluhm 2009; Jochum 1993), intended for exhibition in private libraries.

Against the background of digitization, the analogue book is perceived by connoisseurs to be in danger because it is regarded as increasingly less important for acquiring cultural capital. Connoisseurs struggle to maintain the cultural value of the analogue book and to do this, they need allies who help maintain its status as a medium of distinction and literary quality. They identify established publishers as allies and gatekeepers who ensure that only literary works of a certain standard are published, thereby maintaining the cultural value of the book. This focus on established publishers means that connoisseurs tended to be critical of developments in the book market.

Many of my participants considered the 'liberation' of the publishing market through self-publishing (DeWild et al. 2015; Selzer 2015) to be overriding existing quality controls in the literary market. They questioned the quality of self-published books, especially self-published e-books. Bauer, a former teacher and nurse, explained that these represented a lack of quality control by agents and editors:

> Everyone can just publish what they like. Whether it is good or not. So, there are thousands of [self-published] e-books published. And among them is most likely a lot of nonsense that you don't need to read. I don't want to waste my time going through all that stuff to see whether I find something useful among all these publications.[12]
>
> (Bauer 2018: n.pag.)

Bauer's remark suggests that he assigns the role of the filter or gatekeeper to publishers and assumes that books that have not passed through formal processes are likely not to be worthwhile reading. This view fails to recognize that acclaimed authors such as Thomas Hardy, Alexandre Dumas, Charles Dickens, T. S. Eliot, Ernest Hemingway, and Beatrix Potter self-published their work (Kremer 2013) and that contemporary established publishers also publish e-books.

Bauer's assessment of the literary quality of e-books was shared by Werner, who remembered the moment she received her first e-book reader and described how she downloaded many free e-books because her device could store several hundred (Werner 2018).[13] Later, when she decided to erase many of these, she chose to delete the self-published books first: 'I felt that the books that were published by a publisher were somewhat more valuable. It's hard to explain but I thought it is more likely that I would read these books, than the others' (2018: n.pag.). Brenner, a member of a book club, also felt that, with so many books on the market, books published by a publisher would be of better quality, having gone through a strict selection process. Most participants agreed that publishers were important as filters and editors of literature. Lange summed up this attitude, arguing that the internet had made the book publishing market so crowded and confusing that the editorial work carried by publishers was increasingly important. For her, publishers sift through the volume of texts, choosing what is worth reading.

The perception of the increasing importance of publishers as filters for literary quality also affects authors. Radermacher, an author of crime novels, explained that while it had always been important to be published, in the age of digitization, publication acquires a new meaning for many authors: 'At the beginning [of digitization], the new opportunities for writers were welcomed. Things like BoD [Book on Demand] or publishing online were promising. But now, many have realized that acting as a self-publisher in an overwhelming market is not so fulfilling' (Radermacher 2018: n.pag.).[14] Brenner, also a crime author, described a certain ritual repeating itself on Wattpad, a social platform for aspiring authors:

> The dynamics are always the same. First, everyone pokes at the publishers and assures each other that it would be much better to self-publish. Though, as soon as someone receives an offer from a traditional publisher, most of us are jealous.
>
> (Brenner 2018: n.pag.)

Brenner explained that on Wattpad, where 80 million people read and upload stories and books, receiving an offer from a publisher means being told that among these millions of manuscripts, it is yours that is worthy of being published. It is also crucial that publication is in print form.

As Grant McCracken (1990) argues, printed books legitimize an author and show their belonging to a particular social class. The digital format of the e-book lacks the permanence and durability of printed matter, especially today when digital content can be written, published, and deleted in a matter of minutes. An author named Rhiem declared that he preferred his books to be published in print for this reason; as he wrote on a computer, he knew how easy it was to erase a line or a paragraph – one moment the sentence was there, the next it was gone (Rhiem 2018).[15] He felt the need for his books to be in permanent form. Müller, a bestselling author, said:

> I like the fact that a printed book is a finished product that cannot be changed any more. When I edit my manuscript before I hand it to my publisher, I find it hard to finish. I re-work and edit it repeatedly. But once I hold a printed copy of that book in my hands it's like a relief. That's it! It cannot be changed any more, and it marks a point.[16]
>
> (Müller 2018: n.pag.)

For Müller, the existence of his books in print is an expression of his development as an author.

Hierling, an editor at Hoffmann und Campe, a traditional German publishing house, said that she and her colleagues were aware of this development – the analogue book being of higher value for a certain group of readers and authors – and that publishers increasingly marketed it this way (Hierling 2018).[17] Kress, an editor at Ullstein Verlag, stated '[t]he printed book as an object still enjoys high esteem. This appreciation is growing'(Kress 2018: n.pag.).[18] She explained that Ullstein had 'started to emphasize the objectivity of the book more' and intended to publish more lavishly designed editions of analogue books. Rohn, a publishing director at Rütten & Loening, an imprint of Aufbau publishing group, added: 'Publishers have done a lot to make books more than just containers for the text. That's important because, in our times, books are bought by the people who, if they buy music, go for vinyl' (Rohn 2018: n.pag.).[19] Therefore, such connoisseurs of the analogue book are willing to spend more money if they are offered well-designed editions. Preserving the analogue book is important to them as it is only this hard-copy form that represents distinction, permanence, and literary quality. This may help explain why, during the pandemic, bookshops were allowed to remain open in Germany. The materiality of the books they sold and of the spaces that sold them represented the cultural value of the book in the digital age.

Conclusion

The analogue book does not offer the range of functions offered by digital media such as tablets, smartphones, or laptops. As my research has shown, however, it is precisely these limitations that are becoming more important in the age of digitization. Indeed, the features of the analogue book were not understood by the participants in my study as a limitation but rather as a framework that allowed them to concentrate and focus on the written word. In addition, the materiality of the analogue book aroused feelings of nostalgia. These feelings were focused on the signs of the aging process of books, on the wear and tear of the book's pages and cover. Linked to this was the durability of the analogue book, indicated by the survival of old editions of books. Furthermore, the value of the material book itself played a role, especially for participants who had experienced periods of deprivation and scarcity. Finally, aspects of book design evoked memories and a feeling of nostalgia. Against a background of digitization, some participants were afraid that the existence and importance of the analogue book was becoming endangered. A group of book lovers who I termed the connoisseurs are keen to ensure that the analogue book maintained its status in our society. Overall, my research suggests that the cultural value of the analogue book in the digital age depends precisely on the fact that it is not digital and that its materiality, limitation of function, and design are the things that are valued in a world that is becoming increasingly digitized.

NOTES

1. Bender, interview, 11 May 2018.
2. Brenner, focus group interview, 19 September 2018.
3. Hierling, interview, 24 September 2018.
4. Kuntze, interview, 2 July 2018.
5. Henelink, interview, 25 June 2018.
6. Hochhuth, interview, 21 November 2018.
7. Cramer, focus group interview, 19 November 2018.
8. vom Scheidt, focus group interview, 24 September 2018.
9. Lange, focus group interview, 19 September 2018.
10. Haselbach, interview, 17 October 2018.
11. Haberkorn, interview, 7 November 2018.
12. Bauer, focus group interview, 19 November 2018.
13. Werner, focus group interview, 24 June 2018.
14. Radermacher, focus group interview, 19 September 2018.
15. Rhiem, focus group interview, 19 September 2018.
16. Müller, focus group interview, 19 March 2018.
17. Hierling, interview, 24 September 2018.
18. Kress, interview, 19 September 2018.
19. Rohn, interview, 19 September 2018.

REFERENCES

Baron, Naomi S. (2015), *Words Onscreen: The Fate of Reading in a Digital World*, New York: Oxford University Press.

Bartmanski, Dominik and Woodward, Ian (2015), *Vinyl: The Analogue Record in the Digital Age*, London: Bloomsbury Academic.

Becher, Ursula A. J. (1990), *Geschichte Des Modernen Lebensstils: Essen, Wohnen, Freizeit, Reisen*, München: Beck.

Birkerts, Sven (1994), *The Gutenberg Elegies: The Fate of Reading in an Electronic Age*, London: Faber & Faber.

Bluhm, Detlef (2009), *Von Autoren, Büchern Und Piraten Geschichte Der Buchkultur*, Dusseldorf: Artemis & Winkler.

Bourdieu, Pierre (1984), *Distinction: A Social Critique of the Judgement of Taste*, Cambridge: Mass: Harvard University Press.

Caoduro, Elena (2014), 'Photo filter apps: Understanding analogue nostalgia in the new media ecology', *Networking Knowledge: Journal of the MeCCSA Postgraduate Network*, 7:2, pp. 67–82.

Carreira da Silva, Filipe (2015), 'G. H. Mead', *SSRN*, 6 February, https://dx.doi.org/10.2139/ssrn.2561550.

Comunian, Roberta and England, Lauren (2020), 'Creative and cultural work without filters: Covid-19 and exposed precarity in the creative economy', *Cultural Trends*, 29:2, pp. 112–28.

Coyle, Karen (2006), 'Mass digitization of books', *The Journal of Academic Librarianship*, 32:6, pp. 641–45.

Coyle, Karen (2009), 'Google Books metadata and library functions', *Coyle's InFormation*, 14 September, https://kcoyle.blogspot.com/2009/09/google-books-metadata-and-library.html. Accessed 3 July 2023.

Darnton, Robert (2016), *Die Zensoren*, München: Siedler Verlag.

DeWild, Melissa and Jarema, Morgan (2015), 'Supporting self-publishing and local authors: From challenge to opportunity', in R. P. Holley (ed.), *Self-Publishing and Collection Development: Opportunities and Challenges for Libraries*, Indiana: Purdue University Press, pp. 21–26.

Erler, Ingolf (2005), 'Das Buch als Soziales symbol', MA dissertation, Wien: Universität Wien.

Faulstich, Werner (2004), 'Das Buch im Zeitalter der digitalen Medien. Von den Anfängen bis in die Zukunft', *Communicatio Socialis*, 37:1, pp. 41–56.

Gooding, Paul, Terras, Melissa, and Warwick, Claire (2013), 'The myth of the new: Mass digitization, distant reading, and the future of the book', *Literary and Linguistic Computing*, 28:4, pp. 629–39.

Handberg, Kristian (2015), 'No time like the past? On the new role of vintage and retro in the magazines *Scandinavian Retro* and *Retro Gamer*', *European Journal of Media Studies*, 4:2, pp. 165–85.

Hayles, N. Katherine (2003), 'Translating media: Why we should rethink textuality', *The Yale Journal of Criticism*, 16:2, pp. 263–90.

Jeannotte, M. Sharon (2021), 'When the gigs are gone: Valuing arts, culture and media in the COVID-19 pandemic', *Social Sciences & Humanities Open*, 3:1, https://doi.org/10.1016/j.ssaho.2020.100097.

Jochum, Uwe (1993), *Kleine Bibliotheksgeschichte*, Ditzingen: Reclam

Koh, Byungwan, Hann, Il-Horn, and Raghunathan, Srinivasan (2019), 'Digitization of music: Consumer adoption amidst piracy, unbundling, and rebundling', *MIS Quarterly*, 43:1, pp. 25–45.

Kremer, John (2013), *John Kremer's Self-Publishing Hall of Fame*, Conshohocken: Infinity Publishing.

Lee, Sunjoo (2018), 'Nostalgia films in the post-cinema age: Digital visual effects and the nostalgia for the celluloid cinema', *Contemporary Film Studies*, 14:3, pp. 55–87.

Leonardi, Paul (2010), 'View of digital materiality? How artifacts without matter, matter', *First Monday*, 15:6, https://firstmonday.org/ojs/index.php/fm/article/view/3036/2567. Accessed 3 July 2023.

Lowe, Adam and Latour, Bruno (2011), 'The migration of the Aura – Or how to explore theoriginal through its facsimile', in T. Bartscherer and R. Coover (eds), *Switching Codes:Thinking Through Digital Technology in the Humanities and the Arts*, Illinois University of Chicago Press, pp. 275–297.

Magaudda, Paolo, (2011), 'When *materiality bites back*: Digital music consumption practices in the age of dematerialization', *Journal of Consumer Culture*, 11:1, pp. 15–36.

Mangen, Anne (2016), 'The digitization of literary reading', *Orbis Litterarum*, 71:3, pp. 240–62.

Manguel, Alberto (1996), *A History of Reading*, New York: Viking.

Martins, Angela and Shule, Vicensia (2020), 'The impact of the COVID-19 pandemic on the arts, culture, and heritage sectors in the African Union member states', *International Journal of Cultural Property*, 27:4, pp. 477–80.

McCracken, Grant (1990), *Culture and Consumption: New Approaches to the Symbolic Character of Consumer Goods and Activities*, Indiana: Indiana University Press.

McKenzie, Donald Francis (2002), *Making Meaning: Printers of the Mind and Other Essays*, Boston: University Of Massachusetts Press.

Müller, Marius (2020), 'Corona-lockdown – Warum Bücher keine Lebensmittel sind', *Cicero*, 19 December, https://www.cicero.de/kultur/corona-massnahmen-lockdown-buchhandlung-keine-lebensmittel. Accessed 3 July 2023.

Nunberg, Geoffrey (1996), *The Future of the Book*, Berkeley: University of California Press.

Orlikowski, Wanda J. and Scott, Susan V. (2008), 'The entanglement of technology and work in organizations', LSE Working paper series (168) Information Systems and Innovation Group, London School of Economics and Political Science.

Pickering, Michael and Keightley, Emily (2006), 'The modalities of nostalgia', *Current Sociology*, 54:6, pp. 919–41.

Rashidi, Waleed (2020), 'Young adults' compact disc usage experiences in 2020', *Journal of the Music and Entertainment Industry Educators Association*, 20:1, pp. 127–45.

Rautenberg, Ursula and Wetzel, Dirk (2001), *Buch, Grundlagen der Medienkommunikation*, Berlin: De Gruyter

Reynolds, Simon (2011), *Retromania: Pop Culture's Addiction to Its Own Past*, London: Palgrave Macmillan.

Richardson, Leonard (2015), 'Project Gutenberg books are real', *The Journal of Electronic Publishing*, 18:1, n.pag., https://doi.org/10.3998/3336451.0018.126.

Richter, Felix (2021), 'Chart: E-Books still no match for printed books', *Statista*, 21 April, https://www.statista.com/chart/24709/e-book-and-printed-book-penetration/.

Rosenberg, Simon and Simon, Sandra (eds) (2015), *Material Moments in Book Cultures*, Frankfurt: Peter Lang.

Schweighauser, P. (2020), 'Why does the materiality of books matter', *Future Learn*, https://www.futurelearn.com/courses/reading-digital/0/steps/16848. Accessed 3 July 2023.

Selzer, Brian (2015), 'Thriving among giants: Self-publishing in the digital age', *American Journal of Public Health*, 105:10, pp. 19–56, https://doi.org/10.2105/AJPH.2015.302859.

Singer, Lauren M. and Alexander, Patricia A. (2017), 'Reading on paper and digitally: What the past decades of empirical research reveal', *Review of Educational Research*, 87:6, pp. 1007–41.

Smil, Vaclav (2016), *Making the Modern World: Materials and Dematerialization*, Morrisville: Lulu Press.

Sperb, Jason (2015), *Flickers of Film: Nostalgia in the Time of Digital Cinema*, New Brunswick: Rutgers University Press.

Suominen, Jaakko (2008), 'The past as the future? Nostalgia and retrogaming in digital culture', *The Fibreculture Journal*, 11 November, https://fibreculturejournal.org/fcj-075-the-past-as-the-future-nostalgia-and-retrogaming-in-digital-culture/. Accessed 3 July 2023.

Travkina, Ekaterina and Sacco, Pierluigi (2020), 'Culture shock: COVID-19 and the cultural and creative sectors', *OECD*, 7 September, https://www.oecd.org/coronavirus/policy-responses/culture-shock-covid-19-and-the-cultural-and-creative-sectors-08da9e0e/. Accessed 3 July 2023.

Wang, Amy X. (2019), 'Album sales are dying as fast as streaming services are rising', *Rolling Stone*, 3 January, https://www.rollingstone.com/pro/news/album-sales-dying-as-fast-as-streaming-services-rising-774563/. Accessed 3 July 2023.

Westin, Jonathan (2012), 'Towards a vocabulary of limitations: The translation of a painted goddess into a symbol of classical education', *International Journal of Heritage Studies*, 18:1, pp. 18–32.

Whitten, Sarah (2019), 'The death of the DVD: Why sales dropped more than 86% in 13 years', *CNBC*, 8 November, https://www.cnbc.com/2019/11/08/the-death-of-the-dvd-why-sales-dropped-more-than-86percent-in-13-years.html. Accessed 3 July 2023.

Wolf, Maryanne (2008), *Proust and the Squid: The Story and Science of the Reading Brain*, New York: Harper Perennial.

Yu, Yinan, Chen, Hailiang, Peng, Chih-Hung, and Chau, Patrick (2017), 'The causal effect of video streaming on DVD sales: Evidence from a natural experiment', *Decision Support Systems*, 157, n.pag., https://doi.org/10.1016/j.dss.2022.113767.

Short Take 7

Materialities of Spatial Confinement: Trefeglwys Meets Beirut

Dima Saber

The farmer moved the sheep to the next field up the hill; they have eaten all the grass in the field across the lane since we came here at the beginning of the lockdown. That's how long we have been here.

We only eat chicken now. Meat is so expensive that most people stopped buying it. Soon the whole country will become vegetarian like you.

It was the first time I saw farm dogs herding sheep. It was amazing, they are pretty good at it, and guess what, I saw a hare; a real hare, with long ears and all.

The dollar is trading at 14,000LL on the black market today. Imagine? The Lebanese pound lost about 90 per cent of its value since you were last here in 2019.

A flycatcher bird nested on the house wall. I always wondered if birds left their nests unattended. We set up a nature camera so that we can see the chicks getting fed.

Live rounds were fired last night on old demarcation lines between Chiah and Ain el-Remmaneh. Did you watch the news?

There are estimates of over 140,000 COVID-19 deaths in the United Kingdom and only about 8500 in Lebanon. It is amazing that despite everything, Lebanon has better handled the global pandemic than the United Kingdom.

Has it, though?

I spent the first UK lockdown in a beautiful Welsh village called Trefeglwys – it took me around ten weeks to learn to spell its name. It was like living *in* a postcard, with breathtaking open wide fields, a river, woods, and green hills all around. This was the material reality of my spatial (non)confinement. We got there just in time for lambing season too, so there were lambs jumping around, like in dreamland visions. We lived in a 380-year-old Grade-2 listed Tudor house, which is now part of my British family heritage.

Meanwhile, Lebanon has been going through the worst economic crisis in its modern history, one of the three most severe the world has seen since the mid-nineteenth century, according to a 2021 report by the World Bank.

In Beirut, my parents are buying candles because of power cuts. 'It's more romantic', they jokingly say. 'It's like when you used to do your homework on candlelight, remember?' I do remember, I think. 'The only difference between growing up in the civil war, and now is that there are no bombs and fighting', I tell them, partly to comfort myself that despite the darkness, they are safe. 'Yes, most of the time', they say.

These conversations got me thinking about the ways we will remember these lockdown years; what traces will remain in our everyday lives? What will my 3-year-old daughter remember, if anything at all?

I've recently started rereading Pierre Nora's *Realms of Memory* (1996) for an article I'm writing on the mnemonic potential of crowd-sourced footage from Syria. Despite the shortcomings of his account of archival memory, and his rather elitist conception of history-making processes, I quite like Nora's description of memory; I find it resonates well with how I and my two space-bound families are likely to remember the past two years:

> Memory, being a phenomenon of emotion and magic, accommodates only those facts that suit it. It thrives on vague, telescoping reminiscences, on hazy general impressions or specific symbolic details. It is vulnerable to transferences, screen memories, censorings and projections of all kinds.
>
> (Nora 1996: 3)

Despite the open fields and the wide outdoor spaces, 'secluded' is the one word that comes to my mind when I think of the first lockdown in Trefeglwys. Secluded, and digital, mostly because it involved a lot of screens, and behind those screens, a part of my family which has been living through a social, political, and economic meltdown, haunted by the ghosts of civil war, and an under-reported COVID-19 pandemic.

Screens, voice notes, and short video snaps. That is the symbolic material reality of our 2020 confinement story, so my daughter could remember what our family in Beirut looks like, when being with loved ones is a part of who we are, or what we do, again.

For now, she thinks all those people live on my phone.

REFERENCE

Nora, Pierre (1996), *Realms of Memory: The Construction of the French Past*, New York: Columbia University Press.

6

Essentially (Not) the Game: Reading the Materiality of Video Game Paratexts

Regina Seiwald

Introduction: (Not) the game

I recently wanted to purchase a protective travel case for my Nintendo Switch. I wished to have one that connects to my favourite game series of the Nintendo universe and one that has been part of my gaming life for quite some time: *The Legend of Zelda* (Nintendo EAD et al. 1986–2019). After browsing for a long time, I found the perfect one: a brown leather case depicting Link stringing his beautiful trademark bow and pointing an arrow. For me, this case is a depiction of the game-world Link stands for and which he epitomizes in a timeless manner. This made me think. Why do I want something physically tangible and material that connects to a physically non-tangible, digital world? What impact does this object have on my appreciation of the digital world and, in a sense, my willingness to enter it and become part of it, at least for some time? What is the relationship between this object and the game-world it relates to? And how do other, similar physical and non-physical objects relate to the game (and what is the game)?

These questions circle around ideas concerning the tension between digital and physical materialities as constituted by the text (the game) and its various paratexts (the not-game), which this chapter addresses from various perspectives. In the introduction, I want to unpack the complex relationship between games, materiality, and paratextuality, as well as how these three concepts are embedded in games research, and in media studies more broadly. I continue by demonstrating how the video game relates to its surrounding material through exploring the physical and the digital materiality of games. Next, I will discuss the distinction between paratextual material that is essential and that which is non-essential. Finally, the

ESSENTIALLY (NOT) THE GAME

discussion looks at the kind of paratextual material games are surrounded with, namely gameplay, technological, and marketing paratexts. These sections each address the unique nature of game paratexts and help determine the role they play for the establishment of a coherent game-world. In this sense, the core argument underpinning each section is that the materiality of video games can only be understood as a conglomerate of digital and physical paratextual elements.

Video games open up worlds to us in which we can actively take part. Unlike other media, such as books and films, their interactivity and our subsequent role in shaping the game's story have the effect that game-texts do not exist in a fixed form. The reason for this is that, in a sense, the player creates them in the process of playing the game. This also means that every playthrough differs from the previous one due to the choices players make in their interactive engagement with the game. In *Red Dead Redemption 2* (Rockstar Studios 2018), I can consciously decide how I, Arthur Morgan, am perceived by other characters in the game through not helping those in need or by shooting members of the Pinkerton-gang rather than avoiding them. That way, I, the player, can leave my imprint on the game's story and make the experience I have of it a unique one.[1] Mark J. P. Wolf has synthesized this – potentially problematic – textual nature of video games as follows:

> Whereas works in traditional media are made up of fixed, linear sequences of text, image, or sound (or combinations of them) which remain unchanged when examined multiple times (apart from effects of wear and tear), events experienced in a video game will vary widely from one playing to another.
>
> (Wolf 2001: 14)

A game-text is therefore highly ephemeral because due to the core characteristic of games as media that need to be played, they are, by nature, not fixed. Of course, there are many videos of walkthroughs on YouTube and live streams on Twitch, but the majority of gaming experiences are 'lost' because they are not enshrined in a kind of physical materiality.

This brief discussion and problematization of the status of video games as cultural artefacts already points to a quandary that forms the starting point for the discussion presented in this chapter: What is 'the game' and what kind of materiality does it possess? On the one hand, a game is an object – the cartridge, the disc or, a bit more abstract, the folder stored on a PC or a server – but, on the other hand, it is a non-tangible experience that does not possess any physicality in the real world, while it is the result of digital materiality. If we put a cartridge or a disc in front of a person and tell them 'this is a video game', they will most likely agree with us – provided, of course, that they know in general what a video game is. If you show them an on-screen character and tell them again that 'this is a video game', they will probably challenge this statement. However, both elements – the cartridge/disc/folder and the avatar – share that they are parts of the game but not yet the game itself. This shows that in everyday life, we 'don't require formal criteria in order to enjoy [a] game' (Egenfeldt-Nielsen et al. 2013: 19) because we simply know what it is. In research, however, we need to be more precise and pin down the meaning of 'the game' as used in a specific context in order to address how other material relates to it.

In the comparatively brief history of academic game studies, heralded in 2001 (Aarseth 2001: n.pag.), 'video game' has been defined variously. Markku Eskelinen criticized early on that '[g]ames are seen as interactive narratives, procedural stories or remediated cinema' (Eskelinen 2001: n.pag.) as a result of the colonialization of the discipline of game studies by other, long-established ones. This tells us something about the way we engage with games but not necessarily what they are. Wolf (2001: 14–15) argues that games possess elements such as conflict, rules, player ability, and valued outcome, all of which are presented on-screen. This defines the relationship between the player and the game and determines the individual links made between them. Nicolas Esposito (2005: n.pag.) quite briefly defines the video game as 'a *game* which we *play* thanks to an *audiovisual apparatus* and which can be based on a *story*'. This definition, which maps out the medium, the player, and the content of a game, makes us want to consider 'play' in more detail: It is the active involvement of the player in the game, defined by Eric Zimmermann (2004: n.pag.) as 'the free space of movement within a more rigid structure. Play exists both because of and also despite the more rigid structures of a system'. Roger Callois's (2001: 13, 29–36) definitions of *ludus* (structured, highly rule-based play) and *paidia* (unstructured, spontaneous play) are echoed in Zimmermann's (2004) definition. This focus on 'play' draws our attention to the idea of 'gameplay', for which Dominic Arsenault and Bernard Perron (2009: 113) contend that 'playing a video game is always a continuous loop between the gamer's input and the game's output'. This idea of gameplay emphasizes the link between processual activities and materiality coexisting in the act of playing (Leino 2012: n.pag.), creating a very specific space in which the game exists. This space is filled with various elements, such as characters we encounter, objects we use and landscapes we move in (Bonner 2015: n.pag.). Justyna Janik has recently synthesized those various ideas of gameplay in relation to the artefact game as follows:

[G]ameplay is not something fixed and unchangeable, but rather a performative phenomenon. [...] It is a moment of dialogue between different actants, which takes the form of a spatial communication loop, in which it is very difficult to indicate both the beginning and the end.

(Janik 2020: n.pag.)

ESSENTIALLY (NOT) THE GAME

These definitions of video game and (game)play approach video games from one particular perspective – ludology, narratology, sociology, and media studies, for instance. Yet they do not clearly state how video games relate to elements positioned outside of yet connected to them as well as where (and if) the line between inside and outside can be drawn. For the purpose of the discussion that follows, I will define 'video game' as a conglomerate consisting of all the material associated with a specific game in which a player can actively advance the game in its (narrative or discursive) progression through following a pre-defined set of rules. This means that the act of playing, or gameplay, is the activity associated with this game. The experience of games is therefore characterized by a sense of materiality because every engagement we have with and of it is unique. In order to counter this ephemerality emanating from this uniqueness, paratexts surrounding the game are created. These can be the result of conscious efforts by the game makers, such as promotional trailers, collector's editions or merchandising items, or that of fan endeavours, in the form of fan wikis, 'Let's Play' videos or discussion forums, to name but a few. Both kinds of paratexts share that they add physical and digital materials to the world of the game, simultaneously making the experience we have of it more tangible and less time-sensitive.

Since we now have established what the text – namely the game – is, we can further elaborate on its paratexts. These elements surrounding the game may seem superfluous and appear to be, sometimes ostensibly unnecessary, addenda to it. Examples are allowing the player to design their avatar in *World of Warcraft* (Blizzard Entertainment 2004) as illustrated in Figure 6.1, presenting a playable trailer, such as the game *P.T.* (7780s Studio 2014) functioning as a teaser for the cancelled *Silent Hills*, or sharing your unique stories on forums, such as Reddit, thus inscribing your experience into game history. Video games that were released in the 1980s and 1990s, such as *Pac Man* (Namco 1980), *Tetris* (Pajitnov 1984), or *Tony Hawk's Pro Skater* (Neversoft 1999), presented a very special relationship to the paratexts surrounding them and making them up; many of these games were played on arcade machines or devices that encouraged one-to-one competition, such as the portable Game Boy or the N-Gage, locating the play experience in a less private realm and making high-score lists sharable on physical devices. The 'feelies' these games created by means of the devices they were played on differs markedly from today's experience of playing, which is still sharable, yet mostly through the digital space, even for handheld devices, such as the Nintendo Switch.

As different as these paratexts appear to be, they share that they establish 'a link between a text and the surrounding socio-historical reality' (Švelch 2020: n.pag.), which, in essence, embeds the game in a time and space through digital and physical materialities, countering its ephemerality. This means that paratexts fulfil a threshold function because they build the bridges between the fictive game-world

FIGURE 6.1: Designing an avatar in *World of Warcraft*, Blizzard Entertainment (dev.), *World of Warcraft*, 2004. Available at https://news.blizzard.com/en-us/world-of-warcraft/23737992/shadowlands-an-inside-look-at-the-character-creation-ui-redesign.

and the reality of the player, thus mediating time and space between those two realms (Genette 1997: 2; Mader 2017: 112). However, while paratexts are not the game itself, they nonetheless are central to the creation of the game-world, and some of them are even essential for the game, meaning that without them, the game cannot exist. These elements are bound to different notions of materiality, and each possesses a unique relationship to the game they relate to, which will be the focus of the next section.

Digital and physical materiality between text and paratext

Video games exist in two spatial realms: a digital space, which includes the game-world and other digital elements such as the game's menu, and a physical space, which is materialized in the form of the device the game is stored on as well as the object that allows you to manipulate the game-world, such as the controller or the Virtual Reality headset. When playing a game, the player moves freely between those two worlds and even occupies them simultaneously. This becomes pronounced when playing a multiplayer game, such as *Call of Duty: Black Ops Cold War* (Treyarch and Raven Software 2020), in which players frequently mix game-related comments with real-world banalities when playing with others. These two spaces are bound to two forms of materiality, namely digital and physical materialities (Kirschenbaum 2008: n.pag.; Drucker 2009: n.pag.; Leonardi 2010: n.pag.), which is a distinction that is mostly coextensive with the division between software and hardware. These borders between the digital and the physical are not static or impermeable because the (physical) player's engagement with the (digital) game-world translocates the one into the other. Brendan Keogh's *A Play of Bodies* (2018), for example, studies how players and games connect via the senses by presenting bodily reactions in response to the game, thus combining the physical and the digital world. In a similar vein, Amanda Williams, Lynn Hughes, and Bart Simon (2010) have conducted a case study by developing a game that is navigated by means of bodily interaction in order to determine the role of the physical body in the experience of the game-world. These two key studies regarding the relationship and connection between digital and physical spaces do not necessarily foreground but at least insinuate that the relationship between text and paratext is crucial for physicality and digitality. As will be addressed, this relationship influences the way the game-world is perceived, and hence the different degrees to which they affect the establishment of a game's universe and the player's perception of it need to be discussed in more detail.

Digital materiality is made up of textual and paratextual elements. Textual elements are all those that exist within the game-world, such as characters, objects, weapons, buildings, fauna, and flora. They do not possess physical materiality in the player's reality but they are assigned characteristics akin to this physicality within the digital game-world, while they can also depart from it, for example in fantasy games. This means that the avatar can touch them, utilize them, or form specific relationships with them. Paratextual elements possessing digital materiality are situated outside the immediate game-world but display a strong link to it. Examples are the developer's logo appearing on the screen when the game is loading. Game developer Rockstar has evolved its logo to such a degree that it epitomizes some of the features players can expect from games of the franchise. Those players who have previously played instalments of the *Grand Theft Auto* series (Rockstar North et al. 1997–2013) most likely approach *Red Dead Redemption 2* (Rockstar Studios 2018) with similar expectations towards features they might find in the game, such as strong moral implications associated with the crimes committed by the protagonist, a fetching and detailed storyline, characters with highly elaborated back-stories and a realistic landscape.

Another example of paratexts possessing digital materiality is forums and other discussion platforms, such as Reddit or the Steam community. These spaces afford players the opportunity to exchange their experience of a specific game and any elements associated with it, even beyond the game itself. During the COVID-19 pandemic, *Animal Crossing: New Horizons* (Nintendo EPD 2020) reached a broad audience, and one that spans all age groups. The game's demographics display an equal split between male and female players, with the majority of players in their twenties and thirties (Heather 2020: n.pag.; Gibson 2020: n.pag.), which mirrors global player demographics (UKIE 2020: n.pag.). This resulted in a sense of belonging and the formation of a community in social media spaces. It filled the void left by the inability to meet physically by offering the option of digital meet-ups. As a result, the concept of maintaining existing relationships, forming new ones, and sharing personal experiences shifted to the digital realm. In this sense, these spaces in which players could exchange their perception of the game helped counter the ephemerality of individual gameplay encounters. Therefore, this digital paratext moved the game-world and the player's real world closely together.

Physical materiality, on the other hand, is solely made up of paratexts, unless, of course, the object on which the game is stored is associated with the idea of the artefact 'the game'. Physical materiality is understood here in 'its normal connotation as matter' (Leonardi 2010: n.pag.), i.e. anything that can be touched by the player within their reality realm (and not in the digital space). Components include the device on which the game is played, such as the PC, the console (and the TV displaying the game), the handheld device or the phone, the controller, the keyboard or the touchscreen through and with which the game-world is navigated as well as other physical elements relating to the game, such as merchandizing products. These elements make it possible that the game can be accessed and experienced while simultaneously drawing our attention to it and expanding its realm beyond the game-world. Limited Run Games (2021) is a distributor of physical media of games that were originally only available in a digital format. This has the effect of curatorship because a space that only exists digitally and which is more prone to alterations or even being lost entirely is turned into a physical format that is (seemingly) more stable and less in danger of deletion.

The example of Limited Run Games makes evident that the line between digital and physical materialities in the context of video games is often arbitrary, particularly with regard to paratextuality. The reason for this is that paratexts frequently fulfil the purpose of transforming digital materiality into physical materiality. The post-apocalyptic nuclear holocaust scenario game *Fallout 4* (Bethesda Game Studios 2015) features a device, called a 'Pip-Boy', which the protagonist wears around his wrist and on which all his data and other useful information is stored. The model available in this instalment of the game even allows the player to play in-game video games on it. One of these games is *Red Menace*, which resembles *Donkey Kong* (Nintendo R&D1 et al. 1981–2018) but replaces the gorilla with an alien (Seiwald 2019: 26). *Fallout 4* (Bethesda Game Studios 2015) has been released in form of a collector's edition, for which the game was accompanied by a replica of the Pip-Boy, amongst other items (Hile 2020: n.pag.). By offering a physical manifestation of an item that is so central to the game-world, the player's connection to its digital space is increased. Besides this appearance of an in-game artefact in the player's reality, the two worlds are also linked by items whose connection is less strong. In 2018, Victoria Rosenthal published *Fallout: The Vault Dweller's Official Cookbook* (2018), promising delicious recipes that are accompanied by seemingly handwritten notes making references to the game-world, such as the fact that within the realm of *Fallout*, potatoes, sweet potatoes, and carrots need to be replaced by 'tatos', which have become a staple food after the nuclear blast hit the planet.

The relationship between digital and physical materialities in and for video games can thus be described as one of co-presence. The game-world itself is largely digital, but through material paratexts, its digital universe is supplied with a sense of physicality that potentially increases the player's link to the game. While it has been indirectly contended here that digital materiality is, in a sense, the game, some elements possessing physical materiality are equally essential to the game and make the experience of it possible. The next section of this chapter therefore looks at the distinction between facultative and obligatory paratexts and asks which role different materialities play in the necessity of a paratext for the game-world.

Essential and non-essential paratexts

Earlier on, I mentioned that paratexts are not always needed for a game to be playable but that their function is to make the game visible to the player in the first place (e.g. a trailer for a new game) or to expand the universe of the game beyond its playable content (e.g. through merchandising products). This suggests that the distinction between essential/obligatory and non-essential/facultative paratexts possessing digital and physical materialities needs to be addressed, which is connected to the role these individual paratexts have in the context of creating a game's materiality. For some elements, such as marketing material, it is true that they are not needed by the player to play the game, but these paratexts present the game as an artefact to the player, asserting its existence as a cultural good (Brookey and Grey 2017: n.pag.). At the same time, paratexts often exist before the text itself. For some games, it has even been the case that the paratext has been circulated and still does so today, while the game itself was never realized or realized in a different form to the one originally intended. Above, I already mentioned *P.T.* (7780s Studio 2014), the playable teaser, which survived while the game it should initially introduce, *Silent Hills*, has been abandoned.

A more complex situation arose in 2007, when Blizzard Entertainment announced that they were working on a *World of Warcraft*-esque game called *Titan*, only to abandon it in 2016 (Schreier 2016: n.pag.). As with *P.T.* (7780s Studio 2014), paratexts associated with the game, such as discussions in online forums, news articles, industry media releases and even the trailer, still exist to this day, while the game does not. In other words, the paratexts live on while the text has never existed to begin with. Elements of *Titan*, however, have later been modified and re-used; the result was one of Blizzard Entertainment's big hits, *Overwatch* (Blizzard Entertainment 2016). What we are witnessing here is a postmodern version of Theseus's ship: a collection of paratexts that never had its original text but was instead turned into another text with its own paratexts, while the original paratext still exists. In this sense, *Overwatch* (Blizzard Entertainment 2016) 'possesses nothing but the discrete charm of second-order simulacra' (Baudrillard 1994: 1) in relation to its creational origin.

But let us return to the original focus of this chapter, namely the difference between essential and non-essential paratexts and their relationship to materiality. The excursus to the abandoned *Titan*-game has shown that seemingly facultative paratexts can indeed be the seeds of other texts to the effect that their status needs to be seen as obligatory because without them, the new text would not exist. This suggests that the terminological allocation of essential and non-essential to the paratexts associated with games often has to be made on a case-by-case basis, while some paratexts can be both depending on the perspective taken when considering their necessity for a specific game. I will first consider those paratexts that possess physical materiality. As argued above, their distance to the game itself would suggest that they are not necessarily needed for the game to exist or be played, which is, however, only true to a certain extent. In general, merchandizing products are not essential for the player to play the game, while their role is to make the game visible in the increasingly large pool of new game releases and to invite players into their unique game-worlds. On the other hand, there are also essential components surrounding the game that makes access to the game-world possible, such as the computer, the console, the handheld device or the controller as well as the disc and the cartridge. These objects, however, are not paratexts themselves but make specific paratextual relationships possible through mediating between the physical materiality (and thus the reality of the player) and the digital materiality of the game-world. In other words, without these devices, the game (the text) would not be possible, underlining that specific paratextual relationships are needed to afford the game itself. A look at the history of the first games makes this point evident because the development of the software went hand-in-hand with that of the hardware. Once a memory was added to these early computers, interactivity was made possible and the tic-tac-toe-like game *OXO* (Douglas 1952) made use of this new invention. While today's innovations of digital worlds are also influenced by modifications of physical game-related materials, such as VR-sets, making experiences more immediate, the development of digital and physical aspects of games tends to be independent from each other.

This example illustrates that video games need physical materiality to prevail whereas they themselves and their worlds exist in and of digital materiality. The degree to which this physical materiality is needed, however, largely differs between games. For some games, such as *EVE Online* (CCP Games 2003) or *Pokémon Go* (Niantic et al. 2016), all you need to play the game is the online or downloadable content, a device on which to play the game and internet connection. However, for old console games, such as *Crash Bandicoot* (Naughty Dog 1996), you need to possess the physical disc, have a PlayStation and a controller as well as a television or a screen. This means that while there are games that largely require digital paratexts, others need more physical paratexts, while the fact that all games are digital content played on a physical device suggests that all games need a blend of both forms of materiality.

Similar to physical paratexts, digital ones can also either be essential or non-essential for games. Some digital paratexts can be considered as what Genette (1997: 7) has referred to as 'factual paratexts'. They need to be included for legal reasons and are thus essential in this context, such as the PG-rating or copyright information, but they do not have any effect on the game-world, making them non-essential for the game itself. On the other hand, digital paratexts, such as setting the level of difficulty or creating an avatar, are preconditioned mechanisms for some games. This makes them essential because the choices the player makes in these individual paratextual spaces before even entering the game-world have a strong impact on the game itself. The most conventional way for games to mirror a change in the difficulty setting is to make enemies tougher or to make the avatar more prone to attacks and challenges. Some games, however, have developed rather unconventional ways of picking up the increased difficulty. The first-person shooter *Crysis* (Crytek 2007) draws on Cold War sentiments through placing the player in the role of a US-American soldier who has to fight North Korean forces. By increasing the difficulty, the player is not only faced with stronger enemies, expanded damage, and more complex missions but also with the additional challenge of the enemies speaking Korean. That way, it becomes impossible for players who do not speak this language to react to the game based on intel gathered through secret channels.

A different progression in levels is accomplished by *GoldenEye 007* (Rare 1997). The game comes in three basic difficulty levels, namely 'Agent', 'Secret Agent', and '00 Agent'. With every increase in difficulty, the enemies become tougher, the agent more prone to attacks and armour- and weapon-reload-points are scarce, while the game also offers additional objectives not available in the lower levels.

Once every mission of the '00 Agent'-level has been accomplished, the '007'-level is unlocked, which allows players to design their own difficulty-preferences with regard to their enemies. One player has remarked that this 'increases replay value and depth, making consecutive playthroughs of each level far less repetitive and more interesting' (DdCno1 2016: n.pag.). This mirrors the argument that some digital paratexts are indeed essential if they have an impact on the game-world and the gameplay-experience as does changing the difficulty level for games such as *GoldenEye 007* (Rare 1997). In addition to these essential digital paratexts, there are also many non-essential ones that already give the player a first taste of the kind of game-world they can expect, preparing their mindset for it and inviting them to participate in the illusion (Wolf 1993: 21). In its introductory scene, which follows the developing studio and game director information, *Metal Gear Solid* (Konami Computer Entertainment Japan 1998) manages to draw the player into its world by establishing an intense mood, mirroring that of the game-world itself. The scene introduces the main characters and their voice actors, thus serving the double-role of credits and cutscene, explores the threat the world has to face, and outlines the role the player has to take on in the game. Although the player does not have agency in this opening sequence, it directly speaks to them, preparing them for what is to come in the game itself. This digital paratext is not obligatory, but it nonetheless bears a strong impact on the player's initial experience of the game.

The shifting relationship between digital and physical materialities in the context of essential and non-essential paratexts for video games has recently become evident as the result of two current trends. In 2020, digital sales of games have outnumbered physical sales for the first time in video game history (Roach 2020: n.pag.). Steam sold 21.4 per cent more games in 2020 in contrast to 2019 (Grubb 2021: n.pag.), which had in itself been a rather strong year. The increase in game purchases, particularly downloadable content, certainly has to do with the fact that during the COVID-19 pandemic, people were restricted in their social interactions and games allowed them to connect to other people in a way that is very personalized (as well as to kill time). These contents possessing digital materiality are still in need of a device that allows the player to access the game, and hence the pandemic also brought about a boost for the games industry as a whole. The BBC have reported that '[s]ales of Nintendo's Switch console helped profits to more than triple in the half year to end of September' (Espiner 2020: n.pag.), not to the least because of *Animal Crossing: New Horizons* (Nintendo EPD 2020). The release of the new PlayStation 5 as well as the Xbox Series X and the Xbox Series S have attracted such a large buying power that these consoles were initially mostly available second hand at hugely inflated prices (Davalos 2020: n.pag.). All these devices, which make it possible for players to access the digital world and to meet up with friends in a digital space, thus epitomize the complex pull between essential and non-essential paratexts in the relationship between digital and physical materialities.

However, a trend forming a contrast to the surge in digitally downloaded content can also be observed, albeit one followed by far less people: the urge to have a physical copy of a game. Limited Run Games, described above, is a company that builds on their customers' nostalgia and their sense of longing for a kind of physical materiality of an otherwise digital world although this is not needed for the game to be played. These physical paratexts are therefore entirely non-essential, at least when ignoring the sentimental value they have for a player. These two examples suggest that the distinction between essential and non-essential paratexts having digital or physical materiality is very often related to the role-specific elements that fulfil in relation to a game. The next section will therefore look at three core modes, namely gameplay, technological, and marketing paratexts to determine their relationship to games materiality.

Gameplay, technological, and marketing paratexts

Throughout this chapter, I have argued that paratexts occupy specific spaces in relation to the game and, very often, these locations are formed by groups of elements that share specific features, while individual paratexts can be part of several groups at the same time. The paper map of Los Santos and Blaine County accompanying the physical copy of *Grand Theft Auto V* (Rockstar North 2013), for example, fulfils several functions simultaneously. First and foremost, it aids the player in orienting themselves in the game-world and allows them to map their position in the game against the landscape depicted in the physical map, thus impacting and guiding their engagement with the game. In addition, the map is also a kind of marketing paratext, which allows the player to make their connection to and investment in the game visible by displaying the map. I still remember the framed map hanging on my brother's bedroom wall, neatly annotated with coded symbols, acronyms, and abbreviations. For him, this map was on par with posters, stickers, and t-shirts that were available for purchase, while he personalized it according to his gameplay experience and added value to individual aspects of it.

In this anecdotal example, I have freely moved from in-game (gameplay) paratexts to outside-of-game (marketing) paratexts, which each relate to a different kind of materiality, while actually being the same paratext, namely the physical map. This shows that it is not only important to consider the paratexts themselves, which has been done in the previous two sections, but also the functions they fulfil. The shift away from the (digital or physical) object to its use thus suggests that physical paratexts can encourage or render digital functions. On the other hand, digital paratexts hardly ever lead to physical functions unless they are mediated by another paratext, such as if an increase in difficulty leads to more imprecise controller output. Gameplay paratexts tend to be digital and are located in the same space as the game-world itself, albeit not in the same realm of reference for the player. That is, while these paratexts, such as setting the level of difficulty, creating an avatar or adjusting the brightness, allow the player to manipulate the game-world, this is done from a position of reality, meaning that these are not yet in-game actions. The function these paratexts thus fulfil defines the parameters we want the game-world to have (if the game allows us to do so), which is achieved by the changing aspects located before the game actually begins.

Technological paratexts, on the other hand, appear to possess exactly the opposite characteristics to gameplay paratexts with regard to location. They are much more obviously situated in the player's reality since in many cases, they are of physical materiality and can be touched, or they are consciously crafted, such as the code written for a game. For the first kind of technological paratexts, it needs to be emphasized again that technological paratexts are not the physically material objects themselves but the processes afforded by these objects. Therefore, a controller is not the technological paratext *per se* but the material means through which technological paratextuality can be created, namely the act of pressing buttons and moving joysticks to fulfil certain actions in the game. One of their key features is that the haptic motion executed in reality, such as pressing a button, is translated into something else in the game-world as defined by the rules of the game, such as jumping, climbing, or using a weapon. The act of converting the movement carried out in reality into the action within the game is what technological paratextuality is about. VR has slightly blurred this line because the movements made in reality resemble those made in the digital world much more closely and very often, the two are (more or less) the same. However, while the movements may be exactly the same, the difference between physical and digital materialities clearly points towards the distinction between text and paratexts. I, as the human being in reality, am only a version of myself in the game, hence I occupy two spaces at the same time, which are distinctly different. This means that while the avatar in the VR world is embodied and, in a sense, 'owned' by the player (Kilteni et al. 2012: 373), the player still exists as a real human being outside of the game (Ross 2012: 386–87).

Marketing paratexts are probably the ones that are most diverse because they can take on any form imaginable and be authored by anyone, regardless of whether they are involved in making the game, playing the game or neither of these two roles. These paratexts orbit the game spatially and temporally. They include elements such as game announcements, trailers, game fairs, reviews, interviews, forum discussions, posters, mugs, costumes, and movies or TV shows based on games. While marketing paratexts created by the game makers fulfil very specific functions, such as increasing the visibility of the game and selling it to the potential player, those created by others can have more diverse functions, such as establishing identity, evaluating the game, and reflecting upon it. These non-official paratexts can still be considered as marketing elements because although their aim is not necessarily to sell the game, they nonetheless are 'the activity, set of institutions, and processes for creating, communicating, delivering, and exchanging offerings that have value for customers, clients, partners, and society at large' (Jaworski et al. 2017: n.pag.). In this sense, marketing paratexts of games include any elements that relate to the game based on a sense of (positive or negative) value associated with it. Considering their materiality, it is clear that their versatility implies that 'anything goes' – we have texts on games, paintings, video clips, podcasts, dolls, street art, and many more. Name it and it probably exists.

By considering gameplay, technological, and marketing paratexts, I have introduced three fields to which all paratexts can be assigned to depending on the function they fulfil in relation to the game. This has, in a sense, complicated the relationship between digital and physical materialities because physical elements can have functions that are solely digital, while digital paratexts can be the reason why physical ones are created. Still, this chapter has hopefully also made clear that the tie between digital and physical materialities in the context of video games is a close one, and one that is essential for the game to exist.

Conclusion: What critical work do paratexts perform and why do they matter?

The previous discussion has emphasized the importance of elements that are normally not considered in most critical engagements with video games (and many other media artefacts), namely their paratexts. The introduction has outlined some of the problems this textual type faces in the context of game studies. While some are related to its terminological ancestry grounded in the codex book medium, others have to do with the fact that it is not quite clear how the game, as the text to which these paratexts relate, can be defined. By proposing a definition of 'video game' as the sum total of the playable components, meaning all aspects in which the player has agency and where they can progress the game's story or discourse based on rules, it has become possible to define individual paratexts. At the same time, however, it has been emphasized that the border between text and paratext in the context of video games is not static due to the interactivity afforded to players, which allows them to take agency over the formation of the text, resulting in unique text–paratext relationships. This has been exemplified in recourse to debates surrounding digital and physical materialities and how these relate to the text and its individual paratexts. I argued that our idea of what a game is, namely either the physical object such as a disc or a digital concept, i.e. the code translated into on-screen images with which we can engage, impacts and results in different ideas surrounding physicality and digitality. In response to the definition of video game proposed in the introduction, it becomes evident that the game possesses digital materiality, while paratexts can be realized in the form of digital and physical materiality.

Making this distinction regarding materiality led to the question of requisiteness of paratexts for video games. I emphasized that assigning paratexts the status of obligatory or facultative depends to a large degree on the perspective taken in the discussion of what constitutes the game as a cultural artefact and how its materiality is defined in this context. The examples engaged with in this chapter have demonstrated that this labelling is not binary but instead should be considered as a spectrum, positioning paratexts along a line of essential and non-essential in relation to the game they frame. In the final section, I proposed that paratexts of video games concern gameplay, technological or marketing modes, which each possess different notions of materiality. While gameplay tends to be largely made up of digital elements, technological components afford physical paratextual relationships in connection to the game and marketing paratexts can take on any form the creator chooses. The aim of this critical engagement with the materiality of video game paratextuality has by no means been to propose a taxonomy of video game paratexts in a consideration of the pull between digitality and physicality. I nonetheless hope that the core characteristics of game paratextuality have been addressed in such a way that discussions concerning specific paratexts can draw on a theoretical basis concerning the materiality constituted by the unique text–paratext relationship surrounding video games.

While this chapter focused on video games as the artefacts of study, insights gained from this discussion can also be utilized in other fields of media studies, such as film and television studies. Social media, on the other hand, appear to prioritize the digital over the physical by solely instrumentalizing the physical as a way into the digital, thus making it a means to an end. Nonetheless, physical materiality and the paratexts associated with it are still essential for social media to generate their digital space. These two examples demonstrate that there is much to be taken from discussions of paratextuality and their relationship to materiality, both from the original work developed in literary studies and the ever-developing research conducted in game studies. I therefore finish this chapter with the hope that it is an incentive to swing the pendulum into the other direction by applying game studies research to other areas of media studies.

NOTE
1. The *South Park* episode 'Nobody Got Cereal?' (2018) illustrates the individuality of the game-play experience based on the subjective choices we make in a highly dramatized mode.

REFERENCES
7780s Studio (2014), *P.T.*, Tokyo: Konami.

Aarseth, Espen (2001), 'Computer game studies, year one', *Game Studies*, 1:1, July, http://gamestudies.org/0101/editorial.html. Accessed 3 July 2023.

Arsenault, Dominic and Perron, Bernard (2009), 'In the frame of the magic cycle: The circle(s) of gameplay', in B. Perron and M. J. P. Wolf (eds), *The Video Game Theory Reader 2*, New York: Routledge, pp. 109–31.

Baudrillard, Jean (1994), *Simulacra and Simulation* (trans. S. F. Glaser), Ann Arbor: The University of Michigan Press.

Bethesda Game Studios (2015), *Fallout 4*, Rockville: Bethesda Softworks.

Blizzard Entertainment (2004), *World of Warcraft*, Irvine: Blizzard Entertainment.

Blizzard Entertainment (2016), *Overwatch*, Irvine: Blizzard Entertainment.

Bonner, Marc (2015), 'Ambiguous play pattern: A philosophical approach to the prospect-refuge theory in urban open world games by merging Deleuze/Guattari and de Certeau', in *Proceedings of the 9th International Conference on the Philosophy of Computer Games, Meaning and Computer Games*, BTK – University of Art and Design, Berlin, 14–17 October, https://www.academia.edu/24458160/Ambiguous_Play_Pattern_A_Philosophical_Approach_to_the_Prospect_Refuge_Theory_in_Urban_Open_World_Games_by_Merging_Deleuze_Guattari_and_de_Certeau. Accessed 3 July 2023.

Brookey, Robert and Gray, Jonathan (2017), '"Not merely para": Continuing steps in paratextual research', *Critical Studies in Media Communication*, 34:2, pp. 101–10.

Caillois, Roger ([1958] 2001), *Man, Play and Games*, Chicago: University of Illinois Press.

CCP Games (2003), *EVE Online*, New York: Simon & Schuster and Atari.

Crytek (2007), *Crysis*, Redwood City: Electronic Arts.

Davalos, Jacqueline (2020), 'Sony's PlayStation 5 is beating Xbox in the online black market', *Bloomberg*, 29 October, https://www.bloomberg.com/news/articles/2020-10-29/sony-s-playstation-5-is-beating-xbox-in-the-online-black-market. Accessed 3 July 2023.

DdCno1 (2016), 'What games did increased difficulty levels in interesting and rewarding ways?', Reddit, 7 June, https://www.reddit.com/r/truegaming/comments/4mxpfi/what_games_did_increased_difficulty_levels_in/d3z9g89/?utm_source=reddit&utm_medium=web2x&context=3. Accessed 3 July 2023.

Douglas, Alexander S. (1952), OXO, UK: EDSAC.

Drucker, Johanna (2009), *SpecLab: Digital Aesthetics and Projects in Speculative Computing*, Chicago: University of Chicago Press.

Egenfeldt-Nielsen, Simon, Heide Smith, Jonas, and Tosca, Susana Pajares (2013), *Understanding Video Games: The Essential Introduction*, 2nd ed., New York, London: Routledge.

Eskelinen, Marku (2001), 'The gaming situation', *Game Studies*, 1:1, July, http://www. gamestudies.org/0101/eskelinen/. Accessed 3 July 2023.

Espiner, Tom (2020), 'Covid-19: Nintendo profits triple as games boom continues', *BBC News*, 5 November, https://www.bbc.co.uk/news/business-54813841. Accessed 3 July 2023.

Esposito, Nicolas (2005), 'A short and simple definition of what a videogame is', in *Proceedings of DiGRA 2005 Conference: Changing Views – Worlds in Play*, Vancouver, Canada, 16–20 June, http://www.digra.org/wp-content/uploads/digital-library/06278.37547.pdf. Accessed 3 July 2023.

Genette, Gérard ([1987] 1997), *Paratexts: Thresholds of Interpretation* (trans. J. A. Lewin), Cambridge: Cambridge University Press.

Gibson, Nathan P. (2020), '*Animal Crossing* producer says players are mostly in their 20s and 30s', *Screenrant*, 8 September, https://screenrant.com/animal-crossing-producer-players-age/. Accessed 3 July 2023.

Grubb, Jeff (2021), 'Steam customers purchased 21.4% more games in 2020 than in 2019', *Venture Beat*, 13 January, https://venturebeat.com/2021/01/13/steam-2020-review/. Accessed 3 July 2023.

Heather, Reece (2020), '*Animal Crossing: New Horizon*'s demographic has an even male/female split, with most players in their 20s and 30s', *Nintendo Wire*, 7 September, https://nintendowire.com/news/2020/09/07/animal-crossing-new-horizons-demographic-has-an-even-male-female-split-with-most-players-in-their-20s-and-30s/. Accessed 3 July 2023.

Hile, Bryson (2022), '18 best collector's editions games you need in your library', *Gamerant*, 8 January, https://gamerant.com/best-collectors-editions-video-games/. Accessed 3 July 2023.

Janik, Justyna (2020), 'Negotiating textures of digital play: Gameplay and the production of space', *Game Studies*, 20:4, December, http://gamestudies.org/2004/articles/janik. Accessed 3 July 2023.

Jaworski, Bernard, Lutz, Richard, Marshall, Greg W., Price, Linda, and Varadarajan, Rajan (2017), 'Definitions of marketing', *American Marketing Association*, https://www.ama.org/the-definition-of-marketing-what-is-marketing/. Accessed 3 July 2023.

Keogh, Brendan (2018), *A Play of Bodies: How we Perceive Videogames*, Cambridge: MIT Press.

Kilteni, Konstantina, Groten, Raphaela, and Slater, Mel (2012), 'The sense of embodiment in virtual reality', *Presence*, 21:4, pp. 373–87.

Kirschenbaum, Matthew G. (2008), *Mechanisms: New Media and the Forensic Imagination*, Cambridge: MIT Press.

Konami Computer Entertainment Japan (1998), *Metal Gear Solid*, Tokyo: Konami.

Leino, Olli Tapio (2012), 'Death loop as a feature', *Game Studies*, 12:2, December, http://gamestudies.org/1202/articles/death_loop_as_a_feature. Accessed 3 July 2023.

Leonardi, Paul M. (2010), 'Digital materiality? How artifacts without matter, matter', *First Monday*, 15:6, June, https://firstmonday.org/ojs/index.php/fm/article/view/3036/2567. Accessed 3 July 2023.

Limited Run Games (2021), *Limited Run Games*, https://limitedrungames.com/.

Mader, Ilona (2017), *Metafiktionalität als Selbst-Dekonstruktion*, Würzburg: Königshausen & Neumann.

Namco (1980), *Pac Man*, Tokyo, Chicago: Namco and Midway.

Naughty Dog (1996), *Crash Bandicoot*, Tokyo: Sony Computer Entertainment.

Neversoft (1999), *Tony Hawk's Pro Skater*, Santa Monica: Activision.

Niantic, Nintendo and The Pokémon Company (2016), *Pokémon Go*, San Francisco, Kyoto: Niantic and Nintendo.

Nintendo EAD, Capcom, Grezzo, and Nintendo EPD (1986–2019), *The Legend of Zelda*, Kyoto: Nintendo.

Nintendo EPD (2020), *Animal Crossing: New Horizons*, Kyoto: Nintendo.

Nintendo R&D1, Nintendo R&D2, Nintendo EAD, Rare, Namco, Nintendo Software Technology, Paon, and Retro Studios (1981–2018), *Donkey Kong*, Kyoto: Nintendo.

'Nobody Got Cereal?' (2018), T. Parker (dir.), *South Park*, Season 22 Episode 7 (14 November, USA: South Park Studios).

Pajitnov, Alexey (1984), *Tetris*, USSR: Pajitnov.

Rare (1997), *GoldenEye 007*, Kyoto: Nintendo.

Roach, Jacob (2020), 'What is DRM in video games and how does it work?', *Digital Trends*, 13 October, https://www.digitaltrends.com/gaming/what-is-drm-in-video-games/. Accessed 3 July 2023.

Rockstar North (2013), *Grand Theft Auto V*, New York: Rockstar Games.

Rockstar North, Digital Eclipse, Rockstar Leeds, and Rockstar Canada (1997–2013), *Grand Theft Auto*, New York: Rockstar Games.

Rockstar Studios (2018), *Red Dead Redemption 2*, New York: Rockstar Games.

Rosenthal, Victoria (2018), *Fallout: The Vault Dweller's Official Cookbook*, London: Titan Books.

Ross, Miriam (2012), 'The 3-D aesthetic: *Avatar* and hyperhaptic visuality', *Screen*, 53:4, pp. 381–97, https://doi.org/10.1093/screen/hjs035.

Schreier, Jason (2016), 'Here's what Blizzard's *Titan* MMO actually was', *Kotaku*, 23 May, https://kotaku.com/heres-what-blizzards-titan-actually-was-1638632121.

Seiwald, Regina (2019), 'Games within games: The two (or more) fictional levels of video games', in N. Zagalo, A. I. Veloso, L. Costa, and Ó. Mealha (eds), *Videogame Sciences and Arts*, Springer Communications in Computer and Information Science, vol. 1164, Cham: Springer, pp. 18–31.

Švelch, Jan (2020), 'Paratextuality in game studies: A theoretical review and citation analysis', *Game Studies*, 20:2, June, http://gamestudies.org/2002/articles/jan_svelch. Accessed 3 July 2023.

Treyarch and Raven Software (2020), *Call of Duty: Black Ops Cold War*, Santa Monica, CA: Activision.

UKIE (2020), 'Player diversity & demographics: 2020 stats', *UKIE*, https://ukiepedia.ukie.org. uk/index.php/Player_Diversity_%26_Demographics#UK. Accessed 11 April 2021.

Williams, Amanda, Lynn, Hughes, and Bart, Simon (2010), 'Propinquity: Exploring embodies gameplay', *UbiComp'10*, 26–29 September, Copenhagen, Denmark.

Wolf, Mark J. P. (2001), 'The video game as a medium', in M. J. P. Wolf (ed.), *The Medium of the Video Game*, Austin: University of Texas Press, pp. 13–34.

Wolf, Werner (1993), *Ästhetische Illusion und Illusionsdurchbrechung in der Erzählkunst: Theorie und Geschichte mit Schwerpunkt auf englischem illusionsstörenden Erzählen*, Tübingen: Niemeyer.

Zimmerman, Eric (2004), 'Narrative, interactivity, play, and games', in N. Wardrip-Fruin and P. Harrigan (eds), *First Person*, Cambridge and London: MIT Press, pp. 154–64.

Short Take 8

Materialities and Craft Value

Karen Patel

In my research on supporting diversity and expertise development in craft, I've been trying to think through craft value and how it is racialized, gendered, and classed. Why do the types of craft promoted by my project partner Crafts Council have so much value placed on them, and why craft work and objects created as

FIGURE ST.8: Craftmaking. Author's own image.

part of craft participation programmes and within communities are considered less valuable, and not recognized as aesthetically important? While value judgements do depend on skill and aesthetic expertise, I argue these value judgements are also classed and racialized. There is work on materialities which helps me think through how value judgements can be reframed for a more equitable and inclusive craft ecology.

For example, Fred Myers (2002) explored the trajectory of indigenous Australian paintings and designs as they move through the western art-culture system and as different object ideologies meet. He discussed Aboriginal concerns about copyright and presented three cases of forgery where the designs of Aboriginal artists were copied, culturally appropriated, and used out of context. For example, images put on tea towels and souvenirs in Vietnam. He described the production of 'The Dreaming', which is the revelation of ancestral knowledge or events in material form. The rituals which form them are held within people and communities and are not thought to be the work of an individual. To quote Myers:

> 'The Dreaming' discursively and practically articulates personhood and ontology, mediating the interpersonal relations between people organized spatially (in territorially dispersed groups) and intergenerationally into a system of identity, of similarity and difference, of autonomy and relatedness.
>
> (97)

Myers argues that the art market system detaches signs from those who make them, and the esoteric knowledge developed within families and communities needs to be protected, rather than individual creativity.

Aboriginal painters have drawn on a framework that is not particularly concerned with usual hierarchies of value and categories of what constitutes fine art. Instead 'they use an ontology and set of practices which draw from their own world of production' (99), imagining their circulation in terms of the local economy of exchange. As their work became increasingly situated within the wider art market, Aboriginal artists fought for copyright, to protect their interests and share their stories. As a result, a subcategory of Aboriginal fine art has emerged, which includes white, non-Aboriginal artists. Myers argues that:

> the recognition of Aboriginal objects as art is a material practice – not simply an endorsement of Aboriginal culture, but a recognition of certain forms of its materialisation within a specific institutional form and system of value (involving markets, museums and collectors).
>
> (110)

The subcategory of Aboriginal fine art which has emerged should be better understood as the work of the producers and their social and historical contexts, rather than the judgement of the critics who valorized it. This argument can also be made for devalued craft in the UK context. A materialities approach allows us to think about not only the skills and expertise of makers but their social, historical, and cultural contexts and how they relate to the judgement of craft.

REFERENCE

Myers, Fred (2002), *Painting Culture: The Making of Aboriginal Fine Art*, Durhams: Duke University Press.

SECTION 3

EPHEMERAL MEANING

Introduction

The third and final section of this edited collection turns its attention to the role of media materialities in capturing and mediating otherwise seemingly ephemeral meaning. As Paul Grainge (2011: 3) suggests, 'the ephemeral has become a site for examining the cultural life of media artefacts as they operate within cycles of time and circuits of value'. Whereas the previous two sections have respectively considered the meanings inherent in the physicality of an object at a particular moment in time, and tensions between old media formats and new cultural practices, this final section provides a range of perspectives on material meanings in motion, with contributions which explore the trajectories, boundaries, and persistence of seemingly ephemeral meanings in changing media spaces. The chapters and contributions in this final section do not offer a unified or singular view on the role of ephemerality in understanding the materiality of media. Rather, they explore the ways in which seemingly ephemeral meanings – moments, messages, and experiences created for a time and place that is no longer here, or never came to pass at all – find themselves captured, transformed, and redefined through those 'cycles of time' and 'circuits of value'.

Matt Grimes's short take opens the section. It reflects on his purchase of the album *The Feeding of the Five Thousand* by the anarcho-punk band Crass's and considers how the band's values have influenced his life, politicizing and educating him. Alex Wade and Adam Whittaker's chapter gives a history of the British video game industry, introducing the concept of prosopography to explore a largely undocumented enterprise culture in West Midlands. For them, the Midlands' video game industry demonstrates the relationship between material and immaterial technologies and those who make, play, and distribute games. Martin Cox's material reflection questions the politics of materiality, using the public toppling of Edward Colston's statue into Bristol harbour as an example. Cox draws on John Dewey's idea of experience to consider the changing material contexts of the statute as it becomes a museum exhibition. Also considering the contexts of and for materiality is Rachel Ann Charles and Tim Wall's chapter on podcasting as a material practice. They argue that the material culture resulting from the content of the *Caribbean Diaspora Podcast* is central to the construction of a virtual community, offering alternative stories of Caribbean migrants. Kirsten Forkert provides a reflection upon the spatial geography of the city, and how it operates within those 'cycles of time and circuits of value' that Grainge (2011) describes. Also exploring the transience of material meanings, and their transformation within digital spaces, is Vanessa Jackson's study of the Pebble Mill community archive. Although the digitization of historic photographs for sharing via the Pebble Mill archive alters their material form, Jackson argues that this shift prompts the contribution of new memories and histories. Yemisi Akinbobola's poignant short take discusses the Black Lives Matter protests and how this important moment made her question her material relationship with her African heritage. Finally, we conclude with John Hillman, who uses Lacan's notion of the subject to ponder the philosophy of digital materiality, and the possibilities of the 'material immaterial' as a means of considering the enduring meanings and logic of physical media in digital spaces.

REFERENCE

Grainge, Paul (2011), *Ephemeral Media: Transitory Screen Culture from Television to YouTube*, Basingstoke: Palgrave Macmillan, pp. 1–22.

Short Take 9

Still Angry: Still Feeding

Matt Grimes

I still remember running home from town that Saturday morning, with THAT record tightly tucked under my arm as if it was only yesterday. The rush of anticipation to get back and play THAT record was almost overwhelming, so much so that I had completely forgotten the usual Saturday town centre routine of avoiding particular streets, and keeping a keen eye out for the skinheads that would revel in the oft opportunity to beat the crap out of a 14-year-old punk in town on his own. So, as you can gather, this was most unusual behaviour for me, but this was a most unusual record; a record of mammoth proportions that promised everything I needed at that point in my life and didn't fail to deliver. Actually, that last bit is not quite true, but almost delivered everything and set me on a trajectory that has ingrained itself in my life course.

So, I finally got home, panting, out of breath but very, very excited. I carefully slipped the vinyl out of the gatefold sleeve in anticipation, placed it on my record player dropped the needle into the lead-in groove, turned it up full volume, and waited. I played that record consecutively probably about fifteen times, over and over that day, and, to be frank, I thought the music wasn't all that great. It wasn't the style of punk I was used to listening to but that seemed to pale into insignificance because what that record taught me was a perspective that I was never going to get taught at school.

I became familiar with the band Crass through fanzine articles and I had heard on the grapevine and through the punk 'zines about this record, edgy, dangerous, controversial, blasphemous, lots of swearing; everything a good punk record should contain. One of the many great things about Crass and their records was the importance and aesthetic of the record sleeve as a carrier of meaning. The unfolding multi-layered record sleeve (see Figure ST.9) was illustrated, collage style, with shocking images of war, animal experimentation, and state violence juxtaposed with treatises and statements, questioning power, authority, and encouraging self-autonomy and dissent. But most important were the LYRICS. This was

FIGURE ST.9: Crass's *The Feeding of the Five Thousand* vinyl cover (1978). Author's own image.

raw truth, an exposition, an explanation, and I am not exaggerating when I say that record changed my life, it articulated everything I was feeling at that time as a confused and angry 14-year-old punk. That musical and lyrical epiphany suddenly started to put threads of thoughts, feelings, and ideas into place; into some semblance of cohesive order and importance. How school, your parents, your teachers, and the police were all colluding against you to try to fuck up your life and control you to turn you into a slave to the system. The combination of stark imagery and powerful words was like gold dust to a young boy trying to find his place in all this madness of youth.

That album was vitally important to my education, my politicization, and my life. The values and beliefs I gained and developed from first hearing that record, and my subsequent engagement with anarcho-punk, have mostly remained with me through my life, though as I have got older and more measured, in a less naive and Utopian way. When I am angry and frustrated with the state machine, which is often, Crass's *The Feeding of the Five Thousand* is still my go-to cathartic record.

7

Stamp of Approval:
A Prosopography of the English
Midlands Videogame Industry

Alex Wade and Adam Whittaker

Game before

The United Kingdom and the English Midlands are respective international and national hubs of game development. The United Kingdom's game industry was valued at over £5 billion in 2017 with 2200 active companies. Of these companies, over 10 per cent (250) are situated in the English Midlands with the region accounting for 13 per cent of all videogames ever created in the United Kingdom (DIT 2019). Given their commercial, technological, and critical accomplishment, it is crucial to identify the trajectories of the region to a media which, unlike many others, appears to grow with immunity from economic and biological contagion. In reference to primary data, complemented with material from other sources, this chapter puts forward a prosopographical investigation into the histories of videogames as a future direction, making connections across space and time to examine how distribution has driven the English Midlands' position as a centre for videogame development. Spatially, this is found in the amusement arcade industry which is usually associated with towns and cities dedicated specifically to leisure such as Blackpool, Weston-Super-Mare, and Southend-on-Sea (Downs 2010), or large conurbations such as Manchester, Birmingham, and London, rather than the English Midlands. Temporally, it is found that videogames draw on both pre/post and industrial revolution practices which shape its own industry and its relationship with others, often drawing on the historical geographic centrality of the English Midlands as the 'cradle' of the industrial revolution.

Applying studies of materiality from Harvey (1990) and Hayles (Gitelman 2002), this chapter finds how spaces and times spiral and plait to reveal modes of working in a 'chain of approval' that were presumed incompatible with hi-tech industries, such as fraternal/paternal modes of organization, those which were assumed archaic, such as cottage industries, or are simply barbaric, such as sweatshops. These are found materially in the economic transition from tangible products such as magnetic media (arcade machines, cassette tapes, cartridges) distributed through immaterial networks that existed fraternally, but may have used materiality in their circulation through goods vehicles and high street stores. With this, the chapter offers a new perspective on the liminal spaces that materiality occupies in its histories as well as its current iterations, showing practices in place long before the rise of the internet and network society or the circular economy. For instance, while the monetization of games is seen by many players as a plague on the current industry, it might also occupy an aspirational position in the early videogame industry. This is particularly true of goods released alongside magnetic media, such as artwork and clothing, giving rise to global multi-billion-pound second-hand market trading in rare goods which may or may not be in their original material form.

The nature and complexities of these issues present significant challenges for scholars of game history. Examinations of individual companies, development teams, and purchasers offer one way to understand game histories, but there are hidden hierarchies and relationships that are perhaps more significant in shaping these notions. Capturing these relationships and the flows of information, people, ideas, hardware, and software over time has the potential to offer transformative perspectives on the burgeoning games industry of the 1980s–90s through to the present day. Such a task is made doubly challenging by the often-limited exploration of the institutional histories of some key agents, and the necessity to rely on dispersed testimonies from individuals. Indeed, as this chapter argues, the distributed nature of game development and consumption, means that there are a number of overlapping and intersecting networks at play, in terms of personnel, hardware/software, and places to name but a few parameters, all of which are structured slightly differently.

Rather than see this as an insurmountable issue, however, the geographical proximity of many key stakeholders presents methodological opportunities. A prosopographical inquiry has the potential to better investigate these networks and connect unidentified influences. Prosopography also enables the exploration of material encounters with things no longer present, something that is increasingly important in games histories as hardware and software platforms quickly reach obsolescence with relatively limited infrastructure for preserving and archiving such materials. In short, it enables the mapping of the material conditions of a segment of the video games industry.

STAMP OF APPROVAL

Fielding prosopography

Prosopography is an approach to historiographical research which takes account of lesser-known individuals whose lives may be documented in more fragmentary and sporadic ways than those captured in conventional histories – in scattered records, objects, or testimonies. Prosopography therefore facilitates the investigation of the characteristics of specific populations, often historic, where individual biographies are difficult to trace, or are not well-documented in archival sources. It differs from sociography in that it investigates the characteristics of a specific population, rather than a broad section of society at large, but there are points of overlap. Though it has gained some traction in sociological inquiry in recent decades, it has traditionally been associated with research into the ancient world, where written records about people outside of a ruling elite connected to powerful institutions are scant or fragmentary at best (Broady 2002; Verboven et al. 2007; Rossier 2019). Through combining seemingly insignificant fragments relating to lesser-known individuals, it is possible to identify points of connection between people, events, objects, and places. Through the assemblage of a broad range of evidentiary fragments, coded and tagged to enable large-scale combination, we can unlock the full potential of material that might easily be dismissed as research confetti, revealing insights into individuals, events, and material objects that are otherwise lost.

By focusing on specific population characteristics, bounded in chronology, geography, and/or institution, prosopography enables the combination of large quantities of specific data to better understand a collective biography of a delimited population group. Isolated 'bits' of data, especially about individuals for which little corroborating evidence survives, can be seen as being of limited value to an individual research project. However, when combined, these small fragments can produce a rich map of collective biography, illuminating networks between largely unknown individuals, and demonstrating the significance of events and relationships between institutions which cross disciplinary boundaries. Prosopographical methods allow us to move beyond the systematic compilation of individualized biographical data and towards the study of 'shared biographical details of individuals in aggregate' (Svorenčík 2018: 605). Shapin and Thackray (1974) recognize the value of prosopography as a way to better interrogate notions of the complex networks of activity in the scientific community, offering insight into what it looks like, who participates, and how ideas are shared. In essence, the collective lives of a specialist community are brought together through prosopography, an ambition similar to that of the present chapter. As Andrej Svorenčík (2018: 606) observes, prosopography allows us to identify 'hidden hierarchies or relationships that remain elusive when the focus is on the most prominent members of a group'. To Svorenčík's argument, we would add that prosopography enables us to capture, investigate, and illuminate aspects of materiality which are deeply embedded in these hierarchies that conventional historical inquiry does not bring to the surface. Understanding the true nature of distributed models demands a focus beyond only the most prominent members; we contend that prosopography is part of the solution.

From the perspectives of games history, the interplay between people, technology, and social experiences mean that modes of analysis which permit engagement with different types of evidence are required. The various layers of materiality here, from the interactions between hardware and software through to networks between game developers, promoters, consumers, and wider society, when considered in combination enable insight into material encounters, even when some of the materials themselves have been lost. Indeed, these can lead to a rich understanding of history and structure of a *field*, to borrow from Bourdieu (1984), alongside individual dispositions (Broady 2002; Rossier 2019). Conceptualized this way, prosopography facilitates the dual exploration of common trajectories through quantitative analytical framing, and the qualitative examination of individual cases, encounters, objects, and biographies and the interactions between these. As this chapter makes clear through its analysis, there are numerous threads and models of distribution which run across different evidential sources and are, at present, difficult to consider simultaneously. In the latter part of the chapter, we demonstrate how prosopography provides a way forward by offering a novel way of understanding the materiality of video game histories. In particular, it affords possibilities in mapping the 'double lives' of video games as both sites of activity and material objects (McKeown 2018), which exist in both the social and physical worlds. Indeed, one might also argue that such an approach has applicability beyond games histories, extending into the broad field of creative arts where informal networks operating outside of fixed institutional borders abound and where distributed and diffuse relationships elide easy categorization.

The inland arcade

In an interview in the forthcoming book *Arcade Britannia* (2022), Alan Meades relates how Jimmy Thomas, whose father pioneered the idea of 'inland' amusement arcades, insisted that arcades should be for 'everybody' and especially for 'women who were about shopping or wanted something to do to relax' (Thomas cited in Meades 2022). For the Thomas family, it was crucial that amusement arcades be accessible to all, irrespective of gender or class or proximity to other leisure activities (e.g. fairgrounds, fish, and chip shops) in time and space. Commercially, the inclusive approach was an unqualified triumph, with Thomas Amusements becoming the most successful arcade chain in Europe by the 1960s and introducing a generation of people to games who may have missed out if they were limited to holiday towns and seaside resorts.

The success of the Thomas's firm can be partly attributed to its industrial organization. First, while the use of 'vertical integration', where different specializations of production are brought into one company, were common in Fordist modes of production, they were not common in end-user leisure industries at this time, only becoming so in the silicon revolution of the 1970s and 1980s. The Thomas's brought all functions of amusement arcade production, from the design and sales of machines to shopfitting and building of the arcades themselves, into the Thomas Amusements stable. While it may be tautological to say that older forms of production are copied before being adapted to revised and evolved social and economic modes, Harvey (1991: 152) identifies that older labour systems may revive and thrive in late twentieth century companies. Vertical integration was deployed effectively via 'Silicon Valley' (Hoefler 1971) firms such as Atari, Apple, and Intel. Closer to home it became a conduit for the manufacture of microcomputers in the United Kingdom, including the BBC's highly centralized Reithian model of informing individuals about the existence of computers via TV programmes, educating them as to how to use them by bringing computers into every classroom (produced by Acorn and BBC branded) in the United Kingdom and entertaining them by releasing games for the same computers (Gazzard 2016). This model shows at once how production and distribution, even in its most verticalized forms, becomes wrapped in materialities that exist between the physical world, for example of microcomputers and the social world, for example education (Dale 2005).

Second, the basis of the Thomas's firm in the 'familial' or 'patriarchal' form of company hierarchy is one which leads to the percolation of cultural capital between generations and then structural replication across them. In the interview with Meades (Thomas cited in Meades 2022), Jimmy Thomas assents to receiving a fruit machine for his tenth birthday and through a material – at the physically tangible and economically utilitarian level – relationship with the object, charged both with keeping it in good working order and being able to keep any revenue it produced. Again, although families have been central to economic activity for as long as bartering, trading, or commerce has been a social imperative, this was a model copied by videogame companies setting up business in the Midlands. The division of labour based around the distinct skill-set of the individuals stretched across kin and kith lines to encompass and employ individuals who were as much motivated by matrimony as material rewards.

Third, the Thomas's favoured distribution model was based around testing the popularity of a machine before it was marketed to potential customers. This was a highly localized arrangement. Thomas's company manufactured gambling machines in Quorn, a village north of Leicester, and then deployed the machines to Showboat Amusements in Loughborough, a market town west of Leicester. Showboat Amusements was also owned by the Thomas's as a venue for trialling its success in its target market of inland arcades, far anticipating the weary stories where Atari's *Pong* machine in Andy Capp's Tavern in Silicon Valley malfunctioned after its coin-slot was jammed with a glut of quarter-dollar coins during 1972 (Kent 2001: 43). In a neat parallel which suggests that this hyperbolic tale is not as apocryphal as it sounds, Atari UK's first United Kingdom's headquarters was in Castle Donington, Leicestershire, ten miles north of Loughborough, where *Pong* was manufactured for the United Kingdom market under the parochial title *Wimbledon*. A prototype was sent to a testing-site at the Strathorn Hotel in Nottingham where, as Alistair Crooks, then Director of Atari UK recalls:

> The first night it was in situ I received a call as the machine was no longer functioning. The cash box wasn't big enough and the customers couldn't get any more money in. This was quickly rectified and I hung around for the rest of the evening. It happened a second time too!
>
> (Crooks cited in Drury 2016: n.pag.)

Informal arrangements around the testing and distribution of videogames in the Midlands followed 'chains of approval' familiar to Thomas Amusements and Atari UK. They often drew on the fraternally symbiotic relationship between developers, publishers and videogame magazines, where material goods such as cover tapes would be distributed alongside reviews and advertising for a company's game in the same magazine. The familial ties that bind lead are typical to the 'connected histories' that knit the complex organization of the creation of videogames across space and time at the hyper-local, local, trans-local, regional, national, multinational and global level, leading to surprising concatenations (Swalwell 2021). Through its methodology and exposition, this chapter marks an early attempt at mapping these links, revealing how inauspicious and sometimes overlooked elements of the material and immaterial, formal and informal, economic and social, political can illuminate past and current practice.

Hardwire: Early arcade games in the Midlands

The popular and academic lionization of the United Kingdom's 'home' or 'bedroom' coding scene of videogames (see e.g. Anderson and Levene 2012; Caulfield and Caulfield 2014) is consistent with the material conditions of 'flexible

STAMP OF APPROVAL

accumulation' predicated on new sectors of production and especially 'intensi-
fied rates of commercial, technological and organizational innovation' (Harvey
1991: 147). Despite the United Kingdom's slowness to transition to computers in
a commercial capacity, firms around the Silicon Fen of Cambridge were able to
shift from amateur to semi-professional to professional ways of working in two
short years. In interview, Paul Machacek commented on the rapid development
of the Sinclair home computers in the first three years of the 1980s:

> Look at the ZX80 [1980] which looks like someone made it in the garage and then
> the ZX81 [1981] which doesn't look like a computer, it's got a really wonky keyboard
> and isn't what Joe 90 [Clive Sinclair] promised us, but is clearly at a production
> level much better than the [ZX]80 and then the Spectrum [1982] came a year later.[1]
> (interview with Paul Machacek 2021: n.pag.)

The embedding of production at the domestic, artisanal level is familiar to studies
of British videogames, yet this often focuses on the production of software, not
hardware and distribution. Sinclair were able to minimize consumer costs for their
earlier computers and radionics as they distributed components via mail-order.
Individual hobbyists would then assemble them at home, not just in the purely
clean and domestic spaces of the dining room and the bedroom, but the semi-
industrial, even planned agricultural, arenas of garages, garden sheds, potting
rooms, and workshops. This is important as where faulty components did not
work, finding the tools to enable a 'hack' to take place was a pre-requisite to their
repair. Such practices became common to early software engineers in the United
Kingdom who would almost by default 'wield a soldering iron, several of them
had weird hobbies around lasers and we bought radio-controlled cars and modded
them' (interview with Paul Machacek). Understood in this way, hacking subscribes
to Hayles's ascription of materiality as a 'selective focus on certain physical aspects
of an instantiated text that are foregrounded by a work's construction, operation,
and content' (Gitelman 2002: 9). Materiality is therefore contingent on the action –
the practices – between subject and object, acting as the medium which gives
meaning to form and matter, content and function, becoming close to Latour's
(2005) 'actants' operating at the social level within actor network theory. Bringing these diverse perspectives together through prosopography draws materiality
into dialogue with aggregated experiences.

Indeed, the materiality of education becomes manifest at the sociological level.
The trial and error involved in the heuristic learning of the art and science of
the hack intersects with the trajectory of industrial organization during a time
which drew upon liminal spaces and times of experimentation where a profi-
ciency for elegance in the style of the hack was as important as what it achieved.

165

A well-known instance is in the 1960s use of university mainframe computers built for calculating the megacorpse of the Third World War being adapted by their programmers into machines for playing games. The continued rise of companies with strong familial bonds located within domestic or semi-domestic realms recalls a slight return to pre-industrial – and now post-industrial – revolution cottage industries (Johns 2006). Cottage industries are where firms operate from domestic or commercial premises not primarily designed for this purpose and their use brings an artisanal aspect to hardware production. The extension of cottage industries into the realm of education in the pandemic societies of the 2020s parallels the use of schools as sites where games programming and copying would take place at after-school computer clubs.

Indeed, as heirs to the hacker – or hobbyist – ethic, Tim and Chris Stamper, the eventual founders of Rare, were seen as inventors first and foremost: 'that was the way that I saw them, like the crazy inventors in the shed, making loads and loads of stuff and then they get lucky with something' (interview with Chris Seavor 2021: n.pag.).[2] The role of serendipity or luck, so often seen as the liminal joker in the pack, or the unknown function of games and play, sport, and the ludic, also operates as the unknowable and indeterminate function of the materiality of production as predicates, actions, practices, objects, or subjects. These 'cannot be determined in advance of the work by the critic or even the writer. Rather, they emerge from the interplay between the apparatus, the work, the writer, and the reader/user' (Gitelman 2002: 9), adding further to the mysterious nature of the hack. This also further divines the position of technology in relation to its position as magic when the viewer or audience does not know any better.

The trajectories of a malleable, unknown (perhaps unknowable) flexible accumulation of the future still rely on hard decisions made in the present. Tim and Chris Stamper were Bristolians who relocated with their family to Leicestershire in the English Midlands so the brothers could study software engineering. Paul Machacek recalls:

> [the] family moved to Ashby[-de-la-Zouch] and Tim and Chris attended Loughborough [University] and the reason they dropped out was because they saw the arcade stuff that was going on around them. Chris was a dedicated programmer and he was on a computer software course at Loughborough Uni and basically went 'I know way more than this course is teaching me, that guy over there [the lecturer] knows less than I do'.
>
> (interview with Paul Machacek 2021: n.pag.)

The Stampers' eventual entry to videogame development is consistent with the selective forces of materialities, technologies, and games. First, this is found in the use of their individual spatial and temporal dynamics. As undergraduates, they had time to access Thomas's Showboat Amusements close-by in Loughborough town centre, their test-sites providing access to the latest machines. Their university education would have given them initial access to tools and processes that made modifying hardware easier than in the purely domestic realm: by the end of the 1970s, Chris Stamper had designed and built a computer of his own (Maher 2014). Second, their rejection of formal, higher education in favour of the savviness of soldering irons in sheds embraces the ethos of trial and error associated with material, heuristic learning at the individual level. It also tracks wider social alterations in industrial organization from economies of scale, based around Fordist production methods through to economies of scope, driven by demand-led production.

As seen below, this is a key determinant in the movement towards an industry as much marked by distribution as production and consumption. For the Stampers', this melange of materialities led them to working first with Allied Leisure, whose import/export and distribution business also supported arcade operators in updating printed circuit boards with new games. Following this they struck out on their own with Zilec. Based in the Staffordshire brewery town of Burton-upon-Trent, Zilec was less than 30 miles from Loughborough and was 'one of only two companies in the United Kingdom to 'manufacture and sell *original* arcade games' (Maher 2014: n.pag., original emphasis). For Norman Walker, their manager at Allied Leisure, the importance of focusing on what would be popular in the large markets of Japan and the United States, allowed economies of scope to come to the fore in the circular logic of flexible accumulation, noting 'They [the Stampers] know what a game has to do to make money. In the arcades, a game has to make money or it will almost literally be scrapped' (Walker cited in Maher 2014: n.pag.). The comprehension of the videogame industry as a global business, informed by forces which are as much serendipitous as able to be flexed and flensed, provided the Stampers with a basis to produce videogames for the burgeoning home computer market. This was apcxcd by the Sinclair Spectrum in the early 1980s, famously canted by adverts extolling the capture of the audio-visual extravaganza provided by the arcade experience in quotidian, domestic settings. Less well-acknowledged is the increased awareness that the amusement arcade experience, so readily recognized by the Thomas family, but not widely reckoned within the United Kingdom, had on the importance of distribution to the arcade industry and ultimately to the videogame market more widely.

Centring on software: The arcade comes home

Before becoming Rare, the Stampers used company names that reflected their geographical locality in the Midlands. This was first manifested as Ashby Computer and Graphics, then trading under a moniker closer to their aims as producers of genre-specific (platformers, shooters) titles as *Ultimate: Play the Game*, becoming Rare, an unironic and immodest reflection of their ability, talent, and status in United Kingdom videogame production in 1985. Inserting themselves in liminal spaces between the United States and the United Kingdom, Rare converted famous primetime American gameshows to home consoles to make ends meet, 'at the beginning Rare was making a lot of games that no one knew about, *Spot the Ball*, *Wheel of Fortune*, *Jeopardy* that sort of thing' (interview with Paul Machacek 2021: n.pag.), before starting their own franchises including *Battletoads* and *Killer Instinct*. While the development of videogames was a known quantity in the sense that the individual had complete control over the means of production, publication and distribution was more difficult. Junior developers making contacts with publishers were interactions encumbered with unknown and unwanted outcomes:

> some of it was 'hello I've got a game, can we talk?', and some of them I would put a cassette into a jiffy bag and send it off. I was dealing with a lot of software houses, some of which had ripped me off.
>
> (interview with Paul Machacek 2021: n.pag.)

For the Stampers who desired to have vertical, or at least quasi-vertical integration in terms of design, development, production and distribution, unintended consequences had to be minimized. Achieving this drew on a simultaneous fusion of learning from the past to anticipate the future, a wider practice archetypal to computers which simulated the future based on past models. Historical practices espoused by the site-test model, such as those seen at Thomas Amusements, were combined with new and innovative methods. Individual charisma and the dominion of persuasion coalesced with domestic mobilities (automobiles) and chains of approval to convince store owners to purchase Ultimate videogames. Bound by blood or matrimony, more secure, if broadly informal, materialities of distribution were generated which have the genuine workaround of a 1970s hack, elegantly negotiating the industrial/informational manufacture transition

> They packaged all of this stuff up and Tim and Chris's dad John, and their other brother Stephen drove all around the countryside. John could sell coal to Newcastle, and he would waltz into WH Smith's or John Menzies and just go 'You're going to buy this' and he would talk the store manager into buying a box of stuff from an unknown company and very quickly in a short period of time this stuff was going off the shelves really quickly and then they wanted John to come back with these boxes. They were self-distributing.
>
> (interview with Paul Machacek 2021: n.pag.)

The economies of scope provided by different skillsets were not typically available to individual coders who focused on all aspects of videogame production. While often able to undertake art or audio tasks in the programming of a game, the Stamper brothers, along with the Darling Brothers and Oliver twins of Codemasters in Leamington Spa, were able to split the creation of art and audio with technical tasks. The Stampers, like the Thomas family before them, were able to deploy kith and kin with a spectrum of expertise to exploit materialities of game production. These are concepts common to the present-day industry where the 'twinning of informal and formal modes of videogame production is commonplace' (Keogh 2019: 17) and yet contemporary commentary overlooks, or elides, the historical origin of these types of production, consumption, and distribution. These informal and formal dynamics, both material and immaterial that are widely present in the videogame industry and what is widely understood to be part of the 'circular economy', are clearly evident in the histories of videogame production.

Licence to skill

The videogame industry's early – and enduring – inspiration for licensing games' titles from a variety of media appears common sensical. The ubiquity of screen-based media included high-tech American action fare such as *Knight Rider* and *Airwolf*, where screens themselves were the focus of programme content and lent themselves to the wider inurement of young people into a model of flexible accumulation by the media they consumed. They were able to watch the TV programme and play the game at the same time. While graphical constrictions resulted in some odd manifestations – Elite's *Airwolf* (1984) saw the eponymous helicopter navigating its way through underground caverns in a semi-platform game – they were commercially popular and drew on and revealed the spirit of the time.

The zeitgeist was especially evident in arcade games (Kocurek 2016), while the licensing of Hollywood products was increasingly popular in the 1980s in bringing films to children and young people who were supposedly unable to view them in the cinema or on television given implicit (watershed) and explicit (British Board of Film Classification ratings) age restrictions. Yet licensing also seemed contradictory in an industry which was becoming a victim of its own flexible accumulation in the form of rampant piracy where the ratio between original and copied software was 1:10 in the mid 1980s (Bagnall 2005). This led to a material response from the industry. Ultimate increased the prices of their games to ten pounds, complementing the game with t-shirts, artworks, and big boxes that were not available via pirated copies, the idea being that 'people were less likely to give something away [through copying] if it cost a tenner' (interview with Paul Machacek 2021: n.pag.).

Yet as early examples such as *KikStart* (1985), which included the unlicensed inclusion of the music from the BBC trials bike series demonstrate, copying at the level of consumption was itself being imitated at the level of production, creating an ever-decreasing spiral of distribution and commercial viability to the point where trajectories of materialities converge between these different, but overlapping spheres. For example, Elite Systems, originally involved in licensing TV shows such as *Blue Thunder*, perceived Ocean's *Rambo First Blood: Part II* (1986) as a 'rip-off of *Commando*, a game by Capcom' (Wiltshire 2015: 161), even if the title itself was licensed from the Stallone film of the same name. Seeing this, Elite, founded in Walsall in the English West Midlands in 1984, sensed that there may be market for conversions of the original game of *Commando*. In a neat reversion of economies of scope, Elite signed *Commando* from Capcom for conversion and distribution on the United Kingdom and European home microcomputer market, becoming the template for other Midlands manufacturers, publishers and distributors to follow, with effects that are still apparent to this day. If Zilec were able to use cottage industry forms and Ultimate were able to bring the graphics and audio of the arcade home via familial entrepreneurship, then Elite brought something more immaterial, but arguably more valuable: the semiotics of the brand itself, selling the imagined mystique of videogames produced in exotic locations such as Chicago and Kyoto to domestic computers designed to help with children's homework and family budgeting.

One of the forerunners of the race in licensing Japanese and American arcade-exclusive exotica was US Gold. A development, publishing, and distribution company incorporated in 1982 in the English West Midlands Black Country towns of Halesowen and Tipton began to sign titles from the Japanese arcade company Sega. Their 'rampant commercialism' is widely acknowledged as being responsible for 'transforming the industry' (Wiltshire 2015: 413). The publishing arm of US Gold, Centresoft, which grew so rapidly that it had to repeatedly re-locate around the Midlands (Wilkins and Kean 2015) before ending up Holford, Birmingham to be closer to infrastructure for rapid communication for national and international markets, 'joined forces with Manchester-based Ocean to import, manufacture under licence and market American software under the name of US Gold' (Crash 1984: n.pag.). Now owned by Activision Blizzard, Centresoft continues to trade as a digital and physical videogame distributor from Holford, its historical and contemporary importance to the industry as a distributor overlooked in the glitzy shininess of the latest game from Playground Studios, Rare, Codemasters, or Sumo Digital.

The production of arcade videogames mirrors traditional production-line model objects such as cars. Each unit has the same cost: economies of scale have decreasing returns and economies of scope are minimally applicable when a product requires assembling by hand and then shipping overseas to the geographically and culturally diverse markets of the United States and Japan. The increasing technological demands of arcade-goers also altered the market. They expected machines that offered a fairground ride type of experience and were therefore different to the more traditional games that could be played in the domestic space. Barriers to entry increased. The Fordist model is in distinction to home videogames where costs of each copy were spread across the development and replication process, where the greater the number sold, the lower the cost, imitating the copying/piracy model at the commercial/production level. While operating adeptly within the home market, the financial backing provided by its shared ownership with Nintendo allowed Rare to continue to produce games for the arcade market.

To enable this, Rare adapted the tried and proven method of site-testing used by Thomas Amusements and Atari to gauge the future success of its productions. Reflecting the globalizing of flexible accumulation, the test, and distribution process was deployed at the international, rather than national/regional level:

> One of the Directors at Rare, a guy called Joel Hochberg, was based in America and he started out in arcades in Miami, Florida. He really knew those kind of things, he was that test base, so we would put the units in and see what happened and he would buy the unit and then get all of the cash that comes out of it and it did really well and it was taking around five grand a week.
>
> (interview with Chris Seavor 2021: n.pag.)

While similar in form to previous chains of approval, embedding the process at the globalized level meant that those who were undertaking the development were unaware of its success and not directly rewarded for it. This shows how recognition in the form of knowledge and financial reward for the developer were limited, while maximizing takings through knowledge of the market for the licensee and broker of the machine:

> It was a bit of black arts, how many people bought arcades, who bought them? I don't know what the outcome of that was. I know my bonus wasn't great, wasn't brilliant and then you hear how successful it was in America and it's like 'Oh really?'
>
> (interview with Chris Seavor 2021: n.pag.)

This is a phenomenon common to the revolution driven by an increasing reliance on distribution, as 'capitalism becomes ever more tightly organized *through* dispersal, geographical mobility and flexible responses in labour markets, labour processes and consumer markets, all accompanied by hefty doses of institutional, product and technological innovation' (Harvey 1990: 159, original emphasis).

Centralization of certain practices and materialities, especially knowledge and revenue, runs hand-in-hand with offshoring, subcontracting, and specialization in specific fields. The technologies and techniques that allow for dispersal of information and labour equally permit concentration of knowledge and liquidity. For those employed and working in the area that Harvey terms 'thoughtware' (1990: 156) industries, where there are extraneous and often exorbitant prices placed upon abstract notions of validated knowledge such as licenses and 'intellectual property', a virtuous circle is generated where licensing from arcade machines, which themselves were based on the licensing of famous stars of the time, entered the home market:

> Joel had his finger in a lot of pies. He was running the arcades getting into publishers, Acclaim, Tradewest, LJN, Milton Bradley, others, he just kept signing the rights to things [...]. The first game I wrote [for Rare] was [*Ivan 'Ironman' Stewart's*] *Super Off Road* which came from Joel's links.
>
> (interview with Paul Machacek 2021: n.pag.)

The future of modelling distributions of the past

Taking the cases set out above, which outline approaches ranging from cottage industry, familial entrepreneurship, to brand-centric and licensing models of development and distribution, it is clear that there is a rich, but scattered, evidential trail which, when compiled, has the potential to sharpen our understanding of the wider influences of models of distribution across these different entities and approaches. Through the systematic collation of small fragments of testimony, it becomes possible to consider such data both in aggregation across a larger dataset, or sifted to build up a more detailed biography of a key agent. Essentially, by drawing upon a combination of specific case studies, coded and tagged according to a predetermined schema, it becomes possible to make robust comments regarding networks and relationships that belie generalizable classification. Crucially, it also becomes possible to better understand the materiality of key objects in these networks, and their roles as important nodes in a networked view of games histories.

It is our contention that prosopographical methods have significant potential to transform current understanding of the various past and present (and future) networks at play in the Midlands games industry. There are layers of meaning and connection which can easily escape the grasp of conventional sociological inquiry, especially in connection with the ways material objects are important in networked interactions. Through the collation of such data using key 'tags' across a range of different evidence types to facilitate combinatorial analyses, it becomes possible to consider multiple lines of inquiry simultaneously. There will be additional evidential trails which offer insight into the qualitative experiences of the networks at play, hidden hierarchies within such connections, and the socialized experiences which represent such a crucial part of games history. These survive as an unintended breadcrumb across interview testimonies; prosopographical methods enable us to follow this trail spread across diverse sources and get closer to understanding the materiality of historical games encounters, and the material aspects of games history itself.

For example, although an individual recollection or piece of evidence may be focused on exploring a particular issue or location, it will also likely contain a variety of information which is dismissed as being of peripheral interest for a specific research question, such as names, objects, software, institutions, locations, and opinions. In historical terms, an account may refer to payment to an individual for particular goods and services; this individual is the subject. However, the account may have been witnessed by, or refer to, a number of individuals who, though named, do not actively participate in the event itself, along with objects, monetary values, motivations for purchase, and trading networks. These seemingly peripheral details could, in turn, provide a missing link in a collective biography as evidenced by other sources which do not appear to be connected. Numerous instances like this permit a glimpse at trajectories over time in multiple data sources. What appears as simply a name on a document, or a passing mention in an interview, could be the linchpin in mapping a series of activities for an individual working in a particular role, institution, field, or geographical location. We begin to see some of these connections emerging in the interviews presented here; there is clearly untapped potential if we consider the possibilities of combining hundreds of such testimonies in a rigorous manner.

This process can be applied in a more qualitative sense with modifications. The processing of quantitative data points can be immensely useful in establishing the parameters of the field, key stakeholders within networks, and hierarchies. However, adding qualitative depth enables us to better investigate perceptions over time, as voiced by individuals themselves, lifting the 'lid' on gaming communities over time. It also facilitates the exploration of material encounters through personal recollections, filled with emotional and sensory information, with material objects.

The loom of technology

As noted throughout this chapter, prosopographical approaches provide the opportunity to both look at data in aggregate, and to explore individual cases in greater detail in a qualitative manner, provided that these are 'understood in the framework of the social structure of the field' (Rossier 2019: 11). The precise nature of qualitative investigations may not be immediately clear but approaching data collection as a process of discovery enables inductive analysis of qualitative parameters. Returning to the example of documentary witnesses outlined above, qualitative parameters might include details on the scenario being described, the context in which the record is made, the relationships between different parties involved, etc. As Apperley and Jayemanne (2012: 15) observe, 'the significance of the materiality of games is how they impact on bodies, both individual and collective'. Prosopographical methods enable us to map, and better understand, this significance on individual and collective bodies and, importantly, the connections between these. Recalling David Harvey (1990: 355), 'Aesthetic and cultural practices matter, and the conditions of their production the closest attention'; prosopographical methods could enable us to map these very conditions and offer informed perspectives on the essence of historical materialism, recuperating aspects of social organization within such a frame.

In this increasing abstraction of value, which finds its original form in tangible, material forms, first through gift relations, then barter, then tokens, money, then as credit, shares and stocks, the primary function of knowledge is as a container and harbinger of value. This is a position underpinned, not by its dominion in central banks which control inflation and interest rates, but through the technologies and practices of innovation driven by networks of distribution embedded at the local, regional, national, and global levels. The 'flexible accumulation' common to contemporary societies has to go, has to be *redistributed*, somewhere. In the example of the game economies of the English Midlands, this is in a revolving and spiralling circle of licensing and sub-licensing, based around a studio model where individuals would do little but work to maximize the shares in the firm that were given to them when they commenced employment: both Chris Seavor and Paul Machacek worked long hours, up to '120 per week' (interview with Paul Machacek 2021: n.pag.),[3] reviving notions of sweatshop manufacture (Harvey 1990: 152–53). The links to fraternal modes of working are apparent here: a worker who is 'part of the family' is, for better or for worse, more invested in the livelihood of the company as a financial enterprise than with a contracted, professional, 9–5 worker. That employees were also motivated by the promise of bonuses – whether they were ultimately paid or not – feeds into recent explorations in production studies of 'hope labour' (Ozimek 2019: n.pag.), not on the materiality of a permanent contract, but on the hope that good work will be monetarily rewarded. This is a dynamic, exploited throughout the political economy of media industries which trades on the immaterial hope of a better tomorrow with the material production of the moment. Like the flexible accumulation of Harvey (1990), the future becomes something intangible, which draws on the material, embodied labour of today. In latticing the future into the present, hope is the last thing to die.

Therefore, it is fascinating to note that the culture of crunch, where employees are expected to work punishingly long hours in pursuit of deadlines, has positive connotations historically but is a negative phenomenon in the contemporary industry that continues to this day. It has become so widespread and accepted – even expected – that credits for videogames acknowledge how workers have missed the birth of their children and the growing up of family members, a blatant transposal of the familial bonds that underpinned the early days of enterprise in the amusement arcade and videogame industry found in the Thomas's and Stampers' concerns. Extending this premise, there is an emerging realization that crunch has become outsourced (Bratt 2021) to overseas developers, spotlighting the spiralling, recursive circularity of processes and practices, initially identified in the Midlands videogame industry as broadly positive but are totally abstracted and corrupted over space and time. As distance between people and the effects of practice has decreased technologically, so the speed and proclivity for their disabuse has increased humanly.

It is doubly unfortunate that the region of the East Midlands that Rare hails from has a history of sweatshop practices (O'Connor 2020: n.pag.) tied to the textiles industry. The reveal of shameful, dangerous, working practices show how these are predicates mutual to 'traditional' production-line Fordist industries as well as post/pre industrial modes of flexible accumulation. It is geographically resonant, emanating from the histories of a region which has, for better or for worse, from the looms and Luddites of Leicestershire, had a long-standing, often tense, sometimes tragic, relationship with innovation and technology. It is only through a slowing of the perception of time and space enabled by responses to the global crisis of COVID-19 that the local tragedy was revealed that sweatshops exist in service of the aptly termed pursuit of 'fast fashion'. Harvey (1990: 156) shows that the typical half-life of a Fordist product was 'five to seven years' but 'flexible accumulation has more than cut this in half in certain sectors (such as textile and clothing industries) while in others, (e.g. video games and computer software programmes) the half-life is down to eighteen months'. This may even seem anachronistic now given that videogame licences such as Codemasters' F1 series are released on an annual basis and videogames are given regular updates and patches that were not possible with previous 'material' means of production and consumption, circulation, and distribution. Yet the importance of history is evident in Harvey's insight, the position of videogames in economy and society are as much – if not more – reliant on materialities of distribution as production and consumption. That videogames are able to take from the present as well as the past to mould the future shows how they are both drivers of and driven by change which provides opportunities for some and suppresses others. In its form, social media, perhaps the apogee of the techniques and technologies of the distribution condition, influences the matter and content of Rare's latest releases with *Sea of Thieves* a response to Twitch streamers and influencers becoming 'a social media game as much as a social game' (interview with Paul Machacek 2021: n.pag.). While this chapter highlights some of the avenues to be taken in the historical investigation of the importance of distribution, it is the task of the methodology of prosopography to collect and document these over space and time to reveal where, when, and how the Midlands videogame industry came to be ascendant in its processes and practices, through its histories and futures and where it is positioned in relation to its antecedents and contemporaries both within the games industry beyond.

NOTES

1. Paul Machacek is currently employed at Rare and has worked on a host of different projects in his 30+ years at the company. He was one of the first employees to be recruited to the firm by the Stamper brothers who was from outside of their familial network. The interview was carried out on 9 March 2021 via MS Teams.
2. Chris Seavor was employed at Rare during the 1990s and currently works independently. The interview was carried out on 12 March 2021 via MS Teams.
3. The long hours worked at Rare were verified in an article by Parkin (2012). However, the interviewees for the present chapter doubt the motivation of Parkin's account, even if they agree with the figures presented there. This chapter recognizes the interviewees opposition to Parkin's account, while leaving the reference here as a means of cross-referring the veracity and extent of long working hours at Ultimate and Rare. This is a phenomena raised by the interviewees with the awareness that the choice was made in order to earn money and that working shorter hours would be possible, but with an accordant effect on reward and recognition. It is important to note that while long working hours may have been a common experience in the earlier days of the company during the 1980s and 1990s, this has not been the case for a considerable period of time and is not a predicate of the current/ contemporary Rare set-up.

REFERENCES

Anderson, Magnus and Levene, Rebecca (2012), *Grand Thieves and Tomb Raiders: How British Videogames Conquered the World*, London: Aurum Press.

Apperley, Thomas and Jayemanne, Dharshama (2012), 'Game studies' material turn', *Westminster Papers in Communication and Culture*, 9:1, pp. 5–25.

Bagnall, Brian (2005), *On the Edge: The Spectacular Rise and Fall of Commodore*, Winnipeg: Variant Press.

Bourdieu, Pierre (1984), *Distinction: A Social Critique of the Judgement of Taste*, London: Routledge.

Bratt, Chris (2021), 'The games industry just talked about outsourcing crunch and totally missed the point', *Eurogamer*, 13 May, https://www.eurogamer.net/articles/2021-05-13-the-games-industry-just-talked-about-outsourcing-crunch-and-totally-missed-the-point. Accessed 3 July 2023.

Broady, Donald (2002), 'French prosopography: Definition and suggested readings', *Poetics*, 30:5&6, pp. 381–85.

Caulfield, Nicola and Caulfield, Anthony (2014), *Bedrooms to Billions*, UK: Gracious Films.

Crash (1984), 'US Gold for Britain', *Crash*, October.

Dale, Karen (2005), 'Building a social materiality: Spatial and embodied politics in organizational control', *Organization*, 12:5, pp. 649–768.

Department for International Trade (2019), *Midlands Engine: Video Games*, London: Crown.

Downs, Carolyn (2010), 'Two fat ladies at the seaside: The place of gambling in working class holidays', in R. Snape and D. Smith (eds), *Recording Leisure Lives: Holidays and Tourism in 20th Century Britain*, vol. 112, Eastbourne: Leisure Studies Association, pp. 51–73.

Drury, Paul (2016), No title, *Nottingham Post*, 1 July 2016.

Gazzard, Alison (2016), *Now the Chips Are Down*, Massachusetts: MIT Press.

Gitelman, Lisa (2002), 'Materiality has always been in play', *Iowa Journal of Cultural Studies*, 2:1, pp. 7–12.

Harvey, David (1990), *The Condition of Postmodernity*, London: Blackwell.

Hoefler, Don (1971), *Microelectronics News*, New York, January.

Keogh, Brendan (2019) 'From aggressively formalised to intensely in/formalised: Accounting for a wider range of videogame development practices', *Creative Industries Journal*, 12:1 pp. 14–33.

Kocurek, Carly (2016), *Coin-Operated Americans: Rebooting Boyhood at the Video Game Arcade*, Minnesota: Minnesota University Press.

Latour, Bruno (2005), *Reassembling the Social: An Introduction to Actor-Network Theory*, Oxford: Oxford University Press.

Maher, Jimmy (2014), 'The legend of Ultimate: Play the game', *The Digital Antiquarian*, 14 January, https://www.filfre.net/2014/01/the-legend-of-ultimate-play-the-game/. Accessed 3 July 2023.

McKeown, Conor (2018), 'Playing with materiality: An agential-realist reading of SethBling's *Super Mario World* code-injection', *Information, Communication & Society*, 21:9, pp. 1234–45.

Meades, Alan (2022), *Arcade Britannia: A Social History of the British Amusement Arcade*, Cambridge: MIT Press

O'Connor, Sarah (2020), 'Leicester's dark factories show up a diseased system', *Financial Times Online*, 3 July, https://www.ft.com/content/0b26ee5d-4f4f-4d57-a700-ef49038de18c. Accessed 3 July 2023.

Ozimek, Anna M. (2019), 'Outsourcing digital game production: The case of Polish testers', *Television and New Media*, 20:8, pp. 824–35.

Parkin, Simon (2012), 'Who killed Rare?', *Eurogamer*, 8 February, https://www.eurogamer.net/who-killed-rare. Accessed 3 July 2023.

Rossier, Thierry (2019), 'Prosopography, networks, life course sequences, and so on. Quantifying with or beyond Bourdieu?', *Bulletin de Méthodologie Sociologique*, 144:1, pp. 6–39.

Shapin, Steve and Thackray, Arnold (1974), 'Prosopography as a research tool in history of science: The British Scientific Community 1700–1900', *History of Science*, 12:1, pp. 1–28.

Swalwell, Melanie (2021), 'Heterodoxy in game history: Towards more "Connected Histories"', in M. Swalwell (ed.), *Game History and the Local*, Cham: Palgrave Macmillan, pp. 221–33.

Svorenčík, Andrej (2018), 'The missing link: Prosopography in the history of economics', *History of Political Economy*, 50:3, pp. 605–13.

Verboven, Koenraad, Carlier, Myriam, and Dumolyn, Jan (2007), 'A short manual to the art of prosopography', https://prosopography.history.ox.ac.uk/images/01%20Verboven%20pdf.pdf.

Wilkins, Chris and Kean, Roger M. (2015), *The Story of US Gold: A Very American, British Software House*, Kenilworth: Fusion Retro Books.

Wiltshire, Alex (2015), *Britsoft: An Oral History*, London: Read-Only Memory.

Short Take 10

The Edward Colston Experience

Martin Cox

There is a school of thought, attributable to philosopher John Dewey (1958), that art is experience. While the ongoing conditions of living are continuously passing, 'an experience' has shape:

> We have *an* experience when the material experienced runs its course to fulfilment. Then, and then only is it integrated within and demarcated in the general stream of experience from other experiences ... Such an experience is a whole and carries with it its own individualizing quality and self-sufficiency. It is *an* experience.
>
> (Dewey 1958: 35)

An experience, filtered through perception, always has aesthetic quality. The aesthetic properties of art exist also in 'the sounds and sights of rushing fire-engines' or 'the grace of a baseball player' (Dewey 1958: 5). The art object is not irrelevant. The work of the artist is to embody their material with properties that 'refine' the aesthetic register of experience. Not just ciphering signs and codes but embodying the 'rhythms' and 'energies' of experience.

Perception carries past experience into the present, thus participating in its aesthetic resonance and making every experience unique. For Dewey, an artwork clarifies and purifies the confused meaning of prior experience in the immediate present. The pragmatists turn that Dewey brings is that the symbols and codes refined by the artist must be *experienced* if they are to be of use. The crucial point, experience, is always the vessel of aesthetic appreciation and the aesthetic register of experience unifies its emotional, intellectual, and symbolic agency – the *work* of art is in experience.

The recent spectacle of Edward Colston being despatched into Bristol harbour can certainly be seen *an experience* of the *work* of art. Colston changed (see Figure ST.10). The once proud, legitimate philanthropic role model is now a toppled autocrat. The same material (a bronze statue) carried through a multifarious universe of unique experiences, each transforming it into something new

FIGURE ST.10: Edward Colston's statue at the M Shed in Bristol. Courtesy of Adrian Boliston under Creative Commons Licence Attribution 2.0 Generic (CC-BY-2.0).

and unique. The open sewer that is my social media left little doubt that the effigy of Colston being jettisoning to the depths was experienced differently the world over: Gammon faced supremacists defending dreadful public art from the furious indignation of BLM protesters. Who'd of thought?

And where does this leave the artist? John Cassidy, who designed the statue, took his subject matter and refined its proud stature, elevated above the citizenry, who, under the terms of the commission, were expected to gaze upon it as inspiration for cooperative living. Those aesthetic properties harvested from his experience and worked into form entered into the experience of people the world over. The proud stance, the lofty positioning, the embodiment of the great and the good experienced now as the continuation of that most unacceptable of experience – the horrors of the slaver. Cassidy presumably didn't suppose that economic, geopolitical, and technological progress would land his toil in the murky depths 125 years in the future.

As uninteresting as the statue is, it delivered all the stuff of past experience into the present, carrying it forward through time, symbolic rearrangement, public indecency, resistance and national shame. The statue is clearly more than a public record – a gathering of signs and symbols objectively stating events of the past. Its potency is in experience, bringing forth not only the historical events in which it was forged but the experiences of those who perceive it now, in new consummate experiences that unify new arrangements emotional, intellectual, and aesthetic registers.

It would seem that much of what Dewey theorized holds. Colston changed because perception changed, and perception changed through 125 years of experience.

If the *work* of art exists in experience, it should be no surprise that our feted cultural institutions were not, and have never been the location of art working (in the Dewey sense) in the way Colston just did. Colston worked because he was allowed to exist, decay, offend, and transform through experience, unaided by the cultural sector death star. It's not simply that so often our public cultural institutions remove art (in Dewey's vernacular; refined aesthetic experience) from public view, in buildings often so antiseptic that the uninitiated might suppose they have drifted into a GUM clinic. It's that the experience is infused with all the condescending, pseudointellectual piffle of the curator and further laden with the structural inequality of the cultural sector, which attaches itself to the material in experience. The material changes. It now speaks of the institution to the institution through the institution.

Regardless of the artist's intent, the affect is that material is neutered, rendered static, and stripped of its capacity to transform – curated into oblivion. It is rather like a safari where all the animals have been shot, stuffed, and organized along the roadside in a morbid display of symbolic inertia – all life, movement, and energy drained from experience – dead behind the eyes.

So news that the statue is to be resurrected in a museum is depressing. It's not that this will re-legitimize him – no doubt he would be carefully exhibited to reflect his sullied past. It's that all the inertia, vainglorious platitudes, virtue signalling, and hypocrisy of the cultural institution will attach itself to experience and render the repurposed material lifeless. Colston's current status as the vessel of public experience will be symbolically and experientially appropriated by an institution that can make no claim to the burst of energy that landed it in the sink.

Colston is exactly where he should be, in the harbour depths, where all who have experienced his redeployment as an object of resistance, dissent, and progress can savour what Dewey calls the 'consummator harmony of a complete experience' (1958: n.pag.). The knowledge that he is there, gone but not forgotten (unseen but still perceived), *is* the continuation of that glorious experience – the meaning of the moment lives on uninterrupted. If a visible record of events is required for future perception, let the plinth, absent of its occupant, remain in public view. What better material for retaining the emotion and energy of the moment uninterrupted into the future? The vacant plinth with the knowledge of its former occupant's location is surely the best way to experience Edward Colston.

REFERENCE

Dewey, John (1958), *Experience and Nature*, Mineola: Dover Publications.

8

Reframing Materiality in the *Caribbean Diaspora Podcast*

Rachel-Ann Charles and Tim Wall

Introduction

In this chapter, we explore the way in which ideas of materiality can inform an understanding of podcasting as a cultural phenomenon, with a particular focus on the *Caribbean Diaspora Podcast*. The series focuses on the exchange of migration stories which offer an alternative narrative about Caribbean nationals living abroad. The podcast series, produced by one of this chapter's authors, Rachel-Ann, aims to explore alternatives to historical, mainstream narratives about the Caribbean Diaspora community in the United Kingdom, which mainly provide a negative portrayal often built around themes of illegal residence status, deportation, and criminal behaviour.

Podcasting and podcast listening became one of the boom cultural activities in the lockdown public health response to the COVID-19 pandemic. Podcasters found innovative ways to record their episodes, even using their cars and 'pillow forts' as makeshift studios (Arbuthnot 2020). There has been a growing body of literature that investigates podcast production and listening practices, which includes published works by Berry (2006), Crofts et al. (2005), Menduni (2007), McClung and Johnson (2010), and Markman (2011). However, this literature does not provide us with an agreed definition of the podcast, and we are some way off a developed framework that would allow us to understand the core production, distribution, and listening practices of podcasting.

The *Caribbean Diaspora Podcast* is built around regular audio programmes. Thirteen episodes were produced by Rachel-Ann between July 2020 and January 2021, to engage with this widely dispersed global community. The audio is accessible through online platforms such as Facebook, Twitter, Instagram, Soundcloud, Apple, Spotify, and the website. The analytics overview, from all the online platforms, demonstrates that audiences have been engaging with the podcast content in multiple ways. For example, there have been 545 views, with 180 visitors on the *Caribbean Diaspora* website. These views were made by persons living in the United Kingdom, United States, China, Trinidad and Tobago, Ireland, Netherlands, Guyana, Jamaica, France, Dominican Republic, Belgium, Finland, Russia, and Barbados.

Promotions for the podcast state that the series is:

> centred around all of the things that matter to those within the Caribbean Diaspora community. In each episode, members of the Caribbean Diaspora community talk about their experiences living abroad and discuss topics such as Identity, Belonging, Entrepreneurship, Art, Music, Food, Festivals Publishing, Sexuality, Education and Grief.
>
> (*Caribbean Diaspora Podcast* website n.d.: n.pag.)

A podcast that explores such major ideas has much to tell us about identity in the contemporary society. As Goulbourne and Solomos (2004) argue:

> more than any other part of the contemporary world [...] the Caribbean world has been a precursor of several themes in the energetic pursuit of modernity: capitalism/industrialism, de-tribalization/individualization, plural identities, transnationality, the disruption and transformation of cultural domains and boundaries.
>
> (534)

As Rachel-Ann explains it on the podcast's Soundcloud page:

> Together with highlighting the way that nationals have been representing the Carib bean flag while living abroad, ultimately, the aim of this podcast is to capture the rich history and wisdom within these untold stories through the voice of the person telling the story.
>
> (n.pag.)

In the analysis below, we argue that the *Caribbean Diaspora Podcast* demonstrates the construction of a virtual community through the processes of podcast preproduction and production and that the relationship between listeners and the material culture generated in the content of these podcasts is critical to the formation of this virtual community. As we show, the preproduction and production steps for the podcast are guided, following Whitaker et al. (1997: 137), by the recording of stories as a shared activity.

Testing the insights in wider discussions and between Rachel-Ann's insider status (member of the diaspora culture and producer of the podcast) and Tim's outsider status (white British male, radio studies academic) has been particularly productive. Through emerging themes surrounding podcasting as a form of audio media, and the specific nature of the *Caribbean Diaspora Podcast*, we demonstrate that the materiality of podcasting extends the conventional notions used to discuss such issues in media and cultural studies. This is particularly apt for a media form often seen as ephemeral or immaterial. We present an analysis of both the distinctive cultural materials out of which the *Caribbean Diaspora Podcast* is built, and of the very different pre-production, production, and post-production processes that create both a global virtual listening community and a distinctive material product of black diaspora sound culture.

In the context of this book, the *Caribbean Diaspora Podcast* series enables us to explore four central notions of the materiality of podcasting, which can be generalized into a mature analytical structure to understand this cultural phenomenon. In the first, we critically explore ideas of materiality in relation to attempts to define podcasting as a form of institutionalized media production and distribution. We set out the limitations of such approaches, including the suggestion that the defining quality of sound media is the absence of any materiality and the reductive case that audio media is in essence, determined by its technological form. Second, we also note the neglect of the materiality of listeners and listening in the main approaches to podcasting, radio, and other sound media. When applied to podcasting, we highlight the importance of ideas of virtual communities and how we can move beyond the idea that both sound media and digital media somehow lack materiality. In doing so we trace the emergence of specifically black cultural podcasting. The core area of primary research is set out in an ethnography of podcast production. By focusing on Rachel-Ann's work on the *Caribbean Diaspora Podcast* series, we reveal the distinctive differences of production when compared to mainstream media production processes and the importance of her place within this diasporal culture. In doing so, we open up the final area of discussion: the significant themes of Caribbean diasporal discourse which have emerged in the contributions from a variety of interviewees. We conclude with some suggestions for further work in the materiality of sound media, internet-enabled global communication, and diaspora cultures.

As such, this chapter therefore responds to the need for increased research on podcasts, and theorization of podcasting. As Llinares et al. (2018: 123–45) have identified, we know too little about 'the culture of podcasting, podcast audiences and listening practices, the format's technological properties, and podcast aesthetics and style'. It also focuses our attention on important ideas of diasporal identity, here in relation to these linked to a wider Caribbean culture, and the way practice-based research through podcast production can reveal important aspects of such an identity, especially in the unusual situation of public health lockdown.

The materiality of podcast production, distribution, and listening

Discussions of podcasting, and of the mobile listening associated with podcasts, are rooted in debates about the materiality of sound media in radio studies and sound studies. Over a series of articles and chapters, one of this chapter's authors has established a core argument about these debates (Wall 2004, 2016, 2018; Wall and Webber 2015). We draw on this analysis here, proposing that we need an approach to studying audio media that: (i) integrates the institutionalization of audio media with the experience of consuming it; (ii) is attentive to the historical and cultural locations of podcasting as a media form; and (iii) avoids metaphors from our physical world that privilege the absence of the visual of the immateriality of sound media. In doing so, we need a renewed sense of how podcasts, and other sound media develop notions of time and space.

The Guardian journalist, Ben Hammersley, coined the term podcast in 2004 (Mollet et al. 2017) as a portmanteau word blending the words 'iPod' and 'broadcasting' to signal a medium that enables time-shifting listening of audio obtained via the internet as an alternative to over-the-air radio. In the same article, Hammersley also offered up 'Audioblogging' and 'GuerillaMedia' as alternative terms, although each emphasized very different characteristics of the emerging medium with roots in online citizen journalism and alternative media. Harris and Park (2008) re-enforce the 'iPod' mobile listening/'broadcast' distribution factor when they identify 'audio playback' as the defining material characteristic of this (then) emerging form of audio media. They contrast the fact that listeners can play podcasts at their chosen time with the broadcast model which usually assumed simultaneous distribution and consumption. For Bottomley (2015) and Potter (2006: 97–112), these 'time-shifting' and 'place-shifting' elements in podcasting are differentiating material factors from what they construct as other 'ephemeral' media platforms. Berry (2006) adds an emphasis on the role of subscription, which he sees as transformative of the way listeners access podcast in time and place.

These basic definitional frameworks are useful in recognizing at least some of the characteristics of the *Caribbean Diaspora Podcast* series. The international nature of the audience means that being able to listen at a time chosen by individual listeners is important. For diaspora communities, 'time-shifting' and 'place-shifting' are not just maters of personal convenience, they are central to ways of establishing a shared experience. Likewise, subscription allows geographically and temporally disparate listeners to bring patterns of regularity to their listening.

185

Beyond these basic points, though, by definition of podcasting in relation to over-the-air sound broadcasting, the authors often carry forward many of the essentialist ideas about the nature of audio materiality which have bedevilled our understanding of radio. For instance, scholars in radio studies too often looked for, and crudely applied, materialist metaphors to understand radio, and by extension all audio media. Radio is presented as 'blind' (for instance, Crisell 1986: 3; Chignell 2009: 4), or 'invisible' (Lewis and Booth 1989).[1] Or seen as having an essential material nature that determines not only its form, but by implication, the way it operates culturally for listeners. Andrew Crisell's (1986: 43) characterization of the materiality of radio as 'simply of noises and silence and therefore use time, not space' is a particularly good example of this. We can discern other metaphors of absence in the early days of radio that call on the ideas of 'invisibility' or even 'intangibility' materiality. Noakes (2016), for instance, has pointed to the interest in radio technology amongst early-twentieth-century spiritualists for building 'psychic telegraphs' that it was felt would exploit these shared characterizes of intangibility in radio and the spirit world.

In other approaches, the cultural form of sound is understood to be determined by the materiality of the technologies which enabled its existence. Most studies of both radio and podcasting commence with a historical survey of their enabling technology, presented as the history of the medium (see, for instance Shingler and Wieringa 1998; Berry 2016). This conflation of the cultural form of audio media with its enabling technology is encouraged in the very naming of the media. The term 'radio', for instance, indexes the transmission form used for broadcasting, and 'podcasting' draws on the playback machines used to listen and the use of the internet to disseminate programming from the production centre outwards to those listeners.

As we show in our analysis of the *Caribbean Diaspora Podcast* series, the relationship between enabling technology, material form, and listener experience is more complex than these simple metaphors suggest. For a start, as the programme podcasts of major broadcasting organizations shows, audio media can be distributed at distances as easily along wires of the internet as the radio waves that constitute over-the-air models. Of course, the technology is not irrelevant. However, it is the political economy of audio media enabled by particular technologies, and the political, economic, and cultural priorities, which decide how and for whom these technologies are used; not the other way round. In traditional radio, it is the selection of a central-producer-to-mass-audience model that gives us the 'broadcasting' metaphor. As cell phones show us very clearly, the technology can be adapted for very different relationships between 'producer' and 'listener' up to the point that these concepts become redundant. Likewise, it is the political decision to organize radio at a national level, and to strictly licence who can transmit, that determines the over-the-air form of radio available to us. As we will show, the ability to use the internet as both a distributor of sound programming and a facilitator of interaction *is* centrally important to the potential of podcasting. However, we need to understand these material relationships as opportunities afforded, rather than cultural forms determined, by the available technologies.

As Kate Lacey (2018: 119–20) notes, such positioning often places radio (and we would argue, by extension, podcasting) as immaterial, which ignores 'the materiality of the technologies […] involved in the production, transmission, and reception of radio […] and the ecological implications of airwaves'. But she also counsels caution in constructing this material nature as another form of essence, noting that the term 'radio' (and again by extension, we suggest 'podcasting') is 'called upon to describe any number of different things – material, virtual, institutional, aesthetic, experiential. And, in turn, each of these meanings unfolds over time and in different contexts' (2018: 110).

By contrast, Loviglio and Hilmes (2013: 49) argue that the practices of podcasting, and the material form of distribution of the podcasts themselves, may distract us from the fact that they are based upon the 'serially produced programming' found on radio. Can we, therefore, go as far as suggesting that while materially different in the technologies of distribution, radio and podcasting are not different in material form as programming? In many ways, this would provide a new example of Marshall McLuhan's (1964) proposition that new media take as content the forms of media that preceded them. Berry (2016), in his earliest writing on podcasting at least, provided an extended example of these technologically determining models, suggesting that there would be an explosion of streaming and modern technologies within the radio industry, that there would be a convergence of multimedia platforms, and that this would impact on podcast delivery. Again, such propositions about the materiality of radio usually emerge from the assumption that new technologies drive change and that radio and podcasting are homogenous activities and forms within and across these audio media.

Yet a decade after his original discussion, Berry (2016) reflected that these changes had not been realized. Certainly, major broadcasters like the BBC simply adopted podcasting, along with other forms of audio streaming and downloading as new forms of their previous over-the-air broadcast model. By contrast, the *Caribbean Diaspora Podcast* series, like most podcast programming are of a very different nature: produced from outside mainstream broadcast organizations, often using very different production processes and engaging their communities of listeners in very different ways.

To understand any audio media, we need to move beyond what Sondergaard (2011) has termed a 'pure realist' conceptualization of materiality which relates to a physical matter. Of course, these matters are not limited to discussion of audio media, and there are questions about intangibility in discussions of other digital artefacts. Morizio (2014), for instance, locates digital materiality as an emerging concept within the 'information systems' field, and a series of writers have discussed the digital in terms of immaterial or intangible forms (Latour 2005; Orlikowski and Scott 2008; Suchman 2007). Likewise, Pearce (2010) has noted the way museum studies scholars vary their engagement with the term digital materiality. More productive are discussions in this field of the use of digital technology to access cultural objects. Dudley's (2010) work highlights that materiality is found beyond the physical, when people experience these museum artefacts using their sensory system.

At the same time, those debates about 'form and content' that emerged in the 1960s are still relevant (see Hong 2003), and discussions about connections between content and its underlying structure (McLuhan 1964), as well as the creativity behind the form (Hegel 1998) remain important. Conceptualizing audio media as aethereal distracts us from important questions about the social practice of podcast (and radio) production and the cultural material produced by the listening communities generated by podcasts like the *Caribbean Diaspora*. More helpfully, Leonardi (2010: n.pag) views materiality as both physical and non-physical, which he terms 'practical instantiation and significance'.

More generally, then, technologically determinist, essentialist, and ahistorical approaches neglect the complexity of podcasting (or any other audio medium) as material products of particular cultures. As we go on to show in our analysis of the *Caribbean Diaspora Podcast* series, the materiality of podcasting is to be found in its relations of production and cultural purpose and not in an essence or technological form. Put another way, we need to embrace *Guardian* journalist Hammersley's identification of 'audioblogging' and 'GuerillaMedia' as central parts of what we have called podcasting. 'Audioblogging' certainly signals a form of community-rooted, or citizen journalism, very different from the traditions of radio news journalism established by the BBC or CBS, and adopted and adapted by Caribbean national broadcasters. Blogging of all sorts not only responds to communities of interest, it is central to the formation of those communities and the identities they create. Likewise, the alternativeness (in programme-making practice, content and producer–listener relationship) are seriously neglected, when we solely utilized the technologically materialist concept indexed by 'podcasting' to understand what was new in this new audio medium.

Our study contrasts the material relationship between mainstream radio and podcasting within diaspora communities. The first is built upon a commitment to national identity, dominated by ideas of broadcasting as a distribution metaphor, and still based on over-the-air transmission as their primary artefactual form. The second responds to and creates a diaspora identity within a transnational

REFRAMING MATERIALITY IN THE *CARIBBEAN DIASPORA PODCAST*

community, pushes the broadcast metaphor so that the materiality of the podcast breaks new ground, and uses the affordances of internet distribution. It is to these investigations that we now turn.

The materiality of podcasting in virtual communities

One of the critical components of podcasts, therefore, is their positioning within the logic and organization of online spaces, which alerts us to ideas of virtual communities. Howard Rheingold (1993: 5), pioneer and oft-cited author of this term, defines it as 'social aggregations that emerge from the Net when enough people carry on those public discussions long enough [...] to form webs of personal relationships in cyberspace'. Here, Rheingold alludes to a type of social interaction occurring online between the public and online spaces. Given that radio studies has been a major space for exploring such ideas, most notably in the study of the community radio movement (see for instance, Halper 1991; Lewis and Booth 1989; Partridge 1982; Price-Davies and Tacchi 2001), it is surprising that this aspect of the material culture of podcasting is relatively neglected.

In subsequent years, Dennis et al. (1998), perhaps more straightforwardly, defined virtual communities as people with common interests who interact primarily through electronic means. Whitaker et al.'s (1997: 137) and Preece's (2001: 347–56) characterization of a virtual community as one that has a shared purpose, policy, and computer system deftly links material culture to the materiality of communication technology. In this conceptualization, virtual communities have a 'shared goal' with audiences who actively engage in 'shared activities', they also have access to the focus of the community, 'reciprocity' occurs, and there are similarities in terms 'shared context of social conventions, language, and protocols' (Whitaker et al. 1997: 137). For Ren et al. (2007: 381) and Fonseca et al. (2021: 165), such communities develop common identity and common bond.

Within these frameworks, we need to understand the *Caribbean Diaspora Podcast* series as producing a non-traditional, virtual community, because as Wang et al. (2002) have proposed, they looked beyond meanings of geography, borders, and territories. In this context, the virtual community offers a framework that is quite intimate and personal for understanding the relationships between producer, podcast, and listener. Certainly, Wrather (2016: 43–44) has illustrated the use of podcasts within online spaces such as fora, social networks and blogs. The findings from this research show that podcasts encourage audience participation and promote online and offline communities.

There are, of course, still debates on whether there is a material culture in online spaces. Some, like Barlow (1996), suggest that virtual spaces do not have material culture. However, as Lehdonvirta (2010) has insightfully pointed out, presenting the virtual as devoid of material culture requires that we accept the same sort of essentialist notion of ethereality for that has confounded discussions of the material culture of radio listening. Certainly, as Lehdonvirta points out, virtual spaces contain an architecture that is tangible and that governs how people use online spaces and gain access. Furthermore, they argue that virtual cultures are functional and symbolic. We follow Lehdonvirta, therefore, in working with the notion that the virtual spaces created by the *Caribbean Diaspora Podcast* series create an online community and afford its members the opportunity to engage with 'real artefacts' through the use of 'senses'.

Although an evaluation of the podcast audiences is outside of the confines of this study, material culture is an energizing force within the communication process through its provision for its audiences. Tacchi's (1997: 47) work indicates that radio sound aids in building a social community for listeners. It is through this process that radio sound can contribute to material culture for listeners. Material culture overlaps as it simultaneously provides an architecture for the radio while providing one for audiences. Finally, in exploring ideas of materiality in virtual communities, it is worth noting that the *Caribbean Diaspora Podcast* series is part of the wider emergence of podcasts centred around black sociocultural and political ideologies from 2010. Fox et al. (2020) note the importance of the greater access to new media technologies such as smartphones in enabling the success of these alternative forms of audio media. They include productions such as *This Week in Blackness!* (*TWiB*) (2000), *The Combat Jack Show* (2010), and *For Colored Nerds* (2014). For Giroux (2011: 25), these black podcasts promote representation of 'new voices'. These formats are characterized by humour, discourse on black identity, history, and storytelling. The production formats are typically open-ended, and unscripted, which we contend aims to allow for black audiences to find value in black podcast content. Certainly, Florini (2015) has analyzed black podcasts as performative spaces that complement in-person conversations that are typically heard in black salons or places of worship. The outcomes of these podcasts relate to what Leonardi (2010: n.pag.) refers to as 'materiality seen as practical instantiation and significance'. Essentially, this perspective of materiality explores the ways artifacts impact on cultures or everyday life.

Podcast production and the materiality of diaspora culture

Here we want to make the argument that the *Caribbean Diaspora Podcast* is a conduit for types of material culture which have emerged within the cultural locales of the Caribbean diaspora more generally and that this cultural material is particularly well-suited to the artefactual form of the podcast and the architecture of distribution, most often implied by the use of the term. Furthermore, that the very national, centre-to-periphery, and transmitted-as-live models of traditional over-the-air sound broadcasting are not well suited to deal with global-, time-, and space-shifted diaspora cultures, and so the potential audiences who have been poorly served by more traditional media, most notably over-the-air radio.

In accounting for the distinctive characteristics of programming like the *Caribbean Diaspora Podcast* series as a material product of one diaspora culture, we have taken a broadly ethnographic approach. For Atkinson (1997) and Barnes (1996), ethnography is a careful study of culture, in this case allowing for a view of the podcast through the eyes of those engaged in this study. To achieve this, Rachel-Ann used a virtual ethnographic approach allowing us to deal with a podcast that primarily operates online and allowed her to reconstruct the podcast she had produced, this time through a researcher's lens. In building on this approach, we navigate the roles of researcher, theorist, producer, and audience member. Following Tilley (2001: 262), we have been attentive to the 'space and place and landscape and the way they encode, produce and reproduce, alter and transform patterns of sociability', and from Given (2008: 337) and Hart (2017), we have explored the social interactions occurring in the production of the podcast. In both the wider discussion of podcasting cultural materiality, and this more focused ethnographic exploration of the *Caribbean Diaspora Podcast* series, we have been cognizant of positionality. In particular, we have applied Salazar et al.'s (2015: 458) sense of reflexivity as 'examining both oneself as a researcher and the research relationship'. Being a member of the Caribbean diaspora community herself, this positioning shaped the way Rachel-Ann conceptualized, created, and executed the podcasts, as well as how she conducted the ethnographic research.

We need to understand the pre-production and production of the *Caribbean Diaspora Podcast* as editorial and technological processes that reconstruct pre-existing cultural material into a new form: the podcast episode. And the processes themselves are bound within the overall aim of using pre-existing identities to create media content for the Caribbean diaspora community. For Rachel-Ann, her identity as a podcast producer and a member of the diasporal group informed the planning stages involved in mapping the focus, audience, and the choice of online media platforms for the podcast series. The podcast offers listeners diverse content from Caribbean migrants living around the world. Central to this is imagining the needs and interests of the audience as Caribbean nationals living outside the islands. As a Caribbean migrant in the United Kingdom, Rachel-Ann envisaged that many people within this community are living in a state of uncertainty, a state exaggerated by limitations on social engagement during the COVID-19 global health crisis, and looking for ways that digital platforms can enable them to communicate with friends, families, and colleagues.

Rachel-Ann contacted approximately 30 potential guests, and over half of them confirmed that they would participate. The podcast conversations were semi-structured, with initial conversations with each guest to get background information, which formed the basis for questions for the recording. However, even with the structured questions, interviewees could guide the discussions, too. To improve the quality of the podcasts, Rachel-Ann sought feedback on the concept and the experiences of the participants. To prepare for the recording, Rachel-Ann created a script for each podcast episode which included a list of questions and prompts for the guest. She also briefed the guest(s) about the recording process and the purpose of the podcast prior to the recording session, giving the guest an opportunity to include any additional points for discussion.

The production process determines what finished product is published and audiences have access to. As a first-time podcast producer and with the stay-at-home mandates, Rachel-Ann recorded the interviews at home, which led to several technical challenges. She utilized a headset with built-in microphone when recording the first interview via Zoom, which was easily accessible for the guest and the host. However, the quality was poor, and there was difficulty in retrieving the recording from Zoom. Subsequent recordings were made using a mobile application called Anchor. However, for technical reasons, the audio volume was unbalanced. Fortunately, issues using Zoom were resolved and she returned to that platform to record the remaining episodes in the first season. Whilst recording, Rachel-Ann observed that most of the guests felt more comfortable having the questions ahead of time and doing a pre-interview. One aspect that requires further work is resolving the technological challenges of podcasting to ensure the best quality.

Recording the podcast episodes becomes, in Whitaker et al.'s (1997: 137) words, a process of 'shar[ing] context of social conventions, language, and protocols'. Rachel-Ann recorded thirteen episodes between July 2020 and January 2021. Once the initial episodes were recorded, she then mapped out the order of the episodes, as there were connections across the conversations. The conversations covered issues such as identity, belonging, entrepreneurship, music, food, festivals, publishing, and grief, amongst a few other topics; but these were specific to their country of origin. However, as the conversations increased, Rachel-Ann observed that the Caribbean migrants' dialogues recorded were mainly centred around migration anecdotes. This raises interesting questions about how listeners want to access the conversations.

After much experimentation with structures with the initial recordings, the chosen format for this podcast is a conversational interview featuring a single guest or guests along with the host who also fulfils the role of an interviewer. Rachel-Ann drew on her own experience as a member of the Caribbean diaspora community, and utilized Butler's (2005: 10) notion of 'giving an account of oneself' during the discussions. This allows the interviewer to present the podcast from an insider's perspective, whilst also exploring unfamiliar topics. The format of the podcast also differs from mainstream media which, as with the latter, guests are typically allowed to share their stories for fifteen minutes. Although developing this podcast was very encouraging, one lesson learned, based on the production processes, is allocating time for open conversations and a natural flow outside of the prepared and discussed questions.

All supporting audio was created and edited by Rachel-Ann as the producer. The creative and expressive works used in the podcast, such as the performances and scripts, the interviews, the musical works, and any other type of sound recording were used in keeping with copyright laws, and approvals were negotiated from the interviewees to use the recorded content. For example, the podcast music was purchased from Shutterstock.

Another significant process was the demonstration of power which was negotiated between the producer and interviewees during the production phase of the *Caribbean Diaspora Podcast*; which is another building block of the material culture found in this podcast. In Rachel-Ann's capacity as the producer of the podcast, audience members were given the opportunity to become co-creators. Interviewees were invited to share their full story, understanding all the risks involved and knowing what the role entails. Overall, this podcast is supported by a participatory and community-centred approach that provides participants from the Caribbean Diaspora community with control over the stories they want to share. In this way, the power remains in the hands of those (the audiences) telling their stories. The *Caribbean Diaspora Podcast* focuses on social gain and community benefit; they are owned by, and accountable to, the communities they seek to serve. Although a survey was conducted to understand listening preferences, further work in this area is required to identify the needs of the target group. Drawing on the content the guests shared on the podcast, stories were intense, yet lighted-hearted, and because of this Rachel-Ann felt audiences would prefer to listen to the content in smaller time frames. Therefore, each episode was divided into three or four instalments.

In reflecting on this production process of the podcast, it demonstrates the way a podcast can create a virtual space for the Caribbean diaspora community and its existing material culture, as well as act as a medium for the production of new material culture. Through the host and the guest interviews, as well as the migration stories and topics that are exchanged within this virtual space, both through the discussions and in the minds of listeners, these are connected to offline identities and histories. In many ways, the websites, social media platforms, and other user interfaces through which the podcasts were made available reproduce the space and time coordinates of the Caribbean diasporal experience lived beyond the podcast itself.

Caribbean diasporal discourse

The *Caribbean Diaspora Podcast* series also reveals the significance of the role power plays within the discourse of the contributors. In this sense, audio media like this series offers interviewees new domains through which power can be exercised and demonstrates the way that podcasting production can be utilized to align with diasporal discourse. This alerts us to Foucault's (1972: 49) sense of discourse as 'the production of knowledge through language which gives bonded meanings to material objects and social practises'. Typically, a 'discursive formation' is achieved when language methodically gives meaning to 'material objects and social practises' (Edgar and Sedgwick 1999: 117). This was evident in the way contributors related their Caribbean heritage to their experience of living in other nations, including those that had held imperial power over the islands when they were colonial owners. Particularly interesting were the anecdotes shared by contributors. As part of their stories, most of the interviewees discussed how they integrated Caribbean traditions and cultural objects within their countries of residence, such as the United States, United Kingdom, Japan, Australia, Canada, and United Arab Emirates. Several themes emerged that questioned feelings of belonging. This process is critical in establishing wider knowledge about Caribbean migrants living abroad whilst reliving and constructing past historical moments.

For example, one theme discussed across interviews is having a sense of belonging, particularly as traditions differ between the country of origin and the country of residence. One podcast interviewee made distinctions between 'home' and 'back home' which Grossman (2019) refers to as transnational connections within the diaspora. Matching Grossman's formulation, a podcast interviewee referred to the ways she maintained connections with family members from her homeland and her involvement with the cultural aspects of her homeland. The interviewee also talked about her connection to local activities within her place of residence, particularly volunteering, which has provided a sense of community. The podcast dialogues reveal this constant negotiation of cultural identities and/or dual identities, consistent with the discussions of *Old and New Identities* in Hall (1990: 41–68).

There were some striking similarities across the topics discussed in the thirteen podcast interviews. The discursive constructions of the contributors were primarily built around ideas of representation, identity, gender, race, and equality. Some of the podcast conversations connect to discourses of race and gender inequalities as a political process. Such a framing echoes the discourses Dufoix (2015) found within the African Diaspora community. As such, the podcast series constructs narratives of resistance which are critical to the material culture framework of diasporal identity. There were various calls to action regarding the treatment of social issues in the migration anecdotes. In addressing some issues faced particularly by Afro-Caribbean people, a second-generation Caribbean migrant said:

> It is about self-empowerment and self-determination because I am not waiting for white people to free us. [...] I am not waiting for anybody to stop being racist because [...] we've been waiting for 400, 500, 600, 700 years why is [...] suddenly things going to change [...] overnight.
>
> (Participant 1 2020: n.pag.)

While another Participant 2 (2020: n.pag.) stated: 'I am a black person and if there is brutality in my neighbourhood, I'll be on the streets'. This comment relates to his passion for exercising his human right to resist the racist injustices encountered in his country of residence. As such, he resists the mainstream narratives and methodically reconstructs an alternative narrative about Caribbean migrants living abroad.

The other benefit of this is that wider members of the Caribbean diaspora community can feel represented in the stories which then heightens the material culture. In Tacchi's (1997: 43) work about *Radio Texture: Between Self and Others*, she discusses 'the use of radio sound in the home' which contributes to the material culture through 'social relationships', relating to what Feld (1990) calls a lived work. This also connects with Hall's (1990: 226) work about constructing the past through historical narrative. When applying those collective ideas to the *Caribbean Diaspora Podcast*, it has the potential to strengthen the material culture of the audiences.

Based on the migration stories guests shared, and level of freedom they exercised through co-production, these dialogues reflected a meaningful form of power. In particular, it points to Florini's (2015: n.pag.) discussion of black podcasting as 'alternative media' and 'audio enclaves'. Within these niche communities or closed audio spaces, black podcasters freely discuss the issues affecting them and these issues are told through their lens. There is a similarity as it relates to the intention of the *Caribbean Diaspora Podcast* as the construction of an alternative virtual space that affords its members with the ability to speak on issues that affect them because of the agency that is afforded within the production process. It is through these narrative and co-production discursive practises that the contributors participate in a virtual community. Through the conversations, they move from educational modes, to light humour, and critical discourses emerge, particularly with challenges around Caribbean identities. For Fras (2020: 322–23), this positions such discussions within socio-cultural understanding; exemplified in all of the episodes in the way they represent common traditions, patterns, beliefs, issues, and challenges that the Caribbean community faces within the Diaspora. Listeners, nevertheless, may also take away different messages from the podcast episodes based on their sociocultural backgrounds.

The relationship between the form and the content of the *Caribbean Diaspora Podcast* highlights the technological affordances and material constraints discussed by Fras (2020: 322–23) and Hutchby (2001). Users can access the content on various platforms, and can subscribe, comment, and engage with the podcast and with the production team. However, discoverability of the podcast may not be straightforward for those within the target audience if these platforms are unfamiliar to them. An examination of the podcasts themselves shows a moving away from the physical notions of material as conventionally defined to a wide range of non-physical material. Following Lacey (2018: 119), we need to 'acknowledge the materiality involved in the production and transmission and reception of radio'. This includes the materiality of sound within any audio media. Lacey herself maintains that there is a 'materiality to sound'. Although this argument was posed within a radio context, within the conventional ways of thinking about material, this notion may be problematic as sound requires a medium for its transmission. Perhaps more than in traditional over-the-air radio, podcasts can provide content for audience's interaction.

For example, posts on Facebook reached 700 viewers and 206 users engaged with the content. The podcast clip with the highest engagement on Facebook featured one of the migration stories of a Trinidad and Tobago citizen living in the United States. This post reached 499 viewers with 72 users engaging by clicking, reacting, commenting, and sharing. The post with the highest engagements is on migration stories or facts. On the Instagram social media platform, the comments on Instagram were much more engaging than Facebook. Commenters viewed this podcast as a need in response to the pandemic.

> It is a really wonderful idea. I am now thinking back to when I first moved to the US and that disconnect that I felt [...]. It is good to see other stories to know they did this to make a connection, or they did that to make a connection.
>
> (Participant 3 2020: n.pag.)

The *Caribbean Diaspora Podcast* constructs a virtual community centred around discourses of migration. In thinking about the role of the virtual community as one that promotes a common identity and bond, some comments suggest the podcast content is helping construct such. For example, one commenter on Instagram expressed appreciation for the spelling of a French-Creole term used by Caribbean migrants: 'Thanks. I know the term but did not know how to spell it' (Participant 4 2020: n.pag.). Using French-Creole terms in the Caribbean is a common tradition in many islands. However, most traditions have been dying and weakened within diaspora context.

Conclusion

This chapter has enabled us to explore four central notions of the materiality of podcasting. At the same time, we have used this as an opportunity to critique existing approaches to studying podcasting, expanding beyond the limitations of approaches that connect it too closely to mainstream audio production or essentialist ideas of sound media. In doing so, we return to a developed idea of the way materiality can be useful in the field more generally.

We set out the limitations of approaches that suggest that the defining quality of sound media is the absence of any materiality or the deterministic idea that audio media's materiality is somehow rooted in its technology. We explored the usefulness of ideas of virtual communities for the study of podcasting to replace more traditional models based on centralized models of over-the-air broadcasting. We also located the *Caribbean Diaspora Podcast* series in a wider context of specifically black cultural podcasting. This context is particularly apparent in Rachel-Ann's auto/virtual ethnography of the distinctive differences of production she utilized, and in the differences from mainstream radio production approaches which dominate podcasting. Significantly, this reveals how important discourses of diaspora culture are to the contributors, and to the more open, conversational, shared nature of the discussions.

As a modest ethnographic reflection and deck-clearing engagement with ideas from radio studies, sound studies, digital online media studies within the broader field of media and cultural studies, we seek to open up debate, rather than provide definitive answers. There remains some important work to be done in the materiality of sound media, internet-enabled global communication, and diaspora cultures. In particular, we argue that we need to move away from essentialist approaches to look in detail at the nature of production and the discourses that run through particular examples of audio media programming.

We are also particularly conscious that we did not look at the lived experience of the listener in relation to the *Caribbean Diaspora Podcast*. We hope that discussions of the critical role material culture plays in building a virtual community for diasporal cultures are useful. Producing the podcast series certainly seems to address these matters directly. As one commenter stated: 'this pressure is hard on the mind and soul of the migrant so many times. Thank You for this work' (Participant 5 2021: n.pag.). However, much more of these comments need to be captured to examine the audience reception.

This study set out to determine the relationship between materiality and podcasts using the case of the *Caribbean Diaspora Podcast*. The investigation of the *Caribbean Diaspora Podcast*, through an ethnographic approach, indicates that the podcast allows for readers to imagine materiality beyond the typical conventions. The study has shown that material culture lies at the core and provides structural support for podcasts. These structures appear as human access, input, technological processes, and policies and within processes of discourse and power. Ultimately, the material culture of a geographically and temporally dispersed community united by a sense of diasporal identity forms the content of the podcast and the podcast itself has become new cultural material for, and of, that community.

REFERENCES

Arbuthnot, Leaf (2020), '"We don't want to give up now": Could coronavirus weaken the podcast industry?', *The Guardian*, 22 May, https://www.theguardian.com/tv-and-radio/2020/may/22/we-dont-want-to-give-up-now-could-coronavirus-weaken-the-podcast-industry. Accessed 4 July 2023.

Atkinson, Paul (1997) *Understanding Ethnographic Texts*, California: Sage.

Barlow, John Perry (1996) 'A Declaration of the Independence of Cyberspace', *Electronic Frontier Foundation*, 8 February, http://homes.eff.org/~barlow/Declaration-Final.html. Accessed 4 July 2023.

Brock, André (2009), 'LIFE ON THE WIRE: Deconstructing race on the Internet', *Information, Communication and Society*, 12:3, pp. 344–63.

Barnes, Donelle M. (1996), 'An analysis of the grounded theory method and the concept of culture', *Qualitative Health Research*, 6:3, pp. 429–41.

Berry, Richard (2006), 'Will the iPod kill the radio star? Profiling podcasting as radio', *Convergence: The International Journal of Research into New Media Technologies*, 12:2, pp. 143–62.

Berry, Richard (2015), 'A golden age of podcasting? Evaluating serial in the context of podcast histories', *Journal of Radio & Audio Media*, 22:2, pp. 170–78.

Berry, Richard (2016), 'Podcasting: Considering the evolution of the medium and its association with the word "radio"', *Radio Journal: International Studies in Broadcast & Audio Media*, 14, pp. 7–22.

Bottomley, Andrew (2015), 'Podcasting: A decade in the life of a "New" audio medium: Introduction', *Journal of Radio & Audio Media*, 22:2, pp. 164–69.

Butler, Judith (2005), *Giving an Account of Oneself*, Ohio: Fordham University Press.

Chignell, Hugh (2009), *Key Concepts in Radio Studies*, London: Sage Publications.

Crisell, Andrew (1986), *Understanding Radio*, London: Methuen.

Crofts, Sheri, Dilley, Jon, Fox, Mark, Retsema, Andrew, and Williams, Bob (2005), 'Podcasting: A new technology in search of viable business models', *First Monday*, 10, n.pag., https://firstmonday.org/article/view/1273/1193. Accessed 4 July 2023.

Dennis, Alan R., Pootheri, Sridar K., and Natarajan, Vijaya L. (1998), 'Lessons from the early adopters of web groupware', *Journal of Management Information Systems*, 14:4, pp. 65–86.

Dufoix, Stéphane (2015), 'The loss and the link: A short history of the long-term word "Diaspora" ' in N. Sigona, A. Gamlen, G. Liberatore, and H. Kringelbach (eds), *Diasporas Reimagined Spaces, Practices and Belonging*, Oxford: Oxford Diasporas Programme, pp. 8–12.

Dudley, Sandra (ed.) (2010), *Museum Materialities: Objects, Engagements, Interpretations*, London: Routledge.

Edgar, Andrew and Sedgwick, Peter (1999), *Key Concepts in Cultural Theory*, London: Routledge.

Feld, Steven (1990), *Sound and Sentiment*, Philadelphia: University of Pennsylvania Press.

Florini, Sarah (2015), 'The podcast "Chitlin' Circuit": Black podcasters', alternative media, and audio enclaves', *Journal of Radio & Audio Media*, 22:2, pp. 209–19.

Fonseca, Josélia, Borges-Tiago, Teresa, Tiago, Flávio, and Silva, Sandra (2021), 'Virtual communities in COVID-19 era: A citizenship perspective', in A. Kavoura, S. J. Havlovic, and N. Totskaya (eds), *Strategic Innovative Marketing and Tourism in the COVID-19 Era*, New York: Springer, pp. 163–70.

Fox, Kim, Dowling, David O., and Miller, Kyle (2020), 'A curriculum for blackness: Podcasts as discursive cultural guides, 2010–2020', *Journal of Radio & Audio Media*, 27:2, pp. 298–18.

Foucault, Michel and Sheridan, Alan (1972), *The Archeology of Knowledge*, London: Routledge.

Fras, Jona (2020), 'Unifying voices, creating publics: The uses of media form in contemporary Jordanian radio', *British Journal of Middle Eastern Studies*, 47:2, pp. 320–42.

Freire, Ariana Moscote (2008), 'Remediating radio: Audio streaming, music recommendation and the discourse of radioness', *Radio Journal: International Studies in Broadcast & Audio Media*, 5:2, pp. 97–112.

Giroux, Henry A. (2011), 'The crisis of public values in the age of the new media', *Critical Studies in Media Communication*, 28:1, pp. 8–29.

Given, Lisa M. (2008), *The Sage Encyclopaedia of Qualitative Research Methods*, Los Angeles: Sage Publications.

Goulbourne, Harry and Solomos, John (2004), 'The Caribbean Diaspora: Some introductory remarks', *Ethnic and Racial Studies*, 27:4, pp. 533–43.

Grossman, Jonathan (2019), 'Toward a definition of diaspora', *Ethnic and Racial Studies*, 42:8, pp. 1263–82.

Hall, Stuart (1990), 'Cultural identity and diaspora', in J. Rutherford (ed.), *Identity: Community, Culture, Difference*, London: Lawrence & Wishart, pp. 224–37.

Hall, Stuart (1997), 'Old and new identities, old and new ethnicities', in A. D. King (ed.), *Culture, Globalization, and the World-System: Contemporary Conditions for the Representation of Identity*, Minnesota: University of Minnesota Press, pp. 41–68.

Halper, Donna (1991), *Full-service Radio: Programming for the Community*, Boston: Focal Press.

Harris, Howard and Park, Sungmin (2008), 'Educational usages of podcasting', *British Journal of Educational Technology*, 39:3, pp. 548–51.

Hart, Tabitha (2017), 'Online ethnography', in J. Matthes, C. S. Davis, and R. F. Potter (eds), *The International Encyclopedia of Communication Research Methods*, Hoboken: Wiley-Blackwell, https://doi.org/10.1002/9781118901731.iecrm0172.

Hegel, Georg (1998), *Aesthetics*, Oxford: Clarendon Press.

Hong, JeeHee (2003), 'material/materiality', *The Chicago School of Media Theory*, Winter, https://csmt.uchicago.edu/glossary2004/material.htm. Accessed 7 July 2023.

Hutchby, Ian (2001), 'Technologies, Texts and Affordances', *Sociology*, 35:2, pp. 441–56.

Lacey, Kate (2018), 'Up in the air? The matter of radio studies', *Radio Journal – International Studies in Broadcast & Audio Media*, 16:2, pp. 109–26.

Latour, Bruno (2005), *Reassembling the Social: An Introduction to Actor–Network Theory*, Oxford: Oxford University Press.

Lehdonvirta, Vili (2010), 'Online spaces have material culture: Goodbye to digital post-materialism and hello to virtual consumption', *Media, Culture & Society*, 32:5, pp. 883–89.

Leonardi, Paul (2010), 'Digital materiality? How artifacts without matter, matter', *First Monday*, 15:6, n.pag., https://firstmonday.org/ojs/index.php/fm/article/view/3036/2567. Accessed 4 July 2023.

Lewis, Peter and Booth, Jerry (1989), *The Invisible Medium: Public, Commercial and Community Radio*, Basingstoke: Macmillan Education.

Llinares, Dario (2010), 'Podcasting as liminal praxis: Aural mediation, sound writing and identity', in D. Llinares, N. Fox, and R. Berry (eds), *Podcasting: New Aural Cultures and Digital Media*, New York: Palgrave Macmillan, pp. 123–45.

Loviglio, Jason and Hilmes, Michele (eds) (2013), *Radio's New Wave*, London: Routledge.

Markman, Kris (2011), 'Doing radio, making friends, and having fun: Exploring the motivations of independent audio podcasters', *New Media & Society*, 14:4, pp. 547–65.

Mashall, Dawn (1982), 'The history of Caribbean migrations: The case of the West Indies', *Caribbean Review*, 11:1, pp. 52–53.

McClung, Steven and Johnson, Kristine (2010), 'Examining the motives of podcast users', *Journal of Radio & Audio Media*, 17:1, pp. 82–95.

McLuhan, Marshall (1964), *Understanding Media*, New York: McGraw-Hill.

Menduni, Enrico (2007), 'Four steps in innovative radio broadcasting: From quicktime to podcasting', *Radio Journal: International Studies in Broadcast & Audio Media*, 5:1, pp. 9–18.

Mollett, Amy, Brumley, Cheryl, Gibson, Chris, and Williams, Sierra (2017), *Communicating Your Research with Social Media: A Practical Guide to Using Blogs, Podcasts, Data Visualisations*, London: Sage.

Morizio, Patricia (2014), 'Conceptualising digital materiality and its socio-technical implications through the phenomenon of crowdsourcing', *Journal of Systems Integration*, 5:4, pp. 3–8.

Noakes, Richard (2016), 'Thoughts and spirits by wireless: Imagining and building psychic telegraphs in America and Britain, circa 1900–1930', *History and Technology*, 32:2, pp. 137–58.

Orlikowski, Wanda and Scott, Susan (2008), '10 Sociomateriality: Challenging the separation of technology, work and organization', *The Academy of Management Annals*, 2:1, pp. 433–74.

Park, Juhee and Samms, Anouska (2019), 'The materiality of the immaterial: Collecting digital objects at the Victoria and Albert Museum', *MuseWeb19*, The Sheraton Hotel, Boston, 2–6 April, https://mw19.mwconf.org/paper/the-materiality-of-the-immaterial-collecting-digital-objects-at-the-victoria-and-albert-museum/index.html. Accessed 4 July 2023.

Partridge, Simon (1982), *Not the BBC/IBA: The Case for Community Radio*, London, Comedia.

Pearce, Susan M. (2010), 'Foreword', in S. Dudley (ed.), *Museum Materialities: Objects, Engagements, Interpretations*, London: Routledge, pp. xiv–xix.

Potter, Deborah (2006), 'iPod, you pod, we all pod', *American Journalism Review*, 28:1, p. 64.

Preece, Jenny (2001), 'Sociability and usability in online communities: Determining and measuring success', *Behaviour & Information Technology*, 20:5, pp. 347–56.

Price-Davies, Eryl and Tacchi, Jo (2001), *Community Radio in a Global Context: A Comparative Analysis*, Sheffield: Community Media Association.

Ren, Yuqing, Kraut, Robert, and Kiesler, Sara (2007), 'Applying common identity and bond theory to design of online communities', *Organization Studies*, 28:3, pp. 377–408.

Rheingold, Howard (1993), 'Using participatory media and public voice to encourage civic engagement', in W. Bennett (ed.), *Civic Life Online: Learning How Digital Media Can Engage Youth*, Cambridge: MIT Press, pp. 97–118.

Salazar, Laura, Crosby, Richard, and DiClemente, Ralph (2015), *Research Methods in Health Promotion*, San Francisco: Jossey Bass, p. 458.

Shingler, Martin and Wieringa, Cindy (1998), *On Air: Methods and Meanings of Radio*, New York: Arnold.

Søndergaard, Dorte Marie (2011), 'Virtual materiality, potentiality and subjectivity: How do we conceptualize real-virtual interaction embodied and enacted in computer gaming, imagination and night dreams?', *Subjectivity*, 6:1, pp. 55–78.

Suchman, Lucy A. (2007), *Human-Machine Reconfigurations*, Cambridge: Cambridge University Press.

Tacchi, Jo (1997), 'Radio sound as material culture in the home', Ph.D. thesis, London: University of London.

Tilley, Christopher (2001), 'Ethnography and material culture', in P. Atkinson, A. Coffey, S. Delamont, J. Lofland, and L. Lofland (eds), *Handbook of Ethnography*, London: Sage Publications, pp. 258–72.

Wall, Tim (2004), 'The political economy of internet music radio', *The Radio Journal: International Studies in Broadcast & Audio Media*, 2, pp. 27–44.

Wall, Tim (2016), 'Music radio goes online', in C. L. Baade and J. A. Deaville (eds), *Music and the Broadcast Experience: Performance, Production, and Audience*, New York: Oxford University Press.

Wall, Tim (2018), 'Radio sound', in M. Bull (ed.), *Routledge Companion to Sound Studies*, Abingdon, New York: Routledge.

Wall, Tim and Webber, Nick (2015), 'Personal listening pleasures', in M. Conboy and J. Steel (eds), *The Routledge Companion to British Media History*, London: Routledge.

Wang, Youcheng and Fesenmaier, Daniel (2002), 'Understanding the motivation of contribution to online communities: An empirical investigation of an online travel community, in *Proceedings in the 33rd Travel and Tourism Research Association Conference*, Washington, DC.

Whitaker, Steve, Issacs, Ellen, and O'day, Vicki (1997), 'Widening the net: Workshop report on the theory and practice of physical and network communities', *SIGCHI Bulletin*, 29:3, pp. 127–37.

Wrather, Kyle (2016), 'Making "Maximum Fun" for fans: Examining podcast listener participation online', *The Radio Journal: International Studies in Broadcast & Audio Media*, 14:1, pp. 43–63.

Short Take 11

We're All Victorians Now

Kirsten Forkert

I've been doing cycle journeys for a daily exercise routine, which means I've been going to different neighbourhoods in Birmingham I don't usually visit (prior to this, my movements around the city were quite utilitarian – going between home or work, or various errands, or occasionally gigs). Is COVID-19 inspiring new forms of psychogeography? On these journeys, I've noticed that in the poorer neighbourhoods (Handsworth, Small Heath, Sparkbrook, etc.) few people seem to be social distancing, and you wouldn't know we were in lockdown other than the odd person wearing a mask or gloves; the streets are only slightly less busy than normal. In the whiter, more middle-class areas I pass through, social distancing is adhered to more stringently (is this a certain kind of luxury?) with the exception of Victory in Europe Day when there are street parties with bunting, with mostly white participants (a greater identification with official national narratives?).

Inequality is not only in the streets; it's in the news headlines: COVID-19 deaths are twice as high in deprived areas, ethnic minorities are dying more from this disease, and there is a reluctance to publicly admit how structural racism and class inequality is making people sick.

Beyond the neighbourhood mutual aid groups and #clapforcarers, COVID-19 reminds us of long-standing social divisions and returns us to some older fears, including some Victorian-era paranoias: cities, particularly dense multi-cultural ones, are to be avoided; the wealthy flee to second homes in the countryside. More disturbingly, nineteenth-century eugenics seems to be implicit in the conspiracy theories which attempt to explain the ethnic minority deaths (the latest being that those with darker skin are suffering from vitamin D deficiency, implying they shouldn't be living in 'colder countries'), or the rhetoric around bodily strength and strength of character of populist male leaders as being inherently resistant to the virus, or the more implicit belief that if we end the lockdown quickly we don't have to worry about the vulnerable, as they are the 'surplus populations' which are only a burden on society and a drag on the economy. The nineteenth century was also the era of the rise and consolidation of the nation state. The response to COVID-19 seems fundamentally national; the closing of borders and ending of international travel, the calls to move manufacturing back onshore (instead of the long global supply chains we've become used to) and also the various charts and statistics comparing death rates, the calls to 'look after our own first' and in the very old racist tropes of disease-carrying foreigners. At street level is the equivalent of these headlines the suspicious glances or the wide berth towards the poor, the black or brown, or the different? And conversely, what would be the street-level equivalent of the internationalism and global solidarity we so desperately need?

9

You Can Look, Share, and Comment, But You Can't Touch: The Relationship Between the Materiality and Physicality of Photographs in an Online Community Archive

Vanessa Jackson

Introduction

I scroll through an online folder full of digitized filmic photographs shared with me by a retired television cameraman. Black and white images of performers and crew from long-forgotten programmes stare back at me from my computer screen. I choose a quickly framed snapshot, download it, and copy it across to a Facebook page. I add in text requesting information about the show, the year and who might be identifiable in the photo. Then, with a sense of anticipation, I sit back and wait. Within a couple of hours, I receive comments on my post. These tell me that the photograph is of the Pebble Mill special *Peggy Lee Entertains* (BBC 1981), starring the eponymous American singer. I hear from a former boss of mine that she can see herself in the photograph, seated in the audience. Another previous BBC colleague tells me she vision-mixed the show and that Peggy Lee had difficulty walking and rehearsed using a wheelchair. The production assistant comments that she thinks a man named Bob Langley presented the show. Most surprisingly, a male audio technician, who I do not know, adds that working on that show was one of the most memorable points of his career and that he is in tears now reflecting on it. All this in response to a single digitized, shared, monochrome image; an image which has demonstrated the power to spark collective memories and evoke powerful emotions. Encounters such as these pose questions about how remediating analogue photographs via an online community archive affects their materiality, and what wider implications this might have.

This chapter sets out to explore the tensions between the physicality and the materiality of photographs and how these play-out in relation to digitized photographs displayed on social media. It considers three principle areas: the relationship between the digitized image and memory in the online space, how digitization affects the material properties of the image, and how online spaces present new digital encounters with the material image. There is a wariness amongst some academics regarding the digitization of, and consequent material impact on, photographs. Elizabeth Edwards and Janice Hart (2004: 2) emphasize the importance of photographs as three-dimensional objects, rather than merely images and Patricia Hayes (1998: 6), equates digitization with a probable loss of contextualization and historicization, while Joanna Sassoon (2004: 216) concludes that such moves undermine the nature of the physical archive. In contrast, this chapter adopts Joanna Zylinska's warning regarding anti-digital hysteria (2010: 140) and argues that while the materiality of photographs may be altered, and potentially diminished through digitization and online sharing, that the benefits to online community archives in activating collective memory, through photo-elicitation, outweighs what might be lost in terms of physical material integrity. Challenging Joanna Sassoon's (2004) conclusions, my research suggests that the awakening of collective memory can aid historical contextualization, improving and building online archives.

After setting out the background of the case study project, this chapter explores the place of photographs within material culture thinking, including considering the particular affordances of photographs and discussing the impact on materiality when analogue photographs are digitized and shared online. The focus is around how physicality and materiality are experienced in practice with illustrations from a particular case study: the Pebble Mill project, a community website and Facebook page commemorating the broadcasting history of BBC Pebble Mill. The case study illustrates how online sharing allows for new engagement with the image, providing a different material experience, which affects our thinking of media studies more broadly. A participant observation methodology is applied to the study of the Pebble Mill Studios Facebook page, a site I have operated over the last decade. Specific examples of digitized, shared photographs have been chosen for close analysis, because of how their materiality is affected, through the online experience. Examples of posts featuring digitized photographs have also been included, where the response from users in their comments has relevance to their materiality. The observation and interpretation focuses on the practices of individuals using the Facebook site, including myself as citizen-curator. The Pebble Mill Facebook page is an open group, with all posts published publicly. Despite the fact that all the posts and comments are openly available, I have removed the names of participants, due to the content being considered outside the context the participants had envisaged. The aim of the case study is to illustrate how individuals within communities interact with online photographic stimuli and to draw conclusions regarding the materiality of that photographic stimuli and the implications this has.

The Pebble Mill project

BBC Pebble Mill was the first purpose-built broadcast production centre for both radio and television in Europe (BBC 1962). It was situated on Pebble Mill Road in Edgbaston, Birmingham, UK, opening in 1971, and ceasing operations in 2004, after which the building was demolished, with production moving to other locations in the city. It produced a wealth of television and radio programmes including factual output such as *Pebble Mill at One* (1972–86), *Gardeners' World* (1968–present), *Countryfile* (1988–present), *Top Gear* (1977–present); dramas including, *Gangsters* (1976–78), 'Nuts in May' (1976), *Boys from the Blackstuff* (1982), *The Archers* (1951–present); along with many others.

The Pebble Mill project[1] is an established online community archive consisting of around 1900 posts. Contributors share their photographs and memories of the programmes, people, and the place: BBC Pebble Mill. Attached to the website is an associated Facebook page.[2] The page has over 1700 'Likes', with an active community of contributors, many of whom are former BBC employees. The majority of the interaction around digitized photographs occurs on the Facebook page. Photographs and/or comments are posted on the page, usually by me as the 'citizen curator' of the project, with participants sharing their recollections, and posting their own photographs in response. The site is what Jenny Gregory (2015: 26), citing Hall and Zarro (2012), defines as a social curation site, where personal histories relating to the images displayed are shared, with narrative information added about the images.

Photographs within material culture thinking

It is a useful starting point to situate photographs within existing thinking around material culture. Ian Woodward (2007: 11) tells us that material culture is concerned with the relationships between people and objects, including the uses people put objects to, and what objects do to, and for, people. Scholars in this field also analyze how these relationships work in producing and sharing culture. This is apposite when thinking about photographs and the uses we put them to. Elizabeth Edwards and Janice Hart (2004: 1) explain that photographs are a combination of image and physical object, existing both spatially and temporally and being part of the social and cultural experience. They propose replacing the primacy of the actual image, with an appreciation of its materiality, in addition, arguing that the meanings of both photographic image and photographic object are inextricably linked (Edwards and Hart 2004: 2). They argue that an understanding of the photographic image's materiality is necessary to appreciate it fully.

But what do we mean by the materiality of photographs? Attfield (2000: 3) defines materiality as encompassing all aspects of a physical object throughout its existence, including its 'design, making, distributing, consuming, using, discarding, recycling'. Applying this thinking to a photograph emphasizes how significant considerations of materiality are throughout its life cycle. Whether it is an analogue or digital image, it is framed, taken, printed from a negative or stored as a file, put in an album, photobook, or shared online, before potentially being thrown away or deleted. What we think of as a photograph goes through many forms. As Joanna Zylinska (2010: 148) explains, photographic objects have always been unstable, and liquid, being repurposed in different media forms for cultural purposes.

Material culture has been investigated by scholars from diverse fields, impinging as it does on different disciplines in different ways, rather than being exclusive to any specific one. Anthropologists, archaeologists, designers, and media theorists have developed perspectives around materiality, resulting in a range of approaches from the semiotic to the Marxist, with many others besides. The semiotic view espouses that objects are primarily signs that represent us (Miller 2010: 2), referring to something other than themselves, with material culture being a 'signifier' that communicates some kind of social 'work' (Woodward 2007: 55–56). This is particularly true of photographs because of their indexicality. For instance, Geoffrey Batchen (2004: 40) argues that as a material form, they become virtually invisible, encouraging the viewer to 'see' the subject represented, rather than the photograph itself, as the representation is the product of the actual referent. The physical link between the original scene and the photograph of it – its indexicality – is an important factor in the photographic experience. Janne Seppänen (2017: 122) notes the same phenomenon, explaining that the bodily and emotional aspects of the trace cause research subjects to talk about people in photographs as if they were the people themselves, rather than two-dimensional representations of them. He argues that the power of the agency of the material trace, on the one hand, provides a visual representation of an absent object, while through the material presence of the object in the image, overrides that absence, thus making every photograph a 'multistable and unruly image'. He concludes that this consigns photographic representation to 'an unresolvable epistemological aporia'. This suggests that the agency of the material trace, although paradoxical, is what gives photographs a particular appeal, and makes them so useful in eliciting engagement and evoking memory via social media. Photographs are encoded messages, encoded both mechanically and electronically in the capturing and displaying of the image, and encoded by the photographer in the production of meaning.

Photographs give the illusion of being clear in what they represent, in that they are indexical to their subject matter, and provide documentary evidence of a particular occurrence. Roland Barthes (1964: 44) explains that because an image is 'captured mechanically', [or now electronically], it has the illusion of being an objective record, but as Marcus Banks (1995: 2) notes, photographs are no more 'transparent' than video or written documentation, and are similarly only representations of an event, rather than a 'direct encoding of it'. Photographs mediate their subject, as do written or video material, albeit in a different way. The nature of representations is such that they are subject to their 'social, cultural and historical contexts of production and consumption', a notion which is shared by Sarah Pink (2001: 55), who urges us to take note of the enmeshed nature of 'cultural discourses' and 'social relationships' of individual photographers, in addition to the wider political, economic, and historical contexts. This echoes the conclusions of Charles S. Peirce and Ferdinand de Saussure, that the sign, in this case the photograph, provides coded access to an object (Cobley and Jansz 1997: 29). Photographs are distinct from other signs, such as writing, in that they are 'iconic', and resemble the objects they represent, albeit in a static and two-dimensional form (Cobley and Jansz 1997; Chandler 2002).

Daniel Miller (2010: 10) goes further than objects being signs that represent us and argues that 'stuff actually creates us in the first place'. By this, he means that we define ourselves through the objects we place around us and interact with, they are intrinsically part of our identity and culture. Objects are important symbolically and entwined with ritual and social behaviour, and with ideas around how we shape and depict our identities. Mihaly Csikszentmihalyi and Eugene Rochberg-Halton (1981: 67–69) note that more than anything else in the home, photographs are the prime vehicle for preserving the memories of those close to us, they are imbued with emotion and entwined with our sense of belonging. In their study on the meaning objects held for people, they found that photographs exemplify: 'the importance of tangible artifacts for expressing deep human needs for relationship and continuity, as well as the fragility of the material world we create around us and the people and institutions that make up the world' (224). Regarding the Pebble Mill project, I am constantly surprised about how many photographs BBC staff members took during their careers of the productions they worked on and have kept safe since. They seemed to want to document their working lives, because of the significance the work had for them. This substantiates the point around objects, in this case photographic ones, being used to build and display our identities; they are enmeshed with who we are.

There is an interesting tension between the physical and the virtual in material culture that we can observe playing out in relation to media. Artefacts are not fixed and stable, their forms evolve in different physical and virtual ways. Differences in physical form do not necessarily influence the enjoyment of a cultural artefact. For instance, a piece of music is enjoyable whether listened to via a record, CD or streaming service, although the experience is not the same. For some people, the haptic pleasure of physically handling the vinyl record or CD is an important part of the process of enjoying their music. Digitization has played a significant role in the transference of media from physical to virtual across genres and platforms, affecting its physicality and materiality. The digitization of analogue photographs is a case in point, the transference of the image across forms is relatively straightforward, but the materiality and the physicality are very different. The experience of leafing through a family photograph album is very different from, although analogous to, scrolling through the same images online. Yet there are significant differences in the photographic process between filmic and digital forms. Photography imprints the image of an object through mechanical, chemical, and electronic means, producing a two-dimensional image which accurately represents the object. In analogue film photography, the camera shutter opens and closes, leaving a material trace of light, reflected or emitted from the objects in the frame; in contrast, the digital image translates the trace into an abstract stream of binary mathematical information (Seppänen 2017: 115). With digitization, the analogue image is scanned and ingested as a digital file.

There is disagreement amongst scholars regarding the material integrity of digitized images. As Janne Seppänen (2017: 115) notes, 'it has been suggested that digitization undermines the materiality of the trace'; in contrast, he regards it as an ambiguous process as 'the first form of the digital trace is analogous and invisible and needs to be amplified before its conversion to digital code'. The processes are different, but both signals are physical phenomena, and therefore both indexical and material. Jasmine Burns (2017: 5) emphasizes that the materiality of the original object is not lost but rather translated into metadata and digital information. Joanna Zylinska (2010: 145) warns against anti-digital hysteria, and challenges thinking concerning analogue vs. digital, by arguing that photography has always been essentially digital, consisting of binary data, through the absence or presence of light. This is photography at its most elemental and highlights the fluidity of it as a practice; the technology and apparatus evolve but the fundamental process regarding the interplay of light and the photographic subject remains the same. Joanna Sassoon (2004) sees both advantages and disadvantages in the possibilities of digitization for archival images, on the one hand, she notes the potential of

YOU CAN LOOK, SHARE, AND COMMENT, BUT YOU CAN'T TOUCH

sharing them beyond institutions and the benefits of being able to add hypertext and make new associations but warns of undermining the nature of the archive. This perspective focuses on a broadcast model, of an institution making part of its archives accessible online for the many, rather than considering the advantages of interactivity with a community and the possibilities that sharing digitized images presents in building an online archive. Placing more emphasis on the potential of hypertext, Juliette De Maeyer notes a new turn towards materiality, with digitization providing additional forms of traceability, especially in terms of hyperlinks and metadata, which highlight how tangible and visible our digital world can be. She sees this emphasis on materiality 'as an attempt to reinstate a sensibility to things, and particularly to technology' (2016: 461–62), providing an opportunity to embed journalistic objects with rich networks and associations. This perspective is equally relevant to digitized photographs shared online, where metadata and tags can provide additional information, potentially substantiating authenticity. However, there are counterarguments to this position relating to the ease with which digital artefacts can be altered or tampered with, causing us to question their authenticity.

The Pebble Mill project has taken predominantly historic analogue images and digitally re-mediated them, for virtual secondary consumption in a context which could not have been predicted when they were produced. Elizabeth Edwards and Janice Hart (2004: 3) argue that viewing a historic image online is a very different experience from handling the original, as the 'grammar' of both the image and the object is complex and fluid. Similarly, Andrea Volpe (2009: 13) notes that re-mediation replaces the original terms of the photograph with those of the archive. She argues that the photograph, while its visual rhetoric is preserved, loses its relationship to time, and this becomes heightened through the digitized image often being referred to, rather than the original (Volpe 2009: 16). This re-mediation affects both the physicality and the materiality of photographs. Joanna Sassoon (2004, 200) views digitization as a translation of form, a standardizing process, whereby a three-dimensional object is reduced to a one-dimensional, ephemeral, and ethereal state. Digitization, therefore, encourages an emphasis on the aesthetics of the image, rather than a consideration of its physicality. Patricia Hayes (1998: 6) argues that this risks dehistoricizing and decontextualizing a photograph. Evidence of the photograph's manufacture and patterns of use are lost, with digitization creating a new material object: a digital surrogate (Burns 2017: 2). Through digitalization, a photograph loses some of its aesthetic, and haptic appeal, but gains the possibility of wider, quicker, and cheaper dissemination. Technically, although a digital image does not possess tangible matter, it is inscribed in a file on a computer hard-drive or in the memory of a camera card. It has materiality itself as a digital object, and in relation to the objects it represents, although its physicality is different from a photographic print. Digitization highlights the lack of fixity of images, they are mobile and can change form. For Burns (2017: 6), a digital copy is seen as less valuable than the original, highlighting an 'object-centred culture with a focus on tactility, tangibility, and originality as authenticity'. The privileging of tangible physical objects over digital ones fails to take account of the positive attributes of the digitized images, and the work they can do in terms of stimulating collective memory when shared online.

The Pebble Mill case study

The Pebble Mill case study presents the opportunity to investigate how material culture plays out in practice through an online community archive. This enables an exploration of the three areas of focus mentioned earlier in this chapter concerning, the relationship between the digitized image and memory in the online space, how digitization affects the material properties of the image and how online spaces present new digital encounters with the material image.

The relationship between the digitized image and the memory in the online space

Photographs have both physical and material properties which influence why they are so successful in eliciting engagement and evoking memories. David Bate (2010: 255) likens photographs to memory, in that both are 'fixed and fluid: social and personal'. He explains photographs as mnemonic sites 'upon which a historical representation may be constructed'. Photographs are thus affective and subjective. Karen Cross and Julia Peck (2010: 127–36) also draw similarities between photography and memory, in that they both record images that may be used in recalling the fragmented remains of the past. However, memory obviously lacks materiality, as well as being embodied, in contrast to the photograph's externality. Cross and Peck highlight the paradox, espoused by Barthes (1980: 91), that photographs can actually block memory, becoming a countermemory, which persists and subsumes the original embodied memory. Scholars, such as Connerton (2009: 124), claim that the proliferation of digital images can lead to a cultural forgetting. However, this is open to question, as other academics have noted the positive attributes of social media communities in building a sense of collective memory, through displaying 'fragments from a shared past into a dynamic reflective expression of contemporary identity' (Silberman 2012: 16).

Although photographs (filmic or digital) cannot retrieve the past, they do situate the past in the present, they can stimulate our memories of the past, even if those memories have become muddied by our subsequent experiences, and by details added by others. John Berger (1992: 192) describes the 'thrill' of seeing a photograph that brings an 'onrush of memory', helping us remember what we forget. The use of the word 'thrill' is significant, implying a powerful, and largely positive emotion, whilst 'onrush' suggests that the individual is almost overwhelmed by the sensation of memory. However imperfect photographs might be in their representation of the past, they do seem to be a very valuable medium for memory evocation. In Nancy Van House's (2011: 130) research, she notes that the importance of a photograph was in the memories evoked, and not in its representation and that the quality of the image was irrelevant to its importance. This is a phenomenon that I have observed on the Pebble Mill Facebook page, where the quality of the image itself seems unimportant. Even poor quality or dull images have the power to unlock the memories associated with the subject represented. This is particularly so in the collective context of social media, with other people with similar experiences commenting on the image. I posted the photograph in Figure 9.1 to illustrate a blog, which a retired BBC engineer had written for the Pebble Mill project.

The photograph is not poor quality technically, but it is a seemingly dull image, of an empty institutional workplace restaurant. However, the post reached almost

FIGURE 9.1: BBC Birmingham Canteen 2004. Photograph by Philip Morgan.

MEDIA MATERIALITIES

2000 people – well above average for the page – with 62 'likes' and over twenty comments. Only one comment responded to the blog post itself, with the others all relating to the photograph of the canteen. Several of the comments refer directly to the memories evoked by seeing the image:

> Quite emotional looking at that photo. I loved the canteen and the staff who worked there. They made the best bacon and egg butties! And crumble and custard.

> Ah, a place where many a programme idea would first come to light. Good memories!

> So sad to see the space now. In this canteen, I remember David Hasselhoff coming in for breakfast [...] and Jeremy Clarkson [...]. Amongst many other weird memories [...] I do remember the ladies making the most amazing steak pie for lunch with brilliant pastry.

The comments are illustrative of Seppänen's (2017: 122) point made earlier concerning the 'multistable and unruly image', with one commenter referring to the *photograph*, while the others view the photograph as the place itself, rather than a representation of it. This could simply be a shorthand, in that the commenters know they are responding to a digital image, alternatively, it could demonstrate the power of the material trace in making the form of the image invisible. The commenters concentrate on what Roland Barthes (cited in Pink 2001: 14) describes as the 'punctum', or the 'ecstasy of the image', the factor which gives the photograph an emotive quality, and connects the reader to the image, rather than the 'studium', which encompasses the photographer's skill and technique. It is the emotional connection the image has with the viewer which is significant, rather than the photographic affordances. The restaurant is fondly remembered because of its social connotations, as well as its food. It was an important place for taking a quick break with friends and colleagues, or having a meal during or at the end of a shift, and with the excitement that you never quite knew who you might meet, with the comings and goings of actors and celebrities. Ironically, the fact that the photograph is so seemingly uninspiring may actually be an asset. John Berger (1992: 193) makes a paradoxical comment that the 'sharper and more isolated the stimulus memory receives, the more it remembers; the more comprehensive the stimulus, the less it remembers'. Thus, a black and white image, or a bland image, as here, can provoke more comprehensive memories than a more colourful and lively photograph. This argument is counterintuitive, but it is true of the image above, where the deserted space allows viewers to project their own memories of the institution of the canteen, without the distraction of a particular event to focus their memories elsewhere. What is clear is that the photograph acts as a prompt for

YOU CAN LOOK, SHARE, AND COMMENT, BUT YOU CAN'T TOUCH

users of the Facebook page to reflect on their memories and share those thoughts with others and that the quality of the prompting image is a lower order priority. The sharing of memories on the page becomes a social interaction: the personal memory situated in the collective memory of a particular time and place, tinged with a sense of nostalgia. This process of remembering and sharing those memories publicly has become part of many people's everyday lives, through the proliferation of social media. Photographs seem to be integral to this process, perhaps because of the everyday quality of photography, which we now use habitually to document our daily lives.

The collective sharing of memories on the Pebble Mill sites is the strength of the project, and this is facilitated through the sharing of digitized photographs. When Belfast comedian Frank Carson died, I wrote a post on the Facebook page remembering that he gave an impromptu performance in the Pebble Mill canteen during the staff Christmas lunch after being a guest on the Pebble Mill chat show in the 1990s. In response one of the engineers posted the photograph in Figure 9.2, which had been taken by a colleague. Other former Pebble Mill colleagues added more information: 'He came in through the double doors, saw an audience in party hats and went for it. He was fabulous. It was a real treat. Took our mind off sprouts that had been cooking since September'. The researcher looking after Carson that day wrote: 'When he arrived, he told me his flight back home to Blackpool wasn't until 6 pm, so we had to find something for him to do, the Christmas lunch was a Godsend'. This illustrates how the re-mediation of the photograph elicits nostalgic memory differently from a physical copy because of the ability to activate collective memory, with each comment building on the last. Such a phenomenon has been noted by others, including Jenny Gregory (2015: 42) in her study of the 'Beautiful Old Perth' Facebook group. She concluded that the participants who remembered the lost buildings shown in the digitized analogue photographs, tended to reminisce positively about their experiences of the place, in addition to building considerable social capital through their interactions on the site.

However, not all interactions elicit positive memories. There are certain productions which whenever they are mentioned on the Pebble Mill Facebook page produce a negative reaction. The drama *Witchcraft* (1992), the filming of which is depicted in Figure 9.3, is one such example, with the negativity illustrated by these comments:

[They were] a nightmare bully, sexist and just a complete —. I think that covers that.

Nightmare yes, intense yes, fun in some kind of crazy way, yes; was it worth it, was it a good film? No!

215

FIGURE 9.2: Frank Carson giving an impromptu performance in the canteen in the 1990s. Photograph by Paul Hunt.

These reactions demonstrate that reminiscing on historic photographs is not necessarily all 'rose-tinted' nostalgia, but that the images evoke powerful emotions, whether positive or negative, which individuals want to share with others – a collective venting of feelings which may have lain dormant for many years. Richard McDonald (2015: 28) emphasizes the mnemonic value of heritage-focused Facebook groups. He articulates that the value of images is in the online conversations elicited. He also concludes that membership of a group, such as a heritage-based social media group, enables individuals to recall memories and to develop a sense of belonging which is rooted in material spaces, such as buildings and localities (31–32). The importance of a sense of place, and particularly a lost place, is highly

FIGURE 9.3: Filming on location for *Witchcraft* (BBC 2, 1992). Photograph by Willoughby Gullachsen (Gus).

relevant to the Pebble Mill project, which is centred on the now demolished broadcasting studios.

It is the faculty of sharing, enabling the group interaction which builds social capital. For this to happen, a digitized photograph is not essential, a physical photographic print could be passed round a group of people and the comments written down, but logistically it would be very difficult to bring so many people, who live all over the world, together to do this. It is something which social media can accomplish quickly and easily. The ability to comment, share memories, and stimulate recollection in each other is what makes it a different experience. The fact that we access social media sites individually, often at home, also affects the interaction, making us more likely to contribute more personal recollections than we might in a physical public arena.

How digitization affects the material properties of the image

The photographs on the Pebble Mill project website are a product of their social, cultural, and professional contexts, and this is easily apparent through their nature and qualities. The images themselves tell the social historian much about the means and cultures of production, and the intentions behind their existence. They were produced in different ways, by different groups of people, for different audiences, despite now being grouped together on display for a modern audience which was never envisaged. The photographs would have been taken for professional or social reasons, primarily for immediate use; they were not taken as the historical records they have now become. The photographer would have planned for the use of the image, depending on its context, but unlikely realized its later significance as a historical artefact.

Publicity shots of upcoming programmes are part of the Pebble Mill project's virtual collection. These tend to be black and white images, which were produced to depict an intriguing and creative world for external viewers and were taken on high end professional cameras. Their purpose was to provide privileged access for the public, through the lens of a professional photographer, who witnessed the shoot. The photographer was an outsider, not part of the crew, but accepted by them, usually a freelancer, but employed by the BBC for that day. This relation-ship results in a particular quality of image. As an outsider, the photographer has a degree of objectivity about what is visually interesting about the day's filming; capturing fleeting moments; framing, but not usually choreographing the shot; using the available or televisual lighting, and always during rehearsal, never an actual take. Referring to Barthes (1961: 19), Daniel Chandler (2002: 163) notes that in terms of production, the press photograph is a carefully constructed image which conforms to professional or ideological norms and, in terms of consumption such photographs are read in the context of a tradition of a shared understanding of a system of signs. These photographs provide us, as retrospective viewers, with a rich visual source, perhaps in part because they document the shoot through the eyes of an observer, rather than a participant, and frequently depict the inter-action of cast and crew, which is one of the norms in play. Press and publicity photographs frequently show behind the scenes images, including the camera equipment and the crew, in order to provide a sense of privileged access for the viewer, through the eyes of the photographer, illustrating how the programme was produced. Depicted in Figure 9.4 is a publicity still taken by freelance photogra-pher, Willoughby Gullachsen (Gus), for BBC Pebble Mill of a drama production, *Boogie Outlaws* (1987).

The photograph is taken at night, outside the Princes Cinema; dry ice, creating 'smoke', adds to the atmosphere of the shoot. We can see the grips on the far left, controlling the crane, next to him is the cable basher, with the cable, in his hand, and next to him is probably the sound operator, with the camera operator, above him on the crane. Other members of the cast and crew are not identifiable. The photograph is taken from quite a way back, it, therefore, has an air of observation,

FIGURE 9.4: Crew shooting *Boogie Outlaws* (BBC 2, 1987). Photograph by Willoughby Gullachsen (Gus).

and Gus has cleverly used the lighting and dry ice intended for the shoot, to lend atmosphere to his still. This makes the image of the cast and crew mysterious, dramatic, and exciting, all desirable qualities in a publicity photograph.

Through digitization, the materiality of the photograph has been altered, and the image degraded. I scanned the image from a high gloss filmic print, before posting it online. The way the light reflected from the gloss photographic paper has been lost, and imperfections have crept in, for example, along the top edge of the image you can see the edge of the white strip surrounding the photograph, where I have failed to position it perfectly for the scan. The digital image gives no idea of the size of the original print, nor its weight. In addition, we lose the context of the photograph. It was designed to be viewed alongside an article about the drama, in a listings magazine or a press release. This means that when the image is posted online it benefits from supporting information being added to make full sense of the image and provide details of elements like the drama's title and date. Through digitization, important aspects of its original materiality have been lost, however the aesthetic power of this particular image translates well digitally even without additional information because of the visual norms included in the shot, for instance the camera, crane, and dramatic lighting, signify a behind the scenes drama publicity shot.

Digital remediation online does privilege the visual over other sensory engagement, and this is the case with the majority of digitization. In other contexts, such as in the three-dimensional digitization and printing of replicas of museum artefacts a more multi-sensory, and particularly a more haptic experience would be possible, but this is not the case here. Jasmine Burns (2017: 7) highlights that digitization still equates to preservation, despite the preservation being of the image rather than the form and context of the photographic object; as rather than materiality being lost, there are aspects of substance that cannot be rendered digitally. Digitization does mean that we lose some of the context of use, but this can be supplemented through embedding additional information. There is, however, the danger that additional information may alter the original meaning of the artefact. Jasmine Burns (2017: 6) argues that digital surrogates possess secondary provenance, which is embedded in the custodial history of the original artefact, providing a trace of its past use and material construction. Therefore, the digitized image displays its authenticity through the traces of use and manufacture of the original, and through its custodial record. However, outside an archival institution a custodial record is unlikely. Remediation, as we have observed with the digitized publicity photograph, results in some of the context of use being lost. The authenticity of the artefact is altered and potentially damaged.

Figure 9.5 is a scanned digitized copy of a Polaroid photograph taken by costume designer, Janice Rider, as part of her role on location filming for the drama series *Juliet Bravo* (1980–85). It is part of the collection of artefacts on the Pebble Mill project website. The image shows the lead character, Jean Darblay, played by Stephanie Turner. It was taken for continuity purposes, showing how Stephanie was dressed and what she was holding, so that she appeared the same in subsequent or preceding scenes, recorded out of order and in different locations. Polaroids

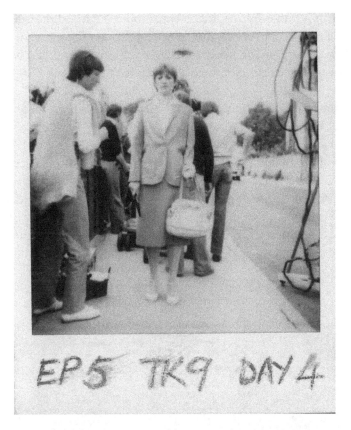

FIGURE 9.5: Polaroid from *Juliet Bravo* shoot (*c*.1980–85). Photograph by Janice Rider.

were ideal for this purpose, as they were processed in the camera and printed instantly. The white area below the image was also useful for recording notes, as we can see here from the hand-written record of the episode, take numbers, and shoot day. We can observe that the writing has been slightly smudged, presumably from being handled before the ink was dry. The colours of the image have faded with age, the red is less present, with a greenish tinge predominating, demonstrating that photographic prints are not fixed and stable objects. The original print has considerable signs of age and use. These signs are also apparent on the digitized copy, although the tangible photographic object is absent, thereby losing its haptic appeal.

In contrast, it can be argued that the digitized version has certain benefits, in that we do not know of any degeneration of digital files with age, and they have the facility to be stored on different platforms, hard-drives, and servers, to prevent accidental or deliberate deletion. If the original print was from a digital file, rather than a filmic source, it could still be re-digitized in order to capture visually the signs of use, for instance written notes on the print, or signs of age and use. However, this is less likely to happen, as a curator would be more likely to return to the source image, rather than scan the digital print.

How online spaces present new digital encounters with the material image

Community-based virtual collections, as observed in this chapter, thrive through the participation of the communities they are part of. This participation can sometimes take unexpected directions. I posted Figure 9.6 in 2021, following the death of the make-up artist shown trimming Brian Glover's hair during the production of the *Play For Today*, 'Shakespeare or Bust' (1973). The degradation of the original filmic image is clear, the colours are faded, there are also imperfections in the digitization, for example the irregular strip of white on the left-hand side. A couple of days after

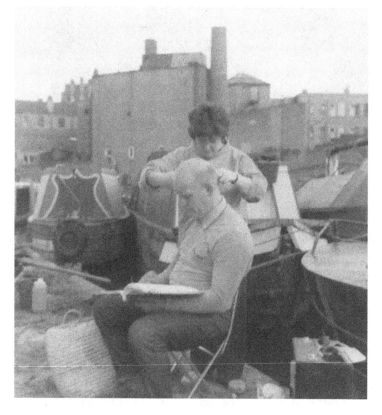

FIGURE 9.6: Brian Glover and Gwen Arthy on *Shakespeare or Bust* (BBC 1, 1973). Photograph by Graham Pettifer.

I posted the image, a regular contributor messaged me privately with a new version, which he had colour corrected (see Figure 9.7). He suggested that I might like to replace the post image with the corrected one, but said he did not want his name mentioning. When I asked why not, he said it was not his photograph, he did not like 'ego-trips' and that the colour correction had only taken him a couple of minutes.

This incident illustrates one way in which social capital is galvanized through social curation sites; expertise as well as information and memories can be shared, which can impact on the materiality of shared artefacts, as seen here. The enhanced image quality also demonstrates some of the benefits of digitization, regarding the restoration of degraded filmic images. A similar restoration would not have been possible from the filmic print, without returning to the negative. It is the sharing of digital, digitized, and physical artefacts that build such collections. Through the sharing of knowledge and expertise from members of the community, information

FIGURE 9.7: Brian Glover and Gwen Arthy on *Shakespeare or Bust* (BBC 1, 1973). Photograph by Graham Pettifer. Colour-corrected version.

that proves the provenance of the digital and digitized artefacts is gathered and added to the collection. Virtual collections benefit from this embedding of information in the digital artefacts, through the use of robust descriptions, metadata, and tagging, which improves the provenance of the collection, as long as it is accurate, as well as making items searchable. In order to maximize their utility, virtual collections should be categorized, not necessarily in the same way as a physical archive, but in a way that makes their digital objects easy to retrieve.

New material encounters become possible because virtual collections make digital artefacts accessible in a way in which physical archives cannot, and often do not want to. Virtual collections tend to privilege access over preservation, while traditional archives tend to restrict access and privilege the preservation of physical artefacts. Virtual collections cannot replicate the haptic experience of visiting a physical collection. In the case of filmic prints, we lose through digitization some of the context of the original manufacture – the expensive high-gloss photographic paper, the size and weight of the print, and some of the signs of use – but the material trace is still present. The visual rhetoric persists despite the change in form, and traces remain of age and signs of use. The encounter with the photographic objects is a different one, beneficial in some ways, detrimental in others. Benefits can include improved access, speed, and searchability, particularly when collections are well categorized. Detrimental factors centre around the lack of tactility and tangibility in an object-focused culture.

Conclusion

What we learn from this case study is that materiality is not a fixed concept, and photographs, as Joanna Zylinska (2010: 141) reminds us, are inherently liquid. The application of technology has the power to alter the materiality of some artefacts, particularly in terms of form, while retaining the visual content of the image. Photographs are sometimes considered as stable objects, but this is not the case. As we observe in the images from *Juliet Bravo* and 'Shakespeare or Bust' the colours of physical prints fade and decay. Careful digital capture is one way of preserving such artefacts, as well as making them more accessible online. Viewing them online adds a further complication, as it relies on a properly calibrated monitor being used for the colours to be correctly received, a factor beyond the control of the publisher of the image. Digitized images can be considered as surrogates of a filmic print, they are not clones, because the form is different, but they are visually closely allied, sharing the material trace of the original subject. Digital surrogates have different material properties. They lack the haptic qualities of the original print but that does not make them less valuable, and the material trace of the original subject remains irrespective of form. The digitized photograph is

YOU CAN LOOK, SHARE, AND COMMENT, BUT YOU CAN'T TOUCH

paradoxically both more fixed and more mutable than the original filmic print. More fixed, in that it is not subject to physical decay and does not display age in the manner of the print, but more mutable in that the image can be manipulated and edited, in a way which can bring its authenticity into question. That is not to say that the filmic print could not have been edited from the exposed negative in the analogue printing process, or in a more modern context, using computer editing software programmes. Neither material form is stable and fixed.

As observed through the examples used in this chapter, remediated digitized photographs are able to elicit nostalgic memories and emotions very successfully through online sharing, meaning that collective memory can be activated, enabling individuals to build social capital through responding to the stimulus of the shared image, or the recollections of other participants. Through this mechanism, a rich context can be aggregated around a digitized artefact. Additional images are likely to be uploaded by contributors in response to the first, in a way which would be practically impossible in an offline situation. In addition, an online community is created. The digitization of media artefacts and their subsequent remediation does have an impact on their materiality. Digital remediation privileges visual over haptic engagement, and some of the context of use may be lost, although traces of age and use can remain. However, there is the ability to add robust description and technical metadata to enrich the user experience and reinforce the authenticity of the digital object. Digitized artefacts should not be viewed as lesser, but as different. There are a number of benefits to them, particularly regarding preservation and accessibility. In the case of virtual community archives, it is the ability to share images and build a collection collaboratively which is their greatest strength. The benefits of sharing digitized photographs on social curation sites, including the building of social capital between participants, the individual and collective memories and emotional responses evoked and the contextualization provided through online comments outweigh the change in physicality from the original photographs.

NOTES

1. http://pebblemill.org.
2. https://www.facebook.com/pebblemillstudios/.

REFERENCES

Attfield, Judy (2000), *Wild Things: The Material Culture of Everyday Life*, London: Bloomsbury Publishing.

Appadurai, Arjun (1986), *The Social Life of Things: Commodities in Cultural Perspective*, Cambridge: Cambridge University Press.

Banks, Marcus (1995), 'Visual Research Methods, Social Research Update', Winter, n.pag., University of Surrey, http://sru.soc.surrey.ac.uk/SRU11/SRU11.html. Accessed 4 July 2023.

Bate, David (2010), 'The memory of photography', *Photographies*, 3:2, pp. 243–57.

Barthes, Roland ([1964] 1977), 'Rhetoric of the image', in *Image Music Text*, New York: Hill and Wang, pp.32–51.

Barthes, Roland (1980), *Camera Lucida: Reflections on Photography* (trans. R. Howard), New York: Farrar, Straus and Giroux.

Batchen, Geoffrey (2004), 'Ere the substance fade: Photography and hair jewellery', in E. Edwards and J. Hart (eds), *Photographs Objects Histories: On the Materiality of Images*, Oxon: Taylor & Francis Group, pp. 32–47.

BBC (1962), Press release, 12 November, M10/23/10, Caversham: BBC Written Archives.

Berger, John (1992), *Keeping a Rendezvous*, London: Granta Books.

Boys from the Blackstuff (1982, UK: BBC).

Burns, Jasmine, E. (2017), 'The aura of materiality: Digital aurrogacy and the preservation of photographic archives', *Art Documentation*, 36:1, pp. 1–8.

Chandler, Daniel (2002), *Semiotics: The Basics*, Oxon: Routledge.

Cobley, Paul and Jansz, Litza (1997), *Introducing Semiotics*, Cambridge: Icon Books.

Colloredo-Mansfeld, Rudi (2003), 'Matter unbound', *Journal of Material Culture*, 8:3, pp. 245–54.

Connerton, Paul (2009), *How Modernity Forgets*, Cambridge: Cambridge University Press.

Countryfile (1988–present, UK: BBC).

Cross, Karen and Peck, Julia (2010), 'Editorial: Special issue on photography, archive and memory', *Photographies*, 3:2, pp. 127–38.

Csikszentmihalyi, Mihaly and Rochberg-Halton, Eugene (1981), *The Meaning of Things, Domestic Symbols and the Self*, Cambridge: Cambridge University Press.

De Maeyer, Juliette (2016), 'Adopting a "material sensibility" in Journalism Studies', in T. Witschge, C. W. Anderson, D. Domingo, and A. Hermida (eds), *The SAGE Handbook of Digital Journalism*, London: SAGE, pp. 460–76.

Edwards, Elizabeth and Hart, Janice (2004), 'Introduction: Photographs as objects', in *Photographs Objects Histories: On the Materiality of Images*, London: Taylor & Francis Group, pp. 1–15.

Gangsters (1976-78, UK: BBC).

Gardeners' World (1968–present, UK: BBC).

Gregory, Jenny (2015), 'Connecting with the past through social media: The "Beautiful buildings and cool places Perth has lost" Facebook group', *International Journal of Heritage Studies*, 21:1, pp. 22–45.

Hartmann, Wolfram, Silvester, Jeremy, and Hayes, Patricia (1998), *The Colonising Camera: Photographs in the Making of Namibian History*, Cape Town: The University of Cape Town Press.

MacDonald, Richard L. (2015), '"Going back in a heartbeat": Collective memory and the online circulation of family photographs', *Photographies*, 8:1, pp. 23–42.

Miller, Daniel (2010), *Stuff*, Cambridge: Polity Press.

'Nuts in May' (1976), M. Leigh (dir.), *Play for Today,* Season 6 Episode 12 (13 January, UK: BBC).

Pebble Mill at One (1972–86, UK: BBC).

Peggy Lee Entertains (1981, UK: BBC).

Pink, Sarah (2001), *Doing Visual Ethnography*, London: Sage Publications.

Sassoon, Joanna (2004), 'Photographic materiality in the age of digital reproduction', in E. Edwards and J. Hart (eds), *Photographs Objects Histories: On the Materiality of Images*, London: Taylor & Francis Group, pp. 196–213.

Seppänen, Janne (2017), 'Unruly representation: Materiality, indexicality and agency of the photographic trace', *Photographies*, 10:1, pp. 113–28.

'Shakespeare or Bust' (1973), B. Parker (dir.), *Play for Today,* Season 3 Episode 11 (8 January, UK: BBC).

Silberman, Neil and Purser, Margaret (2012), 'Collective memory as affirmation: People-centred cultural heritage in a digital age', in E. Giaccardi (ed.), *Heritage and Social Media: Understanding Heritage in a Participatory Culture*, London: Routledge, pp. 13–39.

The Archers (1951–present, UK: BBC Radio).

Top Gear (1977–present, UK: BBC).

Van House, Nancy A. (2011), 'Personal photography, digital technologies and the uses of the visual', *Visual Studies*, 26:2, pp. 125–34.

Volpe, Andrea L. (2009), 'Archival meaning: Materiality, digitization, and the nineteenth-century photograph', *Afterimage*, 36:6, pp. 11–16.

Woodward, Ian (2007), *Understanding Material Culture*, London: Sage.

Witchcraft (1992, UK: BBC).

Zylinska, Joanna (2010), 'On bad archives, unruly snappers and liquid photographs', *Photographies*, 3:2, pp. 139–53.

Short Take 12

Location, Agency, and Hashtag Activism During the COVID-19 Pandemic

Yemisi Akinbobola

I have always been torn between my physical home in the United Kingdom, and my sense of home in Africa. I use 'Africa' deliberately, because in the last few years I have become increasing connected to a continental outlook and not a national one focused solely on Nigeria. While I continue to reflect on the word to describe my identity, I cogitate 'Afropolitan', a word coined by Taiye Selasi (2005), and which Dons Eze (2014: 239) describes as a term used in an 'effort to grasp the diverse nature of being African or of African descent in the world today'. For me, I use it to describe an empowered stance, which does not take its starting point from a resistance to the West, and that rejects notions of victimhood.

The pandemic heightened my sense of responsibility to the continent. Here, in the United Kingdom, I positioned myself as a citizen leaving the responsibility to those in leadership. However, for Africa, I feel I have a responsibility to be part of the leadership addressing the challenges in African countries. I cannot address the challenges faced by everybody, so I concentrate my effort on supporting African women working in media.

All was going well until George Floyd was murdered. The Black Lives Matter protests began, and I am jolted back to seeing myself as Yemisi in the United Kingdom and being forced to reflect on my experiences of racism. I have always resisted seeing myself as subordinate, racialized, and racially observed. In reflecting on this, I begin to remember the biases I have experienced in the United Kingdom, during my education, socially, and in my places of work. It was an emotional thing to do. I wrote a Facebook post about the first time I realized I was black, aged 10 in school, and being told by my teacher 'IF YOU WANT TO BEHAVE LIKE A MONKEY, GO BACK TO AFRICA', simply because I displayed excitement in the only way I knew how. In that same year, I was called a N****r in the playground. The silent complicity of others who have been witness to some of my experiences of racism, including in my workplace, and choosing to look the other way. When I wrote that post, I cried at the acknowledgement that there is a Yemisi in this place in the Diaspora, whose agency is limited. My sense of agency *is* attached to Africa. There I feel as a leader, I feel I have agency, and respect for who I am, and I do not feel that here in the United Kingdom, and that is what the Black Lives Matter debate has really helped me face. I am now challenging myself to do something about this, to take back power!

While the Black Lives Matter discussions were happening online for the global audience, for Nigeria, there was a heightened debate around gender-based violence. The lockdown saw an increase in reports of rape. Yet there is a sense of hope there because ten years ago this would not have been reported. Social media presents an opportunity for it to be reported and debated, much like police brutality in the United States. It is hard to see, but it needs to be seen so that we can do something about it.

REFERENCES

Eze, Dons (2014), 'Nigeria and the crisis of cultural identity in the era of globalization', *Journal of African Studies and Development*, 6:8, pp. 140–47.

Selasi, Taiye (2005), 'Bye-Bye Babar', *The Lip Magazine*, 3 March, https://thelip.robertsharp.co.uk/2005/03/03/bye-bye-barbar/. Accessed 4 July 2023.

10

Thirty-Seven Retweets

John Hillman

Today, the digital world is comprised of groups of individuals who are, increasingly, encouraged to self-organize, publish, share their opinions and express reactions and responses in the form of comments, emojis, or even animated imagery. These varied interactions take place on a range of different digital platforms, such as Twitter, Instagram, WhatsApp, and Facebook, creating a kind of frictionless exchange between people. While there may be conflicts and differences of opinions (e.g. the so-called Twitter pile-on [Delaney 2019: n.pag.] as an expression of group anger and rage), what remains is an underlying process of communication that is structurally robust. Importantly, this system of communicating is simultaneously also a developing knowledge and surveillance system, one that often shifts from its underlying structure in the virtual world to having actual and real-world impacts (Zuboff 2019). The argument I make in this chapter takes as its focus how the rendering of global digital environments tends to obfuscate the material particularities of the personal. In other words, despite many attempts to integrate and mediate lived experience into an online environment, our homogenous online subjectivity still lacks all the individual details which tend to differentiate us in our day-to-day lived reality. This is not to reaffirm an obvious line of argumentation that concludes who we are online is not who we are in real life, nor to claim the digital world is depriving us of any intrinsic subjectivity. Instead, my argument reflects on how our online persona, freed from the constraints of lived reality, seems able to anonymously enjoy an uncontaminated digital fantasmatic real.

The chapter is founded on Lacan's idea of a divided subject, in which there is a disconnection between who we think we are and the world we appear to live our lives in. It is important to note that Lacan's subject is not the same as the subject of post-structuralism, a subject that is caught up in subjective positions and or historical contexts. Instead, Lacan's subject should be thought of as the void that appears when we take away all such subjectivities when there is nothing left. For Lacan, the subject is the empty space left by subjectivity itself. For my argument, this allows the subject to begin at a zero point, a place from which we are unencumbered by material or immaterial conditions. With this in mind, this chapter offers something of a philosophy of materiality that struggles to coalesce with the digital world.

Many of the interactions we have on the internet are unlike their equivalent in real life: people say things they might not usually say in person and users are able to assume new, untried, or different identities. Thus, in many respects, the digital world stubbornly refuses any meaningful infiltration by our material reality. But what happens when the opposite occurs, when material reality seems to be ruptured by our digital experiences? The central question this chapter addresses is what happens to subjectivity when the framework of lived reality begins to be configured by the immaterial experiences of the digital world. I make no attempt to formulate subjectivity as a singularity or something that can be adequately defined since there is no 'real' self that comes out of these new conditions. Instead, what I hope to indicate is how the configuration of our identities in accordance with changing circumstances can be clearly seen when considering the effects of material and immaterial experiences upon us.

Before the rise of digital technology, most of our immaterial experiences were limited to our thoughts, feelings, memories, and fantasies. They resided inside our minds and had little or no expression outside of ourselves. The prevalence of the digital world has meant that many of these experiences can now be realized and articulated externally. In effect, it has never been easier to construct a fantasy world, located at arm's length and mediated by a screen, keyboard, and mouse. Modernity's traditional practices of memory-making are now transferred to transient and traces of lived experience (Hand 2014: 207). In order to consider these kinds of shifts, I will reflect on how subjectivity and the concepts of materiality and immateriality can be understood through a reading of a range of cultural phenomena such as Apple computers, smartphones, Bitcoin, and the TV drama series *Bosch* (2014–20, USA: Prime Video) and *Suits* (2011–19, USA: Hypnotic & Universal Cable Productions). Implicit in my approach is an analysis of the relationship between what I understand as an immaterial, digital world (in all its various forms) and what are the direct experiences we have of material reality and how one has infiltrated the other. Known for his 'medium is the message', Marshall McLuhan (1964: 8) identified how this infiltration extends the term 'media' to include the ways technological developments enhance existing activities. For McLuhan, any infiltration relates directly to a 'change of scale or pace' (e.g. in how mass transport contributes to developing societies). In other words, the material effects of technology actually contribute to changing things in the lived world (Bollmer 2019: 5). There is, then, something performative about media in how some things materialize as an outcome of what media itself does (Bollmer

2019: 173). But before I consider some of the effects of this, I will briefly outline how I am using the terms materiality and immateriality.

For the purposes of some clarity, what is immaterial in 'media' terms is defined by digital or non-tangible experiences. In a contemporary context, it is generally those experiences which tend to be mediated through screens and computers. Conversely, materiality is understood as all the other experiences which are, in some way, dominated by objects or a certain sensuousness that emerges during most of our encounters with the world or with lived reality. Here, sense is a response to a direct encounter with an object or with reality (although clearly sense itself may be an immaterial or non-tangible experience). Nevertheless, the definitions I am beginning with are the binaries outlined above: interactions with material objects emerge from sense experience (such as touch or feeling) in contrast to the abstracted, immaterial experiences of interacting online. It may be important to state here that I believe the 'real' of the world can only be accessed indirectly and certainly not completely. Therefore, despite materiality being consistently the basis of understanding 'things' across a number of disciplines, it is inevitably a mediated compromise of selected experiences. Even our senses are a mediated form of experience. Therefore, if materiality appears to offer a kind of determination, a crude resolving of objects, then it may also be conceived as being little more than a placeholder which fills in a gap created by ideology. Or to put this in reverse, ideology offers a way of completing a representation of material social totality that is essentially unfinished (Balibar 1994: 173). We could then say that ideas need things to finish them or that things are never fully resolved to us without an idea of what they are. Of course, there are always some difficulties in categorizing things in such a binary way. For instance, as well as looking at or through a screen we can also understand a screen to be an object itself and we are aware of it in a material sense. Similarly, the digital world is more than capable of providing experiences that directly also affect our physical senses. The conclusion must be one of recognizing how difficult, given how we appear to be bound up in material and immaterial experiences, it is to tease them apart. Increasingly, the world seems complicatedly entangled and co-created by things we can materially discern and things which have a more ephemeral quality. It may seem logical to imagine we are experiencing something of 'digital materiality' (Pink et al. 2016) – a digital world infused with things. But could it not be equally a 'material digitality', a material world penetrated by digital experiences? The difference being that a digital world, as I have suggested, remains structured in fantasy even when material things appear within it. However, a material world ruptured by the digital has to contend with a direct confrontation with the form of fantasy.

Clearly, there are issues in attempting to define materiality and immateriality in the way I have outlined above. But I hope this initial characterization can develop into a way we can think more complexly about material and immaterial experiences and how each impact the world or has agency. Over the course of this chapter, it is my ambition to refine the basic understanding of materiality and immateriality outlined above and to have moved analysis beyond a brutal choice of tangible and non-tangible experiences towards the question of their entanglement. The wager, then, is to see whether or not materiality can ever truly be possible without some aspect of immateriality. As our everyday lives slowly shift away from direct material encounters with the world towards more digital and immaterial experiences, it appears to be time to consider in more detail how this arrangement and structuring of the world appears to us.

I will take as my starting point an implied tension resonating between the materiality of the physical world and what we describe as our immaterial experiences in the digital world. If our digital persona can and often does take the form of a changeable, anonymous fantasy, then what impact might this have on who we think we are in the so-called real world? First, I claim our subjectivity never aligns itself fully in these material or immaterial worlds; in truth, we are never entirely comfortable in either. This approach, which draws on Jacques Lacan, broadly understands subjectivity as being shaped by the system of symbols that covers experience and which provides it with some kind of meaning (1991: 40). While there is not sufficient space in this section to explain in detail Lacan's ideas around subjectivity, his chapter 'A materialist definition of the phenomenon of consciousness' (1991: 40–52) provides some useful ways to think about how subjectivity emerges. In essence, Lacan maps out a definition of consciousness in which the materiality of the symbolic world shapes the subject. Readers familiar with Lacan will know how desire is also central to his ideas of subject formation. While I shall address some aspects of fantasy (which is usually linked to desire) with respect to our online experiences, the focus of my analysis is not on the desiring subject but on a subjectivity shaped by a symbolic order. Such subjectivity is considered as being both materially and immaterially determined. Today, what seems most interesting is how subjectivity cannot be understood as emerging *primarily* from encounters with the material world. Instead, it would seem to be constructed from a response to how the immaterial and ephemeral properties of the digital world leak into many of our lived experiences. I argue that subjectivity continuously oscillates between these two generalized positions of experience. It is never fully material or immaterial. Furthermore, it seems that many of our contemporary existential problems stem from a difficulty in reconciling how our subjectivity seems to emerge, not from a defined point, a point we can identify, but within the gap or distance between our material and immaterial experiences. To be clear, this gap is not only the space between the materiality of things and the immateriality of the ephemera that surrounds us but also the distance between ourselves and how we experience the world as it is determined by either of these forms. As I explained in the introduction, Lacan's subject is not historically or contextually contingent. The subject is the place where all the formations of subjectivity are abstracted and removed. However, this is not to suggest that there is a 'self' that is in some way independent of experience, rather it is to recognize the ways in which experience is in some way self-forming or self-altering.

In order to think about material and immaterial things together I have drawn, somewhat, on Graham Harman's (2016: 29) writings around objects, his thinking connected to object-orientated ontology and his definitions of what immaterialism is. I use Harman because, by default, objects seem to be the most obvious manifestation of materiality. It may be helpful to briefly recall Harman's definition of immaterialism as being the antonym for materialism. The aspects I found helpful from Harman are how he suggests that essences are not knowable and, in the same vein, that objects should not be reducible to their qualities or to their function, either. This suggests there are additional aspects to objects that contain a surplus we cannot readily access. This elusive sense of there being something 'more than' the object is an implicit rejection of attempts to deconstruct phenomena down to their component parts. Even when we break things down, there still remains something we cannot express that takes the form of this excess in objects. Harman also argues that what an object *is* becomes more interesting than what it *does*. These points of definition require further examination and they suggest that there is more to formulate about the world around us. Thus, I intend to consider what else defines the essence of an object once we abstract its qualities and its function. While Harman rejects what an object does by focusing on what it is, I consider what it *is* an object *does*. To put this differently, I consider something of the ontology of its purpose. The impossibility of thinking through materiality without also thinking obliquely about things and objects means we cannot ignore object-orientated ontology even though it runs counter to my own thoughts about the emergence of subjectivity. The challenge, then, will be to see if these ideas can ever fit harmoniously together and what that model resembles. I do accept I may have to conveniently omit some of the arguments on both sides of the subject/object discussion, but from a buffet of thought, I will take away what I think seems most desirable at this moment.

We tend to accept the relationship between the materiality of objects we touch and the intangible, untouchable, nature of 'stuff' that appears as part of our immaterial experiences. But over time the term materialism has also increasingly been disconnected from ideas about materials or even objects. Materialism is now often understood through historical accounts, cultural practices, and referring to how things are socially constructed. As a result, objects become defined by what they are made up of. However, such definitions are not only limited to the materials used in the manufacture of objects. It is equally as common to define objects through their cultural history or their context. It can therefore be difficult to understand materialism in opposition to a category of immaterialism since immaterial things can equally be historical, cultural, and socially constructed. How then would it be possible, in any meaningful way, to differentiate these terms? We know that when ordering a computer from Apple we hope to receive an object we can touch and use. However, while its build quality, its price, its capability, and design may all connect it with the brand of its manufacturer, we might still reasonably ask what makes an Apple computer specifically synonymous with Apple the brand? Any answer would seem to place material and immaterial relations together in the computer and link these directly with our idea of what Apple is or should be to us. There is probably no doubt that design is a feature of the Apple product range. In this example, design is the conflation of ideas and materials. But what else is there that makes the computer a computer? Along with all the many electronic components, its glass, metal, and plastic materials, there is also the invisible software, written in computer code, which makes up the operating system and the applications that are installed on it. Additionally, as soon as we connect the computer to the internet we receive and send invisible data packets which fundamentally make the computer do more of the things we needed it to do. Once connected to the internet the computer becomes part of a network, linked to servers, other computers, and other objects. It is as if the computer itself almost disappears as soon as we join the nearest WiFi network. In this case, a metaphysics of relations does not take into account the objects themselves and how they make up the relationships (Harman 2016: 31). And is it not the case that even design seems, at times, to be subservient to the relations the computer enacts? So, it seems we cannot easily differentiate between the materiality of objects, their immaterial essences, and the relationships holding them together. While this is true of things it is, of course, also true of people.

Real and digital worlds entwine in season three of the American police procedural drama series *Bosch* (2014–20). In a season in which watching and being watched resonate together, its first episode, 'The Smog Cutter' (2017), depicts how series lead detective Harry Bosch has, illegally, set up his own surveillance cameras in order to watch the apartment of Ed Gunn. Ever since he was unable to convict him of murder Bosch has been fixated with Gunn. During a scene where Bosch watches images of Gunn's apartment, the batteries begin to stop working in each of his hidden cameras. While he is watching the camera feeds close down via the web, Bosch's daughter Maddie calls out from the kitchen, 'Dad you're on the internet'. Bosch apologetically explains to her he is working and immediately closes his laptop. Maddie Bosch enters the room looking at her mobile phone, and she qualifies her statement by saying, 'No, I mean *you*. You're on the internet'.

MEDIA MATERIALITIES

She shows her father her phone as it plays a video of him in a restaurant. Bosch has been filmed arguing and losing his temper with the district attorney, Richard O'Shea. Bosch explains to his daughter what happened and tells her he should not have lost his temper. Sympathetically, she replies that he was lucky because 'It only got, like, 37 retweets'. His daughter then warns him, 'Literally everything is on camera', to which her father replies, 'Ain't that the truth'. Throughout this episode, there is an implicit tension between Bosch as an observer of criminals and the impact the filming and subsequent sharing of his argument in the restaurant may have on his career. When Bosch is watching his suspect, what he is hoping for is that the surveillance cameras will provide him with the evidence he needs in order to, eventually, make a conviction. However, since the surveillance has not been authorized by the police, whatever evidence it produces could not be used in convicting Gunn. What the cameras provide for Bosch is a fantasy support, a way of helping him see visually a reality he is not legally entitled to see. As the batteries fail and the cameras stop transmitting their images, Bosch's visual fantasy disappears before him. We should read this scene as though, for Bosch, there are multiple forms of reality. Firstly, there is the substantial or material reality in which he is looking at his camera image feeds. At the same time, the digital images from the camera feeds constitute a second, essentially immaterial reality, one that is ephemeral and contingently experienced. In this scene, Bosch is the vector for two simultaneous occurrences of reality – one that can be accounted for phenomenologically, while the other appears to exist virtually.

In setting out a materialist definition of consciousness, Lacan (1991: 45) claims our experiences are determined by our ideas about reality. Crucially, we are not directly aware of these ideas. However, he is not suggesting reality exists and we are somehow unaware that within it there are ideas about it. Lacan's point is how ideas, whether they are explicitly known or not, are themselves reality-forming, and they make up the reality we experience. We can understand the point if we consider the way our everyday lives are impacted by the products and services provided by companies such as Google, Amazon, Facebook, or Apple. Even though we seem to have access to these companies we are more generally unaware of the details of the business decisions that help these companies operate: we do not explicitly know what happens in their planning or strategy meetings and we are largely oblivious to their medium or long-term business goals. In their 2012 IPO, Facebook structured the company with different stocks which allowed Mark Zuckerberg to have control of company voting rights (Zuboff 2019: 72). These kinds of internal corporate decisions do have a direct impact on our lives. Our actions and behaviours are shaped by the effects of global strategies created and implemented by corporations. To return to Bosch, there is no easy way to reconcile his material and immaterial realities, instead he remains caught within an 'illusion of his own consciousness' (Lacan 1991: 45), with both realities having different impacts upon him. Throughout the series, the reality of traditional, procedural policing which Bosch understands is frequently ruptured by an advancing and evolving digital world, happening outside. This world simultaneously enables and unsettles him. Throughout the seasons there are numerous references to Bosch not using a smartphone, a shorthand indicating his unwillingness to embrace technology. But by emphasizing this it also, implicitly, highlights our own relationship and reliance on the digital world and mobile technology. Today, the smartphone represents a digital ever-presence, one that appears to have the capacity to 'intervene and interrupt a conversation, regardless of whether it is answered or looked at' (Hand 2014: 221).

In *Being and Time*, Martin Heidegger (2001: 73) explains how we suddenly become aware of a tool when it breaks and it then moves from being unnoticeable to something that is much more 'conspicuous'. For Heidegger, a tool usually remains unnoticed when it is embedded within part of a larger system. Only when it stops working do we become aware of its phenomenological essence, whereas up until that point it is 'silently relied upon' (Harman 2020: 17). Suddenly at this moment of breaking down, the qualities of the tools we usually rely on are revealed. We see this effect when the batteries in the cameras Bosch is using begin to fail. Bosch becomes acutely aware of the technology as it breaks down in front of him. Seconds later, in the same scene, his daughter shows him the video that has been posted online. I suggest this can be read as a point where material and immaterial experiences become confused; the immaterial experience of remote surveillance is contingent on batteries and individual behaviours and emotions are publicly shared in the virtual space of the internet. In the twenty-first century, digital technology is clearly responsible for changing many processes and experiences. In films and dramas, this shift is sometimes articulated in an unexpected way. In crime series such as *Bosch*, old and traditional methods, with which Harry Bosch is associated, are portrayed as being out of date and far less effective. Technology is often used, seemingly, as a shortcut to solve crimes or as a way to avoid the hard work of traditional policing. Inevitably, given Bosch's age and experience as a detective, there is the underlying message that traditional approaches are more reliable. Of course, this position is common to many dramas and films that incorporate older male protagonists (e.g. the James Bond franchise). What these kinds of narratives promote is a humanistic, innate awareness or instinct that emerges as being more dependable than much technology.

As the technology begins to break down, Bosch is caught in a dilemma of knowing something is happening but also ultimately knowing he is unable to fully see or comprehend it. This struggle of not knowing pervades many of our contemporary digital interactions where we are provided with highly filtered and targeted information. Although on a daily basis, we may be overloaded with lots of different information, what it signals is also a lack of connection with what is actually going on. While on one level social media may have an apparent simple purpose of connecting users or as a medium of social communication, it has become more concerned with the visibility and sociability of its data (Manovich 2009: 320). Data from online platforms is instrumentalized and used as part of a suite of analytic tools that account for things like increased surveillance and the commodification of social life (Langlois et al. 2015: 8). The collection of data serves corporations and tech giants, at the same time it also has the effect of the so-called 'end of forgetting' (Mayer-Schonberger 2009) as lived experiences are documented and stored online. With less distinction between private, public, personal, and collective information our lives become permanently stored and remotely accessible. Furthermore, the data associated with this is always in a state of reconfiguration as it becomes continually subjected to algorithmic re-classification. It has become impossible to know exactly where anything is located, instead computers, servers, and the various accounts we connect to organize our digital consciousness.

For Lacan (1991: 46), consciousness is linked to our awareness of an experience such that we cannot grasp a situation without also being aware of our own consciousness. This is to say, our awareness of what is happening requires us to be aware of the process through which the situation is being grasped. In effect, we cannot experience anything without an awareness of ourselves being in that same experience. It is possible to make a link between immaterial thought and materiality through this. If we cannot be objective observers of a reality that we are able to look at from the outside, then we must always be included within the reality we are looking at and experiencing. Crucially, when experiencing reality, we must take into account what seems to be missing. For materialism to do this, it must also contain or indicate a sense of the immaterial. In other words, in order to understand materiality, we have to incorporate something of our own immaterial presence within it. Furthermore, while the phenomenological world we experience contains us within it, as observers, we are unable to ever directly see ourselves as we appear in the world. Instead, embedded within our field of view is an obscured space or blind spot, which signifies our own inclusion in the reality we see (Žižek 2006: 17). I claim, this indication of our own immaterial presence runs through any thinking associated with materiality.

Being included within the reality we see means not only are we subjects making our own reality but we are also subjects who are made by the very same reality. Therefore, what links our abstract, immaterial thought and what we can understand as material experiences is how we are never looking at reality from any outside, objective, position but nor are we simply objects positioned within that same reality. We can see something of this effect in the American legal drama *Suits*

(2011–19). Throughout its nine seasons, the principal characters often quote lines from movies and from other TV series to each other. In season three episode four, the *Suits* characters Mike Ross and Katrina Bennett make a direct reference to the American police procedural drama *The Wire* (2002–08). The scene in *Suits* is a combination of what is often referred to as *The Wire*'s notorious five-minute 'fuck' scene (blended with another reference to the way in which *The Wire* character Clay Davis says the word 'sheeeeit'). The five-minute 'fuck' scene exchange happens in *The Wire* between actors Wendell Pierce and Dominic West. The Lacanian twist occurs in *Suits* when a recurring character, Robert Zane, also played by Wendell Pierce, makes a dialogue reference to the other character that he plays in *The Wire*. What we experience is a reflexive action where actors in one drama expose an awareness of themselves as actors in other series and speak the dialogue of actors from other dramas who happen to also be acting in their own drama. It is this dialogue which indicates to us the Lacanian 'blind spot', the inclusion of ourselves in the reality we are experiencing. We allow ourselves to be, momentarily, reminded of we are watching a drama and that we are a necessary part of its unfolding.

In 'A materialist definition of the phenomenon of consciousness', Lacan (1991: 40–52) describes how subjectivity is not about defining ourselves individually and is not a result of our egos. Instead, for Lacan, subjectivity comes from the direct relation we have to the symbolic world. His argument is that subjectivity is created, not by our past lived experiences or by our close relationships with our friends or parents, but by the way we assume our own symbolic identity. This symbolic identity, shaped by an external world of images (or to be precise the surfaces that produce images), is central to Lacan's materialist definition of consciousness. In this chapter, Lacan considers what happens when we look into a mirror. He explains how reality is apparently relocated onto the plain of the mirror, and what we then see is not the real objects around us but an image of them reflected back in the mirror's surface. The crucial point is that it is only possible to see what we see because of our consciousness, because of our own awareness, this is what he describes as the 'phenomenon of consciousness' (Lacan 1991: 46). As a way of explaining this, Lacan suggests a scenario in which human life no longer exists on the earth. He asks, what would happen if there were no living things left to witness or see any images? He describes how cameras may record images while there are no humans on the planet and how later, humans might return to the world and would then be able to see the images the cameras made. Lacan's scenario blends aspects of the storyline of *Oblivion* (Kosinski 2017) (where humanity is forced to relocate to a new planet) with a Schrödinger's cat thought experiment. But in it, there are three points worth exploring that connect subjectivity to the symbolic world. Firstly, he proposes that an image can be understood as a point of consciousness, moreover images are a consciousness that has no ego. For Lacan (1991: 41), the ego is the 'sum of the prejudices' which make up our individual knowledge. What he is suggesting is a way to think about consciousness as an organizing centre of experience, in a similar way to how images might organize the visual world. He argues it is the ego and not consciousness that makes all humans think they are situated at the centre of the world. What consciousness does is engender a tension with the ego. In effect, the ego is the way we individually parse knowledge. It is an illusion of consciousness that brings about our anthropomorphism and with it the centring of a human perspective on all things. This illusion of our own importance is instigated by our ego. What this results in is a constant mediation of our experiences through ourselves. The second point Lacan makes is about how images provide continuity. They are made and remain regardless of whether anyone looks at them. He describes photographing the world, without anyone being present, as being a 'phenomena of consciousness' (1991: 41). In other words, if we take away any ego then we are left with just consciousness. By taking images without the presence of any humans, cameras function without any intervention of the ego. They are a form of consciousness which is completely unaware of their own presence, and as such they are unable to take account of themselves within their experience. Third, Lacan sets out how the symbolic world is actually a world of machines and by this he means it is a world that has no ego. The materialist subjectivity Lacan is describing is one where neither consciousness nor ego can be located or ever understood. Instead, the materiality of subjectivity comes from a subject shaped by a symbolic order rather than from their ego or their consciousness.

One obvious way digitally immateriality leaks into our day-to-day routines is in the operating systems of the computers and devices we use. User interfaces often deploy anthropomorphic designs which are based on a pseudo or symbolic materialism. Icons and buttons are designed to look as though they resemble something that can be physically clicked, windows have fake shadows, and screen objects are rendered with reflections. What we see on screen alludes to a material existence it does not actually have. In interface terms, this method of designing bridges a gap between material experience and digital immateriality. Although the central function of images is to fill a gap that separates us from the familiar world of objects we can touch (Žižek 2006: 196), there is a more complex relationship that digital images have with data. At some level, digital images are themselves a form of interpreted data, our interactions with images, the ones we swipe, like, or react to all contribute towards a data picture of ourselves. If, as Lacan suggests, the external symbolic world shapes our subjectivity, then what can now be said about how our digital devices are externalizing our actions and registering them outside of ourselves? Today, the symbolic order cannot be limited to the world of visual representation, a world of image. It is clear that abstract data also constructs complex interconnected pictures of who we are. And along with images, this data is always available for permanent and continuous scrutiny (Žižek 2018: 47), which then regulates and controls us. Anyone who owns a fitness monitor will understand how these devices monitor and set targets for us to be active: they literally control how much exercise we take. Combined with tracking our coordinates through GPS, movement is not just monitored but also choreographed on daily basis with constant demands to take more steps. In a similar way to how we try to control our emotions with chemicals and drugs, such as anti-depressants and hormone replacement therapies, we are also involved in controlling our online presence. Since the level of control we are given is limited what we are actually doing is distracting ourselves, while the primary purpose of our activity is to provide a data imprint of our lives for the companies who host the services we are using.

The immaterial nature of a virtual economy brings another problem, specifically in relation to digital currencies like Bitcoin or services which are entirely online and may be rented rather than owned such as music streaming. The advent of adopting virtual money and goods forces us to rethink the Marxist concept of commodity fetishism since this notion is based on there being a solid object (Žižek 2018: 18). Our relationship with the virtual reverses the correlation between objects and ideas, between the material and immaterial. Now 'objects are progressively dissolved in fluid experiences, while the only stable things are virtual symbolic obligations' (Žižek 2018: 18). As the digital world is integrated and embedded into life, its main role is one of mediating social experience. All we are left with is the regular impulse to check in and see what is happening in this immaterial space.

Somewhere in the mix of material and immaterial realities the sense of an individual self has become confused. Identity is clearly constituted from material and immaterial qualities. We know that in the virtual world there are almost no barriers to adopting different identities, yet at the same time there is also something homogenized about how our unregulated online selves are constructed. It seems that rather than providing a place where we can be free of our ideological identity, the internet imposes an even stronger ideological control over us. What sustains ideology is always, in some way, virtual or immaterial in how it operates. Returning to Bosch and the clip that only received only 37 retweets; as soon as it is uploaded the clip joins the millions of other clips of people getting angry that are distributed, shared, and exchanged on a daily basis. This universalizing of our behaviour has the effect of creating a subjectivity devoid of its particularities. At the same time, our immaterial experiences also seem to contain a fictional element to them. Online we can construct whoever it is we decide to be. But who we are online is never totally who we are, as it removes most of the material inequalities that gradate our lives. While we may recognize how repetitive and similar our responses are to the online environment, we continue to interact as if we are able to distinguish ourselves from everyone else. Our immaterial sense of ideology is not a false consciousness, where we are unaware of its influence over us. Instead, we are completely aware of the ideological potency of the virtual world. We upload, share, and comment knowingly and as a symptom of how we are immobilized by the network we are connected to. Fundamentally, the immaterial nature of the digital world seems structured in a materially true manner. We accept it as appearing to be constituted as though it were materially 'there'.

In some sense, what is important is not whether something is true or not, but how we act in relation to it. Even if something is not true, as long as we still act as if we believe it to be true then it will, nevertheless, still function in a truthful way. For Marx, materialism is connected to how ideology permeates and influences the processes of social reproduction, of the perpetuation of our social structures. But this omits how ideology is actualized in the organizations and institutions through their practices and rituals. The emancipatory potential for Bosch's subjectivity is in how he did not realize he would be filmed and how he has no desire to measure the metrics of the limited social reach of 37 retweets. Bosch seems firmly on the outside of the immaterial structures of the internet. Modernity as a period has been defined by increasing degrees of personal freedom as it attempts to establish terms for a less unequal and fairer society. In this quest for freedom, there has been limited attention to wider universal freedoms and a much greater stress on personal or individual freedoms. This formula meant there is, inevitably, less appetite to achieve universal emancipation for everyone and more attention on the particularity of individual identity and the rights they should contain (McGowan 2020). If an immaterial freedom has the effect of feeling exactly like freedom, then it should be understood as only the appearance of freedom. Today, freedom is structured to ensure we accept new and often imperfect conditions. As Frank Ruda (2016: 1) describes, the offer of temporary employment contracts is presented as the freedom to explore other job opportunities. Freedom has now become 'a signifier of disorientation' (Ruda 2016: 2), and the freedom to choose is experienced as having a choice; nevertheless, we then become indifferent to actually making a choice. Zuboff (2019: 29) maps a trajectory of modernity that has two distinct forms, although both track different senses of the individual. For Zuboff, consumers of Ford Motor vehicles are understood to be part of a first modernity, while those who buy iPods and iPhones belong to a second modernity or even third modernity. This transition of modernity is one of evolving individuals who move beyond predefined roles and identities established from groups to being individuals who wish to exercise control over their own lives. Bosch seems to have obtained individual freedom because he does not belong in this second modernity nor does he conform to its expectations. Yet, he is also caught within its mechanisms. If, as Harman (2016) might wish, we think about what immaterial structures of the internet actually are rather than what they do, we would struggle to articulate anything really helpful. I suggest, then, what is needed is a way to understand how the immaterial phenomena we encounter are materially constituted.

In psychoanalysis, all things are important, everything no matter how apparently insignificant deserve to be analyzed and should be taken into account (Ruda 2016: 132). All details, no matter how they are constituted (as slips of the tongue or fragments of dreams, etc.) are all understood 'in their material constitution' (Ruda 2016: 134). This means even immaterial thoughts assume a material importance as everything becomes an object to be analyzed, reflected upon, and considered. Psychoanalysis is nothing if it is not a process of materializing the gaps, ruptures, and absences in experience. These ephemeral occurrences, usually missed or overlooked in day-to-day lived experience, are understood as material objects to which a rational analysis can then be applied. Ruda (2016: 136) identifies the objects of analysis as taking on a kind of 'immaterial materiality'. But it is material immateriality that best describes how our experiences are now constructed. The question I framed at the beginning of this chapter considered what happens when the material reality is ruptured by our digital experiences? My suggestion is that we find ourselves in material immateriality. Running alongside this response is also the sense that material immateriality ushers in a distinctively different subjectivity.

Part of the new subjectivity that emerges within material immateriality can be seen in how our bodies are reconfigured. As lived reality continues to be shaped by the immaterial experiences of the digital world our bodies have become increasingly restrained. We may move but only if we take our devices along with us. In support of this, digital immateriality is constituted by de-materialized social relations and their production of data. While the means to produce, distribute, and disseminate is disaggregated and given over to users what surfaces is a false sense of ownership of the intrinsic means of production. We install applications on our devices and browse the internet from our homes. Yet the real mechanisms of production are situated on the servers and in the computer algorithms that orchestrate our interactions, and at all times we are expected to remain connected. Paradoxically, even though our bodies are no longer visible in the same way we continue to be encouraged to enhance ourselves by joining the gym, with Botox beauty treatments, implants, or procedures like laser eye surgery (Žižek 2008: 172). It is as if we are expected to reshape our bodies even though we know we are becoming increasingly invisible to each other. This then is the basic contradiction; material immateriality needs to always maintain appearance despite the disappearance of substance. This shifting of our bodies forms part of how we are expected to work more flexibly and how we are now encouraged to acknowledge more fluid identities.

It is clear that terms like fluidity and flexibility are used across different contexts to describe our current social conditions or the strategies needed to adapt to them. These descriptors, along with the continual repositioning of phenomena are a feature of capital and define how new issues and crises continually appear and in themselves enable the evolution of capital (Harvey 2010: 117). In recent decades, we experienced the financial crisis of 2008, the 'dot com' bubble, global terrorism and a global pandemic. In the context of subjectivity, we confront a crisis of our identity, not because identity has suddenly become increasingly fluid and flexible but because we have only recently become aware of that its inherent instability is the feature that defines it. There is probably no one less fluid or flexible than Bosch operating as he does as a kind of buffer to the changes around him. Despite resisting it, he embodies a subjective loneliness in his reactions to the digital world. For many people, the paradox is that at a time when we are most connected there remains a pervading sense of alone-ness. No matter how connected we are, we remain in the same space looking at the same screen even though our computer links across a network covering the entire globe. Screens provide the ultimate local-ization of all external experiences, where the world is brought to us, on our desks, and in our rooms. Through his surveillance cameras, Bosch was allowed to watch over the criminal he wanted to convict. For a moment, he was free to see anything he wanted to see but the material reality of failing batteries meant his immaterial fantasy would have to end. When his daughter confronted him with the video, the situation is reversed, and Bosch's own day-to-day experience becomes mediated and redefined by the digital domain. Today, it is not uncommon for so-called viral videos to result in a call from social media for those portrayed to lose their jobs. Certainly, such videos can cause significant reputational damage. How then can we think about material immateriality?

Material immateriality cannot be reduced to its qualities or its function; it is undoubtedly more slippery than either of these. Of course, if we cannot under-stand what it is, then we will inevitably try to understand what it does. If material immateriality ushers in a very different mode of subjectivity, then I suggest *how* it does it gives us inroads into understanding what it is. The *how* question could be addressed by its limitations and inconsistencies. As Lacan might express it, when we reach the limits of the material world all we then experience is its immaterial counterpart. When the Lacanian subject is unknowable, it is not because it has no material form, but because it is in some way absent from its own presence. As we consider the details of experience, we will eventually come up against a formal inconsistency, such as when Bosch illegally watches others and is also himself unknowingly watched. At the level of a subjectivity emerging from material imma-teriality, we should consider whether it is ever reasonable to be reducing ourselves to retweets, likes, or follows. The freedom to be anything online provides an immaterial freedom that leads us to imagine ourselves as being neither materially present nor fully cognisant of the entirety of something like the internet. At some point, all we can hope for is that we make some meaningful and useful interventions as we grapple with the material immateriality of our experience. Perhaps then, what Maddie Bosch really meant to say to her father was: 'No, I mean *you*. You are the internet'.

REFERENCES

Balibar, Étienne (1994), *Politics and Truth: The Vacillation of Ideology*, New York: Routledge.

Bollmer, Grant (2019), *Materialist Media Theory*, London: Bloomsbury.

Bosch (2014–20, USA: Amazon Studios and Fabrik Entertainment).

Delaney, Brigid (2019), 'It's the era of the Twitter pile-on. Isn't there something healthier we can do with our rage?', *The Guardian*, 19 November, https://www.theguardian.com/media/2019/nov/19/its-the-era-of-the-twitter-pile-on-isnt-there-something-healthier-we-can-do-with-our-rage. Accessed 4 July 2023.

Hand, Martin (2014), 'Digitization and memory: Researching practices of adaption to visual and textual data in everyday life', *Big Data? Qualitative Approaches to Digital Research*, 13, pp. 205–27

Harman, Graham (2016), *Immaterialism: Objects and Social Theory*, Cambridge: Polity Press.

Harman, Graham (2020), *Art and Objects*, Cambridge: Polity Press.

Harvey, David (2010), *The Enigma of Capital*, London: Profile Books Ltd.

Heidegger, Martin (2001), *Being and Time*, Oxford: Blackwell Publishers Ltd.

Kosinski, Joseph (2017), *Oblivion*, USA: Universal Pictures.

Lacan, Jacques (1991), *The Seminar of Jacques Lacan, Book II: The Ego in Freud's Theory and in the Technique of Psychoanalysis 1954–1955* (ed. J. A. Miller, trans. S. Tomaselli), New York: Norton & Company, Inc.

Langlois, Ganaele, Redden, Joanna, and Elmer, Greg (eds) (2015), *Compromised Data from Social Media to Big Data*, London: Bloomsbury.

Manovich, Lev (2009), 'The practice of everyday (media) life: From mass consumption to mass cultural production?', *Critical Inquiry*, 35:2, pp. 319–31.

Mayer-Schonberger, Viktor (2009), *Delete: The Virtue of Forgetting in the Digital Age*, Princeton: Princeton University Press.

McLuhan, Marshall (1964), *Understanding Media: The Extensions of Man*, Cambridge: MIT Press.

McGowan, Todd (2020), *Universality and Identity Politics*, New York: Columbia University Press.

Pink, Sarah, Ardèvol, Elisenda, and Lanzeni, Débora (eds) (2016), *Digital Materialities: Design and Anthropology*, London: Bloomsbury.

Ruda, Frank (2016), *Abolishing Freedom*, Lincoln: University of Nebraska Press.

Suits (2011–19, USA: Hypnotic & Universal Cable Productions).

'The Smog Cutter' (2017), A. Davidson (dir.), *Bosch*, Season 3 Episode 1, 21 April, USA: Prime Video.

The Wire (2002–08, USA: Blown Deadlien Productions and HBO Entertainment).

Žižek, Slavoj (2006), *The Parallax View*, Cambridge: MIT Press.

Žižek, Slavoj (2008), *The Plague of Fantasies*, London: Verso.

Žižek, Slavoj (2018), *Like a Thief in Broad Daylight*, London: Penguin.

Zuboff, Shoshana (2019), *The Age of Surveillance Capitalism*, New York: Hatchette Book Group.

Conclusion:
Shifting Horizons of Possibility

Susanna Paasonen

When I was a sharply green first year student of film and television, an art school friend of mine told of her teacher, an award-winning animation filmmaker who had once been part of Andrey Tarkovsky's crew, explaining that the reason that this renown auteur used so much silence in his work – think *Stalker* – owed to his privileged access to Kodak film. Being able to use imported Western rather than Soviet film stock, it was explained, Tarkovsky did not need to fill up his soundtracks in order to distract the audience from unwanted noise: this possibility then opened up the possibility to think of the sonics otherwise.

Many have since snorted at this anecdote, labelling it an urban myth disrespectful of artistic vision. For some three decades now, I have nevertheless wondered, 'why not'? If technology presents a material, ever-shifting horizon of possibility for what can or cannot be done at any given point in time, as is fairly standard a view in media studies, how would not such techno-material horizons directly impact the aesthetic choices made? And, furthermore, why should the ability to consider available forms of expression in tandem with the technological tools at hand eat away at the value of the work produced? Is this not a standard issue of professional skill? And is not film history the stuff of such shifting technological horizons – from film formats, sound and colour to transformations in camera technology from the fixed to the very much portable, or from analogue to digital post-production practices, special effect techniques, storage and distribution formats?

It is not a controversial claim to make that materiality has always been key to media, whether this be the case of production practices (not limited to Tarkovsky's), storage, retail and distribution formats, networks and platforms, or the cultures of consumption, from the mundane-casual to the aficionado-committed. As the chapters in this book illustrate with great nuance and contextual care, media becomes perceivable – and in this sense materialises (Paasonen 2011: 100–05) – through objects that are both mass-produced and unique in how we relate to them. We live with devices and media objects marked by signs of their use so that the abstract question of form versus content fails to operate as a binary in how we make sense of the mediated everyday. To deploy analytical insights from science and technology studies, and from actor-network theory in particular, as nonhuman actors, media devices and media objects impact that which we can record, depict, revisit and do, and how. This was the case with the qualities of film stock that Tarkovsky could operate with, just as it is the case with aspiring TikTok influencers and the videos they can craft, or with the mediated forms of remembrance that are available through slides, digital files, 8mm films, or VHS tapes dependent on the necessary playback devices (that one may or may not have access to).

Media Materialities makes strikingly clear the gap that exists between haptic interactions with media and the relatively lukewarm interest with which questions of materiality have generally been received in media studies to date. This gap, which this book sets out to bridge, presents nothing less than a paradox in terms of understanding lives lived in and transformations occurring in mundane media environments: in how music is made and listened to, in what kinds of games we have played and continue to play, or in the importance of the technologies of writing and reading to how we focus, think and make sense of the world. As Eve Kosofsky Sedgwick (2003: 17–19) points out, the term 'feeling' entails the sense of proximity, contact and touch so that the haptic and the affective come entangled. Following this line of thought, media formats and devices need to be thought of not merely in terms of what they store or mediate but also in terms of how this happens: a swipe on the smart phone's streaming playlist; the press of 'play' button on a cassette player; the careful placement of a record needle on an LP and the personal histories involving the devices, tapes and records. Listening to a Sex Pistols track on Spotify may not sound too different to listening the same song on a C-tape bootlegged as a teenager. But does it feel the same, or matter in the same way?

The relatively scarce interest towards such material attachments presents a paradox also given the importance of technology within both historical and contemporary media research, and the extent to which any historical research is directly dependent on storage formats and archival access that directly impact, and even condition the forms of analytical inquiry available. This is not to say that such interests do not exist – considering, for example, strands of media ecology and media archaeology, studies of media collecting, the field of platform studies and, of course, the width of scholarship both cited in and developed in the edited collection at hand (see also Bogost and Montfort 2007; Parikka 2012; Gillespie, Boczkowski and Foot 2014). Some scholarship on media formats and platforms has in fact turned the emphasis on content over form inside-out, or upside-down.

CONCLUSION

For media theorist Friedrich Kittler (1999: xl), for example, what 'remains of people is what media can store and communicate'. Furthermore, what 'counts are not the messages or the content with which they equip so-called souls for the duration of a technological era, but rather ... their circuits, the very schematism of perceptibility' (Kittler 1999: xl–xli). Kittler's argument is for the primacy of media and storage formats over that which is being mediated, and what one might subsequently make sense of.

To make an argument for the centrality of materialities in media research however by no means necessitates such prioritisation or boundary work between that which is considered essential or trivial. Rather, a focus on media's materialities as issues of infrastructure, manufacture and production, transmission, consumption and archiving helps make evident the possibilities and constraints that exist in any given time and place. It also makes it possible to expand reflections on the fundamental 'worldliness' of cultural inquiry from semiotic messiness to the material – plastic, metal, carnal, pulpy – mess that makes the mediated everyday (Hall 1992). This further helps in mapping out the ecological toll of this everyday – a quest that has grown increasingly acute with the energy demands of server farms and the extraction of natural resources necessary for the manufacture of devices in our so-called 'immaterial' digital culture. Here, the foci of media ecology extends beyond mundane environments and object-worlds to the circuits of production and waste preceding and following our lives with media devices (Jucan et al. 2019).

There is nothing simple to the questions of how materiality matters, how media matters, how media materializes or, indeed, to how the materialities of media matter. Yet none of this is trivial. What was the case again for that Sex Pistols C-tape?

REFERENCES

Bogost, Ian and Montfort, Nick (2007), 'New media as material constraint: An introduction to platform studies', *Electronic Techtonics: Thinking at the Interface. Proceedings of the First International HASTAC Conference*, pp. 176–93.

Gillespie, Tarleton, Boczkowski, Pablo. J. and Foot, Kirsten A. (eds) (2014), *Media Technologies: Essays on Communication, Materiality, and Society*, Cambridge, MA: The MIT Press.

Hall, Stuart (1992), 'Cultural studies and its theoretical legacies', in L. Grossberg (ed.), *Cultural Studies: A Reader*, London: Routledge, pp. 277–86.

Jucan, Ioana B., Parikka, Jussi, and Schneider, Rebecca (2019), *Remain*, Minneapolis: University of Minnesota Press.

Kittler, Friedrich (1999), *Gramophone, Film, Typewriter* (trans. G. Winthorp-Young and M. Wutz), Stanford: Stanford University Press.

Paasonen, Susanna (2011), *Carnal Resonance: Affect and Online Pornography*, Cambridge, MA: The MIT Press.

Parikka, Jussi (2012), *What Is Media Archaeology*, Cambridge: Polity Press.

Sedgwick, Eve Kosofsky (2003), *Touching Feeling: Affect, Pedagogy, Performativity*, Durham: Duke University Press.

Contributors

YEMISI AKINBOBOLA is a senior lecturer at the Birmingham Institute of Media and English, and an associate director of research at the Birmingham Centre for Media and Cultural Research, Birmingham City University. Her research is focused on the intersections of media development, women's rights, and African feminism. Yemisi is an award-winning journalist and co-founder of African Women in the Media (AWiM), an international NGO that aims to create enabling environments for African women working in media industries.

* * * * *

OLIVER CARTER is a reader in creative economies at the Birmingham Centre for Media and Cultural Research, Birmingham City University. His research focuses on alternative economies of cultural production; informal forms of industry that are often removed from a formal cultural industries discourse. His research into Britain's pornography business has informed the award-winning documentary series *Sexposed* as well as the second episode of the 2021 BBC series *Bent Coppers: Crossing the Line of Duty*. His latest monograph *Under the Counter: Britain's Illicit Trade in Hardcore Pornographic 8mm Films* was published in 2023.

* * * * *

RACHEL-ANN CHARLES is a lecturer in media and communication and the BA (Hons) Journalism Deputy Course Director at Birmingham Institute of Media and English. She lectures across undergraduate courses within the School of Media at Birmingham City University. As a member of the Birmingham Centre for Media and Cultural Research (BCMCR), she has made contributions to the study of social action community media within a Trinidad and Tobago context. She is currently exploring the practice of podcasting within the Caribbean Diaspora community.

* * * * *

HARRISON CHARLES is currently a Ph.D. researcher conducting his doctoral study at Birmingham City University. His project is exploring the genre of gay adult video games and the concept of sexual play, considering to what extent these games structure sexual agency and sexual conducts, focusing on queer player perspectives. His research engages with discourses surrounding the explicit constructions of sex and sexual content in games, queer sexual representation, queer gaming cultures, sexual scripting, gay pornography, and the use of autoethnographic approaches in conducting research.

* * * * *

SAM COLEY is an associate professor for the Institute of Media and English at Birmingham City University, where he teaches a range of audio production modules. His book *Music Documentaries for Radio*, published in 2021, explores how the genre has developed technically and editorially and provides an overview of practical production processes. Coley has produced several radio documentaries and presented conference papers about the musicians Prince and David Bowie. He continues to work as a freelance radio documentary producer and has served as a Grand Jury member of the New York Radio Festival since 2012.

* * * * *

MARTIN COX completed his doctoral studies at the Birmingham Centre for Media and Cultural Research, Birmingham City University in 2023. He has twenty years' experience of working in the cultural sector as an artistic director, creative producer, programmer, and artist. His research explores alternative resourcing models for arts activity in urban environments, critically examining the effects of cultural mediation on practice and outcomes.

* * * * *

KIRSTEN FORKERT is a professor of cultural studies at the Birmingham Centre for Media and Cultural Research, Birmingham City University. She is the author of *Artistic Lives* (2013) and *Austerity as Public Mood* (2017), and co-author of *Go Home? The Politics of Immigration Controversies* (2017). Kirsten was a Principal Investigator on the AHRC-funded *Conflict, Memory, Displacement* project (2016–17), and a book based on this research entitled *How Media and Conflict Make Migrants* was published by Manchester University Press in 2020. Kirsten is a member of the *Soundings* editorial collective.

* * * * *

CONTRIBUTORS

NICHOLAS GEBHARDT is a professor of jazz and popular music studies at Birmingham City University. His publications include *Going for Jazz: Musical Practices and American Ideology* and *Vaudeville Melodies: Popular Musicians and Mass Entertainment in American Culture, 1870–1929*. He is the co-editor of *The Cultural Politics of Jazz Collectives* and *The Routledge Companion to Jazz Studies*, and also co-edits the Routledge book series *Transnational Studies in Jazz* with his BCU colleague Tony Whyton.

* * * * *

LEE GRIFFITHS is a doctoral researcher at the Birmingham Centre for Media and Cultural Research, Birmingham City University. His current research explores the relationship between music and words in contemporary jazz practice. Lee is also a saxophonist and promoter who is actively involved in the improvised music scene in the West Midlands.

* * * * *

MATT GRIMES is a senior lecturer in music industries and radio at the Birmingham School of Media. Matt's research and research interests include anarcho-punk and DiY punk scenes; ageing within popular music scenes; popular music memory and nostalgia; DiY music cultures/subcultures and scenes; and music industries entrepreneurship. Matt has several publications in those research fields and has a forthcoming edited collection titled *Punk, Ageing and Time* published through Palgrave Macmillan in winter 2023. Matt is the general secretary of the Punk Scholars Network and is an associate editor for The Punk Scholars Press and *Punk and Post-Punk* journal.

* * * * *

JOHN HILLMAN is an associate professor and head of film, media, and english at the University of West London. He is an educator, writer, and practitioner. His interests lie in philosophical approaches to contemporary culture and understanding how images and media technologies shape our experience. His research is interdisciplinary in form and covers the social, political, and philosophical dimensions of contemporary experience. What unifies his interests is the exploration of how theory can enrich and offer new insights into creative practice and lived experience. His approach is distinctive in its foregrounding of theoretical ideas and in how it attempts, not to explain phenomena through theory, but to elucidate theory as it appears within contemporary culture.

* * * * *

VANESSA JACKSON is an associate professor in enterprise and employability at the Birmingham Institute of Media and English at Birmingham City University. She is a television practitioner with a wide range of production experience at the series producer level, including constructed and observational documentaries, lifestyle and makeover shows, magazine shows, and live studio and outside broadcasts. Vanessa completed her practice-based Ph.D. at Royal Holloway in 2018, exploring how multimedia online platforms provide new opportunities for historiography. Her work focused on how to create purposeful online histories of television production.

* * * * *

CHRIS MAPP is a bass-playing improviser who completed his doctoral studies at the Royal Birmingham Conservatoire, Birmingham City University in 2022. His practice and research focuses on the use of electronics in improvised music.

* * * * *

CHRISTIAN MÖRKEN worked in the German music and publishing industry before he completed his doctoral studies at the Birmingham Centre for Media and Cultural Research, Birmingham City University in 2022. His research focuses on the cultural value of the printed book in the age of digitization, looking at how producers of books (authors and publishers), consumers of books (readers), and intermediaries (booksellers) value the book in the digital age.

* * * * *

SUSANNA PAASONEN is professor of media studies at University of Turku, Finland. With an interest in studies of sexuality, media and affect, she is most recently the author of *Dependent, Distracted, Bored: Affective Formations in Networked Media* (MITP 2021), *Technopharmacology* (with Joshua Neves, Aleena Chia and Ravi Sundaram, Minnesota/Meson 2022) and *Yul Brynner: Exoticism, Cosmopolitanism and Screen Masculinity* (Edinburgh UP, 2023).

* * * * *

KAREN PATEL is an AHRC Leadership Fellow based at the Birmingham Centre for Media and Cultural Research, Birmingham School of Media. Her current research focuses on diversity and expertise development in the contemporary craft economy, in collaboration with Crafts Council UK. She is particularly interested in issues around diversity and inequalities in craft work and the wider creative industries. Her previous work with Crafts Council UK looked at how social media platforms could support diversity in the craft economy.

* * * * *

DIMA SABER is an independent researcher. Her research is focused on media depictions of conflict in post-war and post-revolution contexts, and on the role of archival records in identity-building processes. She is responsible for leading and delivering projects in citizen journalism in the North Africa Western Asia region (NAWA), exploring ways digital literacy can foster social impact and enhance the work of political activists in post-revolution and conflict countries such as Lebanon, Egypt, Syria, Yemen, and Palestine.

* * * * *

REGINA SEIWALD is the German subject lead in languages for all at the Department of Modern Languages, University of Birmingham. Regina's research interest lies in video game studies as well as literary theory and narratology in English and German literature. In her Ph.D. thesis, she researched metafiction in the postmodern British novel based on a comparative analysis of English-speaking and German-speaking theories of narratology. During her three-year post-doctoral fellowship at Birmingham City University, she studied the textuality of video games and Cold War narratives in games.

* * * * *

E. CHARLOTTE STEVENS is a lecturer in media and communication at Birmingham City University. She earned her Ph.D. in film & television studies at the University of Warwick (2015), and her thesis monograph, *Fanvids*, was published by Amsterdam University Press (2020). She has published articles in *Transformative Works and Cultures*, *Alphaville*, and *Feminist Media Studies*, as well as chapters about vidding, video game fans, historical precedents of binge-watching, and representations of archaeology in Chinese dramas.

* * * * *

IAIN A. TAYLOR is a senior lecturer in music and programme leader for BA Commercial Music at University of the West of Scotland. His research is concerned with the changing materialities of music forms, formats, and spaces. Iain is the co-managing editor and lead designer of *Riffs: Experimental Writing on Popular Music*, a peer-reviewed interdisciplinary journal which provides a space for experimental ways of thinking and writing about popular music research. Prior to entering academia, Iain worked variously in events marketing and PR, music tuition, and as a multi-instrumentalist musician.

* * * * *

TIM WALL is a professor of radio and popular music studies at the Birmingham Centre for Media and Cultural Research, Birmingham City University. His books have become widely used in universities across the world. He is an AHRC Strategic Peer Reviewer, a Trustee of the National Jazz Archive, and a member of the editorial boards for *Radio Journal*, *Jazz Research Journal*, and *Popular Music Matters*. His co-edited book, *The Northern Soul Scene*, was recently published by Equinox, and he is currently writing the history of *Jazz on BBC Radio from 1922 to 1972* for Equinox, and co-editing a book *Rethinking Miles Davis* for OUP.

* * * * *

ALEX WADE is a senior research fellow at Birmingham City University. Trained as a sociologist he has written widely on media histories, mental health, young people, and media and French social theory. He was Chair of the Histories of Games Conference Committee (2018–22) and is Work Group 1 Lead for the Co-operation on Science and Technology project 'Grassroots of Digital Europe' (2022–26).

* * * * *

NICK WEBBER is an associate professor in media, and director of the Birmingham Centre for Media and Cultural Research, at Birmingham City University, UK. He is co-convenor of the Historical Games Network and his research focuses on (video)games, cultural history, and identity. His recent work explores the historical practices of player and fan communities, the impact of games and virtual worlds on our understanding of the past, and the relationship between national cultural policy and video games.

* * * * *

HILARY WESTON JONES is a lecturer in professional and academic development at the Birmingham Institute of Media and English, Birmingham City University.

CONTRIBUTORS

Hilary specializes in embedding employability within modules across all years and supporting students with securing work placements. Having spent 24 years working as a television production manager (BBC and Independents), Hilary teaches and mentors students within this area.

* * * * *

ADAM WHITTAKER is the Head of Pedagogy at Royal Birmingham Conservatoire, Birmingham City University. He researches music education and musicology and has been involved in research projects examining traditions of exemplarity in medieval and Renaissance musical theory, the reception history of early music, and music education in the modern world. He is interested in the ways in which musical pedagogies have changed over time, and what these changes can tell us about our current pedagogical approaches. He co-edited *Recomposing the Past: Representations of Early Music on Stage and Screen* (2018) and was a co-investigator on an AHRC network exploring the representation of/in classical music.

* * * * *

PHILLIP YOUNG is a senior lecturer in media studies at the Birmingham School of Media, Birmingham City University. Before moving into academia he was an award-winning journalist and owner of a successful PR agency. Philip has been investigating the impact of social media on PR theory and practice since 2005, as a lead researcher on the pioneering EuroBlog project and then as project leader for NEMO: New Media, Modern Democracy at Lund. He co-authored *Online Public Relations* and contributed to *The Public Relations Handbook*. His other research interests include science communication, activism, and the portrayals of PR in fiction.

257

Index

ill refers to an illustration; *n* to a note

8mm Magazine 28
1975, The (rock band) 97

A
Aboriginal art 152–53
Ackermann, Claire-Lise 80, 82–83
Activision Blizzard Company 170
Actor-Network Theory 6
Adventures in the World of Wearth (game) 54
Africa and Africans 228–29
Age of Empires (game) 49
Agfa film company 37
Ahmed, Sara 49
Airwolf (game) 169
Akinbobola, Yemisi 251
Ala-Fossi, Marko 80
Alilunas, Peter 25
Allied Leisure Company 167
Amateur Cinema World 28
amusement arcades 159, 162–64, 167, 169, 170–71
analogue books 115–25
    design of 121
    nostalgia for 115–16, 120, 125
Anderson, Benedict 49
Animal Crossing: New Horizons (game) 138, 142
Apperley, Thomas and Dharshana Jayemanne 174
Archers, The (radio programme) 207

Arneson, Dave 43
Arsenault, Dominic and Bernard Perron 134
Ashby Computer and Graphic Company 167–68
Atari Company 164, 171
Atkinson, Paul 191
Audio Technical Services company 75
audioblogging 185, 188
Auna Radios company 83–84
Auronlu (map game) 54

B
bakelite 78
Baker, Stacey Menzel and Patricia Kennedy 85
Bandcamp (streaming platform) 102
Banks, Marcus 209
Barber, Mark 79, 82
Bard's Tale (map game) 53, 55*ill*
Barlow, John Berry 189–90
Barnes, Donelle M. 191
Baron, Naomi 116
Barthes, Roland 209, 212, 214, 218
Batchen, Geoffrey 208
Bate, David 212
Batenburg, Willem van 33
Battletoads (game) 168
Bauer (focus group member) 123
Bauhaus movement 77
Baxter, Weston [et al.] 74, 76–77
Beaudry, Mary 8
Beautiful Old Perth (Facebook group) 215

259

Belle Epoque radios 83, 84*ill*
Berger, John 213, 214
Berger, Joseph [et al.] 4
Berry, Richard 185, 187
Betts, Raymond 72
Bicknell, Jeanette 74
Birkerts, Sven 116
Birmingham Centre for Media and Cultural Research xiii, 3, 11
Bitcoin 241
Black Lives Matter (BLM) 228–29
Blackburrow (map game) 53
Blackman, Merric 56
Blackmoor (roleplay game) 43–44
Blessing publisher 118–19
Blizzard Entertainment company 140
Blue Thunder (tv programme) 170
Boggs, Dan 43–44, 46, 54, 60
    'The Oldest Dungeon Maps in D&D History' 43–44
Bollmer, Grant 9
Bolt-Wellens, Camille 37
Bomback, R.H. 27–28
Bonini, Tiziano 78, 79, 80
Boogie Outlaws (tv programme) 218–20, 219*ill*
books 114–25
    connoisseurs of 116, 122–25
    digitization of 116, 117
    self-publishing of 123, 124
    see also analogue books; e-books; Kindle books
Borschke, Margie 98
Bosch (tv programme) 235–37, 241–42, 244–45
Bottomley, Andrew 185
Bourdieu, Pierre 162
Bowie, David 'Cracked Actor' (CD box) 95, 96*ill*
Boys from the Blackstuff (tv programme) 207
Braudel, Ferdinand xiii

Brenner (focus group member) 118, 123
Britain: games industry in 159–76
    see also Midlands
British Film Institute (BFI) 37
British Phonographic Industry 97
Burns, Jasmine 210, 212, 220
Bussey, Gordon 81
Butler, Judith 193

C
calculators 67*ill*, 68
Call of Duty: Black Ops Cold War (game) 136–37
Callois, Roger 134
Cardoso, Daniel and Susanna Paasonen 23
Caribbean Diaspora Podcast 182–98
    Facebook posts on 196
Caribbean migrants 191–97
Carlsen publisher 119
Carreira da Silva, Filipe 116, 117
Carson, Frank 215, 216*ill*
Carter, Oliver 17–18, 251
cassette tapes 97–110
    nostalgia for 105–06
Cassidy, John 180
Cattaneo, Eleonora and Carolina Guerini 70, 85
Cave, Nick 1–2
Centresoft Company 170
Chandler, David 218
Charles, Harrison 18, 41–42, 252
Charles, Rachel-Ann 182–84, 191–93, 251
Chez M. Pirgeon (film) 18, 23–37, 30*ill*, 31*ill*, 33*ill*
    title cards 35*ill*
Chignell, Hugh 82
Church, David 22–23
Cicero (magazine) 114
Classic Gold radio station 74
Climax Films 25–26, 34

INDEX

Codemaster Company 169, 175

Coley, Sam 11, 18, 252

colonialism and mapping 49–52

Colston, Edward: toppling of statue of 179–81, 180*ill*

Combat Jack Show, The (podcast) 190

Commando (game) 170

commodity fetishism 241

compact discs (CDs) 82, 94, 97, 103, 115

Connerton, Paul 212

consciousness 233, 236–37, 238–40

Cook, Ivor 37

Coroama, Vlad [et al.] 3

cottage industries 166

Countryfile (tv programme) 207

COVID-19 pandemic 130–01, 137–38, 142, 175

    and Caribbean migrants 191–92

    impact on cultural sector of 114

    response to 182, 203–04

Cox, Martin 252

crafts 151–53, 151*ill*

Crash Bandicoot (game) 141

Crass (rock band) 157

    The Feeding of the Five Thousand (album) 155, 157–58, 158*ill*

Crisell, Andrew 186

Cross, Karen and Julia Peck 212

Crysis (game) 141

Csikszentmihalyi, Mihaly and Eugene Rochberg-Halton 102, 110, 209

D

Darling, David and Richard 169

de Maeyer, Juliette 211

de Saussure, Ferdinand 209

Dennis, Alan [et al.] 189

Destiny Quest (game book) 58

Detroit Becomes Human (game) 59

Dewey, John 179

Di Lauro, Al and Gerald Rabkin *The Adult Loop Database* 37

digital currencies 241

digitization 114–15, 116–17, 210, 220, 224–25

Dire Straits (rock band) 113

Dolce Vita, La (film) 36–37

Donkey Kong (game) 138

Droemer-Knaur publisher 121

Dungeons and Dragons (game) 43–44, 45*ill*, 51

    'Tomb of Horrors' 61*ill*

Dunton, Davidson 71

E

e-books 116, 123–24

Eastronic radios 74–75, 86, 87*ill*

Ecko radios 78

Edwards, Elizabeth and Janice Hart 206, 208, 211

Elite Systems Company 170

Ellis, Warren *Nina Simone's Gum* 1, 12

Erotic Film Society 34

Eskelinen, Markku 134

Esposito, Nicolas 134

Etrian Odyssey (map game) 53

EVE Online (game) 141

Everquest Map Preserve (database) 53

Eze, Dons 228

F

Facebook 196, 205, 236

Fallout 4 (game) 138–39

fanzines 91

Fickers, Andreas 69, 77

Fighting Fantasy (game book) 44, 58

film laboratories 27

films

    cleaning of 29

    digitization 29–30

    title cards for 35*ill*

    see also pornographic films

Final Fantasy (map game) 53–54

Florini, Sarah 190, 195
Floyd, George 228
fog of war 51
For Colored Nerds (podcast) 190
Forkert, Kirsten 252
format theory 93–94, 100
Fort-Rioche, Laurence and Claire-Lise
    Ackermann 80, 82–83
Forty, Adrian 78, 79, 84, 85, 86
    Objects of Desire 77
Foucault, Michel 48, 194
Fox, Kim [et al.] 190
Frankfurt Book Fair 115
Fras, Jona 196
Freeman, Mike 33, 28
    I Pornographer 26–27
Frith, Simon 73
Fuchs, Michael [et al.] 51

G
game books 44, 58
Game Boy 135
Game Boy Color (game) 18, 41*ill*
games 132–46
    agency in 48–49
    arcade games 169, 170–71
    licensing of 169–71, 174
    ludus and *paidia* play 134
    multiplayer games 136–37
    nostalgia for 41–42, 143
    roleplay games (RPGs) 43, 51, 56
    sales of 142
    see also specific games
games industry 159–76
employment in 174–75, 176*n*3
flexible accumulation in 164–65, 174–76
vertical integration in 163, 168
Gangsters (tv programme) 207
Garcia, Antero 51
Gardeners' World (tv programme) 207

Gazi, Angeliki and Tiziano Bonini 78, 79, 80
Gebhardt, Nicholas 253
Geddes, Keith and Gordon Bussey 81
Geller, Valerie 77
Gerd, Leonhard 99–100
German book market 114, 118–19, 121, 124–25
Geveart film company 37
Gibson, James 46
Gillespie, Tarleton [et al.] 9
Giroux, Henry 190
Giruvegan (map) 54
Given, Lisa 191
GoldenEye 007 (game) 141–42
Google Books 116
Google Scholar 116
Gorfinkel, Elena 22, 37
Goulbourne, Harry and John Solomos 183
Grainge, Paul 155–56
Granby, Martin 25
Grand Theft Auto (game) 137, 143
Greadio Radio company 83
Gregory, Jenny 207, 215
Griffiths, Lee 17, 19–20, 253
    notebook 19*ill*
Grimes, Matt 253
Grossman, Jonathan 194
Guerilla Media 185, 188
Guerini, Carolina 70, 85
Guild Wars (game) 56
Guitarist (magazine) 113
Gullachsen, Willoughby 218
Gutenberg Project 116
Gutowski, Andy 85
Gygax, Gary 43

H
Haddon, Leslie 77, 78
Hall, Catherine and Michael Zarro 207
Hall, Stuart 4, 195
    Old and New Identities 194

INDEX

Hammersley, Ben 185, 188
Harman, Graham 234, 242–43
Harrer, Sabine 52
Harris, Howard and Sungmin Park 185
Hart, Janice 206, 208, 211
Hart, Tabitha 191
Harvey, David 163, 171–72, 174, 175
Hayes, Patricia 206, 211
Hayles, Katherine 115, 165
Heidegger, Martin *Being and Time* 237
Hidden in Shadows (blog) 43
Hilderbrand, Lucas 22
Hillman, John 253
Hilmes, Michele 70–71, 79, 82, 187
Hoffman und Campe publisher 118, 124–25
Hornby, Nick *High Fidelity* 105
Hotel Sexi (film) 36–37
Hutchings, Timothy 53

I

Ilford film company 26
immateriality 231, 232, 234, 235, 243, 244
Independent Communications and Marketing
   Unlimited 101
Ingram, Andrew and Mark Barber 79

J

Jackson, Vanessa 254
Janik, Justyna 134
Japanese game market 53, 80, 167, 70–71
Jayemanne, Darshana 174
Jeopardy (game) 168
Jones, Hilary Weston 11–12, 18, 67–68, 256–57
Judges Guild (game publisher) 43
Juliet Bravo (tv programme) 220–22, 221*ill*,
   224

K

Kallinikos, Jannis 17
Keith, Michael 69

Kennedy, Patricia 85
Kent, Alexander 47, 49
Keogh, Brendan *A Play of Bodies* 137
KikStart (game) 170
Killer Instinct (game) 168
Kindle books 115
Kinsey Institute 37
Kittler, Friedrich 5–6, 249
Knight Rider (game) 169
Knopfler, Mark 113
Kosinski, Joseph *Oblivion* 239–40
Kuchera, Ben 60
Kusek, David 99–100

L

Lacan, Jacques 230, 233–34, 236, 238–40,
   244
Lacey, Kate 78, 187, 196
Lady Gaga 97
Lange (focus group member) 120–21, 123–24
Langley, Bob 205
Latour, Bruno 6, 7, 48, 114
Lavabora (film) 35, 36, 37
Law, John 6
Law, John and Annemarie Moll 2
Lebanon 130–01
Lee, Peggy 205
Legend of Zelda (game) 132
Lehdonvirta, Vili 190
Leonardi, Paul M. 10–11, 46, 47, 115, 188,
   190
Leonhard, Gerd 99
Lester, Jo-Anne 46, 48
letterzines 91–92
Limited Run Games (distributor) 138, 143
Lipa, Dua 97
Llinares, Dario [et al.] 184
Lloyd, David 69
Loviglio, Jason and Michele Hilmes 187
Lowe, Adam 114

263

MEDIA MATERIALITIES

M

Machacek, Paul 165, 166, 174, 176*n*1

Magaudda, Paolo 109

Mangen, Anne 116–17

Mapp, Chris 11, 254

maps and mapping 43–62, 50*ill*
    hand-drawn maps 59–62, 61*ill*
    materialities of 45–48
    medieval maps 56–57
    nodal maps 56–57
    nostalgia for 59–60
    pointcrawl in 56, 57*ill*

Mapstalgia (game collection) 60

Marsh, Calum 106

Marsh, Julian 34, 37

Marx, Karl 242

material culture studies xiii, 8–9, 23, 60

materialism 242

materiality 2, 4, 7, 46, 47–48, 114–15, 232
    ephemerality of 155–56
    philosophy of 231–45
    see also immateriality

McCracken, Grant 124

McDonald, Richard 216

McEwan, Rufus 82

McKenzie, Donald 114, 116

McLeish, Robert 69

McLuhan, Marshall 4–5, 6–7, 13, 187, 231
    Understanding Media 5–7

Meades, Alan *Arcade Britannia* 162

Megarry, David 43–44, 45–46, 54, 59–60

Meltdown Festival 1

Ménage à Trois (magazine) 23

MetalGear Solid (game) 142

Metropolitan Police. Obscene Publications
    Squad 21, 25

Midlands (UK) 159, 164, 166–67, 170,
    175

Miller, Daniel 8, 47–48, 71, 209

Moll, Annemarie 2

Moore, Thurston *Mixtape: the Art of Cassette
    Culture* 105

Morizio, Patricia 188

Mörken, Christian 254

Müller, Marius 114

Murray, Janet 48

music
    audience participation in 107–09
    digital music 100–01
    hybridity of formats of 99–110

Myers, Fred 152

N

Noakes, Richard 186

Nora, Pine *Realms of Memory* 131

nostalgia 105–06, 120
    see also cassette tapes, radios, etc.

novels 115

Nuts in May (tv play) 207

O

Obscene Publications Act (1959) 27

Orfanella, Lou 72

Organization for Economic Co-operation and
    Development (OECD) 114

Orlikowski, Wanda and Susan Scott 115

Overwatch (game) 140

OXO (game) 140–01

P

Paasonen, Susanna 13, 23, 254

Pac Man (game) 135

paidia (structured play) 134

Paillard Bolex cameras 33

Palmer, Catherine and Jo-Anne Lester 46, 48

paratexts 133, 135–36, 137–38, 139–46
    digital paratexts 141–43
    and marketing 144–45

Park, Sungmin 185

patch leads 112–13, 112*ill*

INDEX

Patel, Karen 254–55
Pebble Mill At Once (tv programme) 207
Pebble Mill Facebook page 206, 207, 213, 215–6
Pebble Mill Studios 206–07, 211
    canteen 213–14, 213*ill*
Peck, Julia 212
Peggy Lee Entertains (tv programme) 205
Peirce, Charles S. and Ferdinand de Saussure 209
Perron, Bernard 134
Pew Research Centre 84–85
Phantasy Star (map game) 53
Phile (magazine) 23
Philips radio catalogue (1959) 73*ill*
Philips radio recorder 81, 81*ill*
Phillips, Evan 'Big Jeff' 25–26, 27
photographs 205–25
    digitization of 206, 210–12, 220–02, 224–25
    and memory 209, 212–17
    press photographs 218
Pink, Sarah 209
Play Generated Map and Document Archive (PlaGMaDA) 53, 59
PlayStation 5: 142
podcasts and podcasting 182–98
    Black cultural podcasting 184, 190–95
    materiality of 184, 197
Pokémon Go (game) 141
Pong (arcade game) 164
PopMatters (online magazine) 106
pornographic films 21–37
    orphaned films 18, 22, 25, 36
    packaging of 25–26
    smuggling of 38*n*2
pornographic magazines 23
pornography 21–38
post-structuralism 230
Potter, Deborah 185

Pound, Ezra *Lustra* 121
Priestman, Chris 79
Pritchard, Brian 28
prosopography 160–62, 172–73, 174
psychoanalysis 243
P.T. (game) 135, 139, 140

Q

Quiet Year, The (map game) 44, 52

R

Rabkin, Gerald 37
racism 228–29
    in games 51
Radermacher (focus group member) 124
Radiant Historia: Perfect Chronology (game) 58–59
radio presenters 72, 73–74
radio-cassette players 81–82
radio and radios 69–87, 186–88, 195
    clock radios 81
    design of 77–87
    digital radios 79–80
    emotional impact of 71, 73–74
    impact of internet on 82
    intimacy of 71–72
    listener participation in 79
    nostalgia for 74, 80, 84–85, 86
    retro revival in 70–71, 80–87
    transistor radios 79
Rambo: First Blood (tv programme) 170
Random House publisher 115, 118
Rare Company 166–68, 171, 175, 176*n*3
reading
    generational differences in 118–19
    impact of digitization on 116
Red Dead Redemption (game) 133, 137
Red Menace (game) 138
Resident Evil V (game) 52
retromania 105–06

265

Reynolds, Simon 105–06
Rheingold, Howard 189
Rider, Janice 220
Roberts radios 82–83
Rochberg-Halton, Eugene 102, 110, 209
Rockstar (game developer) 137
Rosenthal, Victoria *Fallout: the Vault Dweller's Official Cookbook* 139
Rowland, Thomas 56–58
Royal Danish Library, Copenhagen 1
Ruda, Frank 242, 243
Rütten & Loening publisher 125
Ryuutama (map game) 44, 52, 56

S
Saber, Dima 255
Saint-Exupéry, Antoine de *The Little Prince* 121
Salazar, Laura [et al.] 191
Sassoon, Joanna 206, 210–11
Scheidt, Jürgen vom 120
Schweighauser, Philip 121
Scott, Susan 115
Sea of Thieves (game) 176
Seavor, Chris 174, 176*n*2
Sedgwick, Eve Kosofsky 248
Sega Company 170
Seiwald, Regina 255
Selasi, Taiye 228
Seppänen, Janne 208, 210, 214
Shakespeare or Bust (tv programme) 222–23, 222*ill*, 223*ill*, 224
Shapin, Steve and Arnold Thackray 161
Sharma, Sarah and Rianka Singh 6
Sharp, Sharon 85
Shingler, Martin and Cindy Wieringa 79
Showboat Amusements Company 164, 167
Sid Meier's Civilization (game) 49
Siegert, Bernard 58
Silent Hills (game) 135, 139
Silverstone, Roger and Leslie Haddon 77, 78

Simone, Nina, chewing gum relic of 1–2, 12
Sinclair home computers 165
Sinclair Spectrum 167
Singh, Rianka 6
Slade, Joseph 25
smartphones 190, 237
Soho, London 21, 23
Soho Bibles 23, 32, 37
Soho Postcards 30, 32, 34, 36, 37
Solomos, John 183
Søndergaard, Dorte Marie 187
Sony CRF-150 radios 75–76, 76*ill*
South Park: Nobody Got Cereal 147*n*1
Spot the Ball (game) 168
Spyri, Johanna *Heidi* 121
Stamper, Chris and Tim 166–69
Starkey, Guy 80
Steepletone radios 83
Sterne, Jonathan 6–7, 93, 99–100
Stevens, E. Charlotte 18, 255
Stiernstedt, Fredrik 72
Stone, Alison 78
Stranger Than Kindness (exhibition 2020) 1
Strong National Museum of Play, NY 53
subjectivity 231, 239, 240, 243–44
Suits (tv programme) 238–39
Svorenčík, Andrej 61–62

T
Tacchi, Jo 70, 73, 74, 190, 195
    Radio Texture: Between Self and Others 195
tactility 47–49
Tandy, Lester 75–76
Tarkokvsky, Andrey 247
Taylor, Iain A. 255–56
Taylor, 'Skinny' Ken 37
Tetris (game) 135
textile industry: employment conditions in 175

INDEX

Thackray, Arnold 161

This Week in Blackness (podcast) 190

Thomas, Jimmy 162, 163

Thomas Amusements Company 163–64, 167, 169, 171

Thorpe, Leonard 37

Tilley, Chris 8–9, 191

Tischleder, Babette and Sarah Wasserman 10

Titan (game) 140

Tony Hawk's Pro Skater (game) 135

Top Gear (tv programme) 207

Tuan, Yi-Fu 56

Tulloch, Rowan 48

Turner, Stephanie 220

Turquier, Barbara 33

Twitter 280

U

Ullstein Verlag 125

Ultimate Company 168–70

Ultimate: Play the Game (game) 168

US Gold Company 170

V

van House, Nancy 213

videogames *see* games

Vintage Erotica (digital archive) 22

virtual communities 189–90

virtual reality (VR) 144

Vismann, Cornelia 49

Volpe, Andrea 211

W

Wade, Alex 256

Waldroup, Heather 36–37

Walker, Norman 167

Wall, Tim 184, 256

Wang, Youcheng [et al.] 189

Wasserman, Sarah 10

Wattpad (reading and publishing platform) 124

Waugh, Thomas 24–25

Webber, Nick 18, 256

Westin, Jonathan 117, 119

Wheel of Fortune (game) 168

Whitaker, Steve [et al.] 188, 189, 192

Whittaker, Adam 155, 257

Wickstead, Helen 23, 36

Wieringa, Cindy 79

Wilson, Janelle 105

Wire, The (tv programme) 239

Witchcraft (tv programme) 215–16, 217*ill*

Wolf, Mark J.P. 133, 134

Wolf, Maryanne 116

Woodward Ian 207

World of Warcraft (game) 56, 135, 136*ill*

Wrather, Kyle 189

X

XBox series 142

Y

Young, Philip 12, 257

Z

Zarro, Michael 207

Zhuhai Ge Ge Lan Technology company 83

Zilec Company 167, 170

Zimmermann, Eric 134

zines 91–92

Zuboff, Shoshana 242

Zuckerberg, Mark 236

Zylinska, Joanna 206, 208, 210, 224

www.ingramcontent.com/pod-product-compliance
Lightning Source LLC
Chambersburg PA
CBHW060835070425
24454CB00035B/16